A Journey of a New Person

HARDEN NOT YOUR HEART

A Journey of a New Person

of a

HARDEN NOT YOUR HEART

Robert W. Spruce and Sherri C. Petrek

TATE PUBLISHING
AND ENTERPRISES, LLC

Published by Tate Publishing & Enterprises, LLC
127 E. Trade Center Terrace | Mustang, Oklahoma 73064 USA
1.888.361.9473 | www.tatepublishing.com

Tate Publishing is committed to excellence in the publishing industry. The company reflects the philosophy established by the founders, based on Psalm 68:11,
"The Lord gave the word and great was the company of those who published it."

Book design copyright © 2015 by Tate Publishing, LLC. All rights reserved.
Cover design by Samson Lim
Interior design by Jomar Ouano

Published in the United States of America

ISBN: 978-1-68142-642-6
1. Religion / General
2. Religion / Christian Church / General
15.07.03

Acknowledgments

The authors would like to thank their spouses, families, and friends for allowing their spiritual friendship to develop and to result in the writing of this book. We would like to thank all the members of our Catholic parish, St. Anthony of Padua Catholic Church of The Woodlands, Texas, who have encouraged and supported the writing of this book with their words and their many prayers.

We would like to thank those employees of the Chick-fil-A store at the Alden Bridge Shopping Center in The Woodlands, Texas, who have been so gracious and kind to us during the hundreds of hours we spent in their store discussing the topics in the book. We would like to specifically acknowledge Romi, Virginia, and Andy for their hospitality.

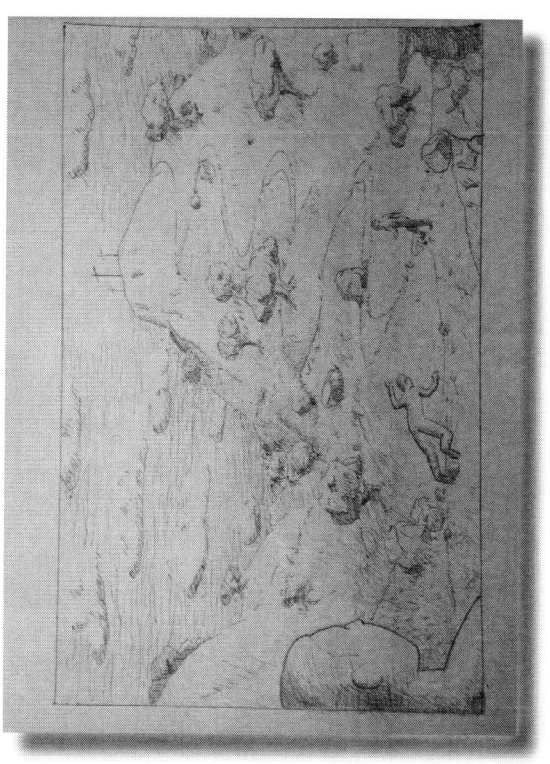

Contents

Foreword

The authors suggest that the reader read the "Vocabulary of Terms Used" section prior to the reading of the first chapter of the book. The "vocabulary" and then the "phrases used" sections provide summary of the ideas of the book and build upon one another resulting in a knowledge level that should allow the reader to more readily understand what the authors' are saying in the remainder of the book.

In Conversation at Chick-fil-A

Bob: So, Sherri, as I mentioned to you, I have been active in some church all my life. But recently, I have begun to feel a calling through so many different ways to examine my relationships—my relationship with God, with my friends, and with people I come in contact, if even briefly. Above all, I have spent a good part of my life sizing people up for business purposes, analyzing them, and drawing conclusions about them. And what is often disturbing, I am often wrong about them as a person and as a child of God. I feel there might be more to people, more to God, than I have been willing to notice. I feel...I feel well, like I need to really follow Christ at a deeper level and do His will always, maybe for the first real time. I need to...maybe...become a new person!

Sherri: Bob, Christ in the Sermon on the Mount and the Beatitudes told us, almost ordered us to become new persons under the guidance of the Holy Spirit. We are to be radically transformed, to become new persons, to be His disciples and have the right relationship with God.

Bob: How does one become this "new person"?

Sherri: Well, I am not sure we can help one another understand what all is involved in just a few minutes. Let's maybe discuss this more. I also need to understand more about relationships in my life and particularly my relationship with God.

Bob: Why don't we meet here at the Chick-fil-A each Tuesday morning before Mass and just talk about what is all involved in becoming this "new person."

Preface

Jesus tells us in Mark 12:31 that the second greatest commandment is "To love your neighbor as I have loved you"—an abstraction, a theory, a moral goal, or a command? With His further statements in the Beatitudes, Jesus would seem to be saying very directly to us that His Gospel is not a philosophy of life, but the only singular way to live life, if we are to be in true harmony with our purpose for being born, which is to love and serve God and prepare ourselves for eternity with Him. There are no other options for anyone and certainly understood to be so by a Christian. It is a direct command from God Himself. It is not to be considered an unobtainable goal but the only proper focus and exercise for all the human faculties that God has given us. Only when we are trying to be in ordered alignment with this divine directive are we in harmony with God and our physical and the supernatural world. Christianity is experiential, not a theory. No theory leads to eternity. Only truth leads to eternity.

Each human has been given the opportunity through grace to choose to accept the call of the divine directive to love God with all your heart, mind, and soul and to love your neighbor as yourself. Through free will, we can either choose to prepare for and spend eternity with God and fulfill our purpose for being, or reject Him and live in a disordered way with our physical world and our fellow men.

If we choose through free will to respond to the Triune God through Jesus's command then we find ourselves on a life-long "journey" of conversion to love God and our neighbor. This grace of preparation to meet God can only be achieved through our active pursuit of a true relationship with the Trinity. But the pursuit is more of a continual response on our part to the conversation with our companions: the Father, the Son, and the Holy Spirit of the Trinity.

Understand, my fellow sojourner, there is no one moment of conversion in which we are suddenly transported to our destination with greater knowledge of God and our exercising of our love for our neighbor. We do not immediately stop sinning, and we do not cease to be responsible for our sins. Christ has died for our sins to give us the ability to love Him and obey Him. It is a long and arduous journey for each person. We have huge mountains in ourselves and others to overcome and particularly so with those who are not on the journey and never will be. We have to learn to live with and overcome these obstacles while on the journey. It is we who must make our own journey. But that journey can carry with it many companions that are right there with us every step of the way—the persons of the Holy Trinity, the Church, the blessed sacraments of Eucharist and Reconciliation, our fellow Christians, the Angels and the Saints, and our Blessed Mother, Mary (i.e., the community of Christians).

From a Marian viewpoint, we are particularly called to understand and exercise the role of the Blessed Mother not only in salvation history but also in our journey and the journey of those we encounter. Since self-centeredness is the route of all sin, we turn to the most important fully human Christian companion that will ever exist, born without sin and forever without sin, the Virgin Mary, model, guide, and helper in our journey to God.

The purpose of the following discussion is to help any of us on the journey to understand the journey, its blessings and difficulties, challenges and mysteries, to understand our commitment to God and others as we prepare for eternity with our Lord and Savior. Through Marian Spirituality, we will find our companion Mary with us at all times, showing us how we move beyond ourselves so that we may have joy in this life and eternity loving God with all our might and our neighbor as our self. This is "our Savior's *command*"!

Introduction

"Teacher, which commandment in the law is the greatest?" He said to him, "You shall love the Lord, your God, with all your heart, with all our soul, and with all your mind. This is the greatest and the first commandment. The second is like it: You shall love your neighbor as yourself."

—Matthew 22:36–40, NRSVCE

"Which is the first of all the commandments?" Jesus replied, "The first is this: 'Hear, O Israel! The Lord our God is Lord alone! You shall love the Lord our God with all your heart, with all your soul, with all your mind, and with all your strength.' The second is this: 'You shall love your neighbor as yourself.' There is no other commandment greater than these."

—Mark 12:29–31, NABCE

"There was a scholar of the law who stood up to test Him and said, 'Teacher, what must I do to inherit eternal life?' Jesus said to him, 'What is written in the law? How do you read it? He said in reply, "You shall love the Lord, your God, with all your heart, with all your being, with all your strength, and with all your mind, and your neighbor as

yourself.' He replied to him, "You have answered correctly; do this and you will live."

—Luke 10:25–28, NABCE

"I give you a new commandment: love one another. As I have loved you so you also should love one another."

—John 13:34, NABCE

"The community of believers was of one heart and mind…"

—Acts 4:32, NABCE

In these well-known verses, Jesus verifies the already accepted Jewish commandment, "To love the Lord your God and love your neighbor as yourself." What Jesus meant continues to entice our intellects and our hearts thousands of years later as it did the intellect and the heart of the first century Jew. Why was the question even asked of Jesus anyway? Was it just to try to entrap Him? Or was it a daily struggle to understand at that time and in our own time what is really meant. Did the Gospel community of the book of Acts understand what this prime directive of Jesus really meant to allow them, "to be of one heart and one mind"? As with so much of the Jewish law, those pursuing the will of God were trying to understand what was really being asked of them. Jesus in the Beatitudes helps us to begin that thought process by showing that in fulfilling this commandment it goes far beyond just the execution of the letter of the law. It moves the focus from the intellect to the heart.

He enters new thought into the interpretation of the law with the authority of God incarnate. No longer was there a need for prophets to speak for God or Scribes to interpret the law as they think God meant it. There was no longer an interpretation. It is now the commandment from God Himself.

As the greatest commandments, our fulfillment is fundamental to our salvation. Yet the command often alludes even the most pious in practice. In the eyes of our minds, thousands of years later, we are still challenged with Jesus' meaning—was He speaking abstractly about something we should conceptualize as the north star for all of humanity, was He giving us a goal of perfection for those whose lives are lives of prayer in monasteries and convents and an unattainable goal for those of us in this world or was this a command directly from the Triune God, incarnate, that must be obeyed without equivocation and with all of our strength and might, attainable, and expected.

Our purpose here is to remove the abstraction of conceptualization, to remove the idea of a goal obtainable or not obtainable, and to make the clear declaration that this is the command from God that is possible and can be obtained and is demanded by those who say "yes" to the pursuit of God. We can under the right leadership and graces, love the Lord our God with all of our heart, soul, and mind, and our neighbor as ourselves. And as with others before us, we can actually do this with the graces of the Triune God, the direction of the Holy Spirit, and the model of the one human being who from eternity is destined to lead us to Jesus and by that model the one who is in the "right relationship with God" who is righteous, our Blessed Mother Mary.

A Marian view would suggest that we live this commandment because it is all about relationships and along with all of the evangelization and educational effort of a Marian approach, the fundamental foundation of Mary is relationships. Not that deep prayer, or education, or the poor are not important and are not an importance of a Marian approach, but Mary is all about relationships.

Relationships are so key to our existence as children of God. She is the one and only one who has the "right relationship with God," and who unencumbered by sin is able to say with a clear head, "love thy neighbor as thyself." She is without the root cause of all sin, self-centered, and egocentric behavior.

Certainly, Catholic Christianity is all about relationships, our relationship with God, with our Gospel Community of Christ, The Church, with our fellow man and woman in marriage, in unique Trinitarian Communions, in our relations with other Christian communities and in our relationship with secular society. And Mary as our model leads us to having the "right relationships" that allow us to love the Lord our God and our neighbor as ourselves.

In this book, we will look at what Jesus meant when He commanded us to love our neighbor as ourselves, which implies a commandment relationship with God, the many influencers that determine our relationships with God and others, obstacles that we and the evil one place in our way and the illusion that it cannot be done in the first place. We will go at this discussion from a distinctively "Mary" perspective. Mary is just not some invention of The Church in the Middle Ages but is the mother of the entire Church of Christ, like it or not, and she is the one that will follow her Son's direction in leading all mankind back to a righteous relationship with God and our neighbor. She is the Star of the Sea that leads all who are on the path of the journey as we pursue God on our road to eternity.

> *So be perfect, just as your heavenly Father is perfect.*
>
> —Matthew 5:48, NABCE

We pursue in living out the commandments of love of God and neighbor through a response to God's calling us on a journey to pursue Him. A journey that finds prayer as the "executor" of our lives and the manager of our journey, a journey to be holy and return to the Garden. This is a journey that often takes a path that is not straight but meandering and is often long as we struggle with the obstacles to our right relationship with God and others. We may even fall off the path on the way. But we are responding to God's call, not our own initiative. We continue on the journey and the path because the Holy Spirit has in-planted in us an increasing hunger for a relationship with God. Certainly we can only respond to His commandments regarding Him and our neighbor through Jesus' other commandment, "To be holy as your father in heaven is holy," as He commands us in the Beatitudes. Only through this desire for virtue are we able to obtain the fulfillment of the greatest commandments. Always, we must remember that our own egocentric selfishness is the root cause of all sin and that this selfishness is used against us in brilliance by the evil one who disorders all of the influences and will run us off the path and make us give up on the journey to eternal life with God, our only reason for being.

It all starts with our view of God and whether it is ordered or disordered! We seek unity with the Divine on the journey, not perfection and He does ask us to try.

> *Jesus was not satisfied with destroying sin and meriting only a sufficient amount of grace for our salvation. He did much more and He Himself declared it, "I am come that they may have life, and may have it more abundantly" (Jn. 10:10). This plenitude of life is the plenitude of grace, the supernatural life which causes sanctity to blossom.*
>
> *Sanctity is not reserved for a few; Jesus, by His Incarnation and by His death on the Cross, merited the means of salvation and sanctification for all who believe in Him. He, the All-holy, came to sanctify us, and has*

taught us, "Be you therefore perfect, as also Your heavenly Father is perfect" (Mt. 5, 48).

Jesus did not give this precept to a chosen group of persons, nor did He reserve it for His Apostles and close friends; He proclaimed it to the multitude who were following Him. St. Paul received His message and announced it to the Gentiles, "This is the will of God, your sanctification" (I Thes: 4:3). And in our times the Church, speaking through the great Pope Pius XI, has repeated it strongly and on many occasions to the modern world: "Christ has called the whole human race to the lofty heights of sanctity… There are some who say that sanctity is not everyone's vocation; on the contrary, it is everyone's vocation, and all are called to it…Jesus Christ has given Himself as an example for all to imitate." And elsewhere: "Let no one believe that sanctity belongs to a few chosen people, while the rest of humanity can limit itself to a lesser degree of virtue. Everyone is included in the law; no one is exempt from it."

Jesus comes not only to save me, but to sanctify me. His is calling me to sanctity and has merited for me all the graces I need to attain it. (Divine Intimacy)[1]

Vocabulary of Terms Used

When we use these words or phrases we mean:

Adaptability. Able to adjust oneself readily to different conditions. Makes us aware through ordered comparison of how we are same or different from the characteristics of the new person as well as how we are different from others on the journey and from others in general.

Admonish. To reprove a fellow Christian in a mild and good-willed manner regarding conduct that is opposed to loving thy neighbor as thyself and the loving of God.

Authentic. Truthful, honest, real, not false in behavior, reliable; being who one is.

Beauty. The individual acknowledging in their own unique way the qualities in another person that gives intense pleasure and satisfaction in the other by realizing the creative presence of God in the physical, spiritual, and other characteristics of another person. Beauty is truly in the eye of the beholder and what is considered beauty is unique for each individual.

Betrayal. To compromise one's self or other's trust in what is ordered in God's way.

Charism. A divinely (Triune God) conferred gift or power. In reference to Catholic religious orders, each order's charism seeks to explain how they in their order live out the Gospel.

Charitable Interpretation. Interpreting the other's statements with respect and agreeing that to the other they are rational, truthful, of interest and that we *migh*t believe the same if we were in the other's circumstances.

Christhole. A Christian that sees nothing wrong in threatening and or killing another who disagrees with their beliefs or opinions.

Christian Catholic woman. A woman of the Roman Catholic Christian faith who attempts to live her life in accordance with the tenants of that faith.

Church. The Roman Catholic Church, the Church founded by Christ in which the full truth of Christianity resides and where Christ is found and represented on earth.

Commitment. An unwavering pledge or promise to another person, a group, or an action.

Companionship. The true nature of what God intended for the relationship between a woman and a man exemplified in the Garden of Eden. There is no hierarchy, and there is complete equality with the unique feminine and masculine gifts and qualities molded into one relationship making for an integrated whole of the woman and man.

Competition. Attempting to achieve the same objective with different but ordered modus operandi.

Concupiscence. The tendency of all human beings toward sin as a result of original sin even after baptism.

Consistency. Repetitive predictability particularly in actions and words.

Conversion. The spiritual transformation of an individual in thoughts, words, and actions in surrendering to God and obeying Him accompanied by a response to the call from God and the individual moving into a journey back to God. This is a lifelong journey of transformations with Jesus and Mary as the guides and prayer as the executor of the individual.

Cross-Gender Trinitarian Communion. An isosceles triangle depiction of the relationship between the two different genders and God with God at the apex of the triangle and each different gender at the two base angles.

Discerning. The process of listening to God through prayer, readings, discussion, and through the input of others to determine God's will in a certain situation or to determine one's vocation in life.

Discernment of Spirits. Ignatius's fourteen rules to determine if a spirit is from God or the evil one during periods of spiritual desolation and consolation.

Disordered. Actions that are not in the proper right relationship with God.

Dogma. A specific tenet or doctrine authoritatively laid down by the Roman Catholic Church.

Dualistic Conscious. Separating the good from the bad in exact distinction in philosophy, theology, and world view. Everything is clearly black or white; there is no room for gray.

Exercising an idea. Living the idea in heart, head, and action.

Experiential. Derived from experience.

False self. Who we are led to believe that we are by the evil one. This persona may be exterior or it may be internal. Either way, it may negatively affect our view of ourselves in relationship to God and our fellow man.

Fear. Reverential awe for God as the Almighty creator of heaven and earth; to include adoration of God.

Freedom. The power to determine action to do God's will without the constraint of sin.

Garden. The Garden of Eden, i.e. the perfect, righteous relationship with God as it was meant to be in the Garden of Eden before the Fall. The Garden is also Heaven.

Gifts of the Spirit. Wisdom, understanding, counsel, fortitude, knowledge, piety, fear of the Lord.

Greed. Excessive desire, especially for material things.

Inclusive. A characteristic meaning we accept all no matter how marginalized to the Church or in society. It should be reflected in the characteristics of the Marian Church (world-wide and local) and in each of us as new persons.

Invisible Church. Attributed to St. Augustine of Hippo who may or may not have believed it to include the elect who are known to God. In Catholic doctrine, the one true church is the visible society founded by Christ, namely, the Catholic Church. An exclusively mystical church would be one that deified its members and mean that the acts of Christians are simultaneously the acts of Christ.

Justice. The cardinal virtue concerned with rights and duties and what is due to those within relationships; the commitment, as well as the actions and attitudes, that flow from the commitment.

Lectio Divina: Divine reading by letting the Word rise out of scripture—reading, reflecting, praying, and receiving divine strength conversion and change through rest with Scripture.

Loving honesty. Dealing with the other in a manner that always exudes love for the other but deals with truthfulness and honesty in any situation.

Lukewarm. To show a lack of enthusiasm for one's faith and to lack zeal for the Church and its mission.

Lust. Intense sexual desire or appetite. Disordered sexual desire of "use" in marriage, cross-gender spiritual friendships, or in intergender relationships of singles.

Mariology. The study of the person and nature of the Virgin Mary, especially in reference to her role in the incarnation of God in Christ.

Marriage Trinitarian Communion. An isosceles triangle depiction of the relationship in a marriage between the man and the woman and God with God at the apex of the triangle and each different gender at the two base angles.

Mary's role in salvation history. Mary was uniquely given a singular grace and born without original sin and never sinned. Thus, she was the only human being capable of inviting God to become a creature and dwell in her by free will because she could say "yes" to Him because sin would not skew her thinking.

Name for devil. The evil one.

Neighbor. Every person other than yourself.

Neopagans. Members of contemporary society who do not believe in the personal Triune God of Christianity.

New Adam and the New Eve. Jesus and Mary. Adam and Eve failed God and mankind by disobeying God. Jesus and Mary obeyed God and established the new covenant.

New Garden. The New Heaven and the New Earth of the Book of Revelation.

New person. There are those individuals who hear God's call, embrace his invitation, say "yes" to his invitation, and pursue Him back to the Garden. They are transformed, converted into new people, and live it in their hearts, minds, and bodies.

Non-dualistic conscious. Defined by Rohr as a panoramic, receptive awareness whereby you take in all that the situation, the moment, the event offers without eliminating anything. He also defines "contemplation" as the same thing.

Nouwen's view of God. God is always with us. He never leaves us. He is always forgiving us. We are His Beloved as if we were the only one in the world. He accepts us just as we are.

Nuptial. Of or pertaining to marriage.

Obedience. The willingness to try to totally surrender to God and do His will in a continuous way.

Ordered. Actions that are in the proper right relationship with God.

Passive-aggressive behavior. A common defense mechanism among adults who see passivity or aggressiveness as beneath them. Instead of a direct attack on the perceived enemy, I quietly sabotage his efforts.

Passive hostility. Inappropriate disposition toward another not openly acknowledged.

Prayer. Communication with God in all possible ways by humans initiated by God.

Prayer as the Executor. In the person who is being transformed as a new person and clearly seeking God, the new person is completely enveloped directly in all aspects of life by prayer and from directions no matter how obtained from the Holy Spirit in prayer. Prayer is transformed from a set activity at a particular time and place into a total way of living, a lifestyle without an end either in this world or the next.

Radical feminism. The doctrine advocating social, political, and all other rights of women equal to those of men allowing and advocating a woman's right to complete control over her body to include the right to on-demand abortion, lesbian legal marriages, women priests, etc.

Righteous. In the right relationship with God.

Secularists. A spirit or tendency, especially a system of political or social philosophy that rejects all forms of religious faith and worship.

Schema. In psychology, a conceptual framework or script of how things are supposed to happen.

Self-centeredness. Selfish; concerned solely or chiefly with one's own interests, welfare, etc.; egotistical.

Solitude, community, service. From Henri Nouwen. As Jesus went into solitude to pray then went into community with his disciples and then went in service to others we are to pray, work within the community of the Church, and go serve.

Spirituality. Of or pertaining to interfacing with the Holy Spirit person of the Triune God as seen in the affective side of the human person. Spirituality involves more than just God and me alone with the inclusion of others and a compassionate concern for them, using of the gifts of the Holy Spirit as personal charisms always related to life.

Spontaneity. The immediate response to another person. The response may be based upon positive or negative frames of reference regarding all the physical, cultural, and other characteristics of the person in the initial meeting.

The curse, the Fall. The fall from Grace of Adam and Eve in the Garden of Eden in their exercising of free will to disobey God and fracture the divine righteous relationship between God and man. This incursion of original sin on the part of man due to the Fall brought sin and death into the world.

The journey and the path. The journey is our response to God's call to begin a journey with Him back to the Garden of Eden (New Heaven and the New Earth). The response is to continually strive to become the new person and to think, speak, and act accordingly. The path is the often circuitous plan that God has for us with its many stumbles and falls, diversions, sins, and graces. The journey and the path always lead to God and require us to surrender to Him and do His will. Jesus and Mary are our principal guides with the saints/ Saints and life as our guide.

The Nazareth years. Those years lived by Jesus in Nazareth until the beginning of His mission. The image invokes the image of Jesus, the incarnate God, existing in the normalcy of human life as one of us.

The new community. In the context of this book, the term refers to the Roman Catholic Church of the future with unchanged dogma and hierarchy that incorporates the new persons, the new man and the new woman defined as companions with the characteristics outlined in this work.

The new person. One who has listened to the call of the Triune God and as a result made the commitment to surrender to the Triune God and to obey Him and begin the journey back to the Garden as a true disciple of the second person of the Trinity, Jesus Christ, to obey the Holy Spirit through prayer and to make prayer the executor of the new person's life.

Third Order. A mostly pre-Vatican II term for a confraternity or order of the Roman Catholic Church such as the Jesuits or the Marists.

Tradition. The living transmission of the message of the Gospel in the Church. The oral preaching of the Apostles, and the written message of salvation under the inspiration of the Holy Spirit (Bible), are conserved and handed on as the deposit of faith through the apostolic succession in the Church.

Transparency. To the degree that it is possible to provide complete truthfulness, honesty, and openness in our interaction with others. Transparency leads to trust.

Trinitarian Communion. An isosceles triangle depiction of relationships with God at the apex and humans at the two base angles.

Unworthy. We are all not worthy to serve our Triune God but through Grace the same God through Christ makes us worthy to do so. The evil one especially uses the disordered view of women by certain men and society to make the woman feel that she is unworthy and a failure in her relationship to men and to God.

Vocation apostolate. Each lay Christian is asked to be an apostle for Christ in the world within the context of his vocation in the world, i.e. in his place of work, no matter where it is or what his job is.

Vocation. Marriage, vowed, consecrated single, spiritual friendship, a chosen state in life with all the commitments associated with the state.

What we call Mary. Mary is the Mother of God, the Spouse of the Holy Spirit, the Mother of the Church, our mother, our mediator as a helper of Christ, our advocate.

Will of God. What God has planned for us which we believe to be what is best for us in the context of eternity making us the best version of ourselves possible. We are asked through free will to obey His will for us.

Vocabulary of Phrases Used

"God comes to man (male) through the woman (female)." A woman is equal to a man intellectually and spiritually and they have characteristics that are more God-like than those of the man. When her unique God-like characteristics are ordered verses disordered they include a greater range of capacity for love, nurturing, compassion, humility, emotion along with its different approach to logic. The man learns love from the woman.

"Perception divides, honesty unites." Our perceptions of others and particularly our initial conception of others may be incorrect and cause us to conduct ourselves in a way that is not totally honest and transparent. When we care about the other and are less self-centered we are able to find out about the other and relate ourselves to the other in a spirit of truth, honesty, and transparency. This unites people.

"Take captivity captive." Captured by sin as new person's we ask our Triune God to give us freedom to not sin and be captured by God for Himself and hold us captive to His love, mercy, forgiveness. This gives us true freedom to do God's will and be happy.

"Solitude must always lead to community and community to service." As Jesus did, we must go be alone and pray, but we cannot stay there. He leads us, as He himself did, to go from solitude to community, the Church, where we are to worship and witness and then go out and serve others in the community.

"Christianity and Church are experiential." Most of us are not called to stay walled up and selfishly want only our God in solitude. As did God Incarnate in our Lord Jesus Christ we are told by our faith to as individuals and in community (the Church) serve God by bringing others to Christ and loving them as our neighbors and therefore as we love ourselves.

"Moving beyond ourselves." Self-centeredness is the root of all sin, and therefore, we are asked to care more about others than ourselves as Christian disciples and to move out beyond ourselves and our own little sphere of interests.

"Hidden and unknown in this world." The Charism of the Marists (The Society of Mary) which exemplifies our Tri-une God's call to make a difference in the world for Christ through works in which we are exemplary but without the gratitude of others. We wish to not be tempted to be egotistical and think that we are the ones doing the work when all glory is to be given to God who works through us as the Holy Spirit.

"Self-centeredness is the root of all sin." All sin comes as a root of our own selfish and disordered egotistical nature. We are asked to overcome this as Jesus teaches us in the Beatitudes and from the Sermon on the Mount.

"When I am weak, I am strong." Paul was so right! The new person is humble, compassionate, etc. and wins the hearts and the minds of the other. This makes relationships better and actions more easily accomplished in an environment of love and respect. This is true strength that endures.

"I am the Beloved of God." Each one of us is God's Beloved, and in that uniqueness, we find God who always loves us, never leaves us, always forgives us, and if we allow, leads us to eternal life with Him.

"You are not able to be God to me." To paraphrase Henri Nouwen, you as another human cannot be everything to me and always fulfill my every need, want, and desire. If I think you can or if I have expectations of this nature about you, then I will be disappointed. Only God can be God. In Him, in God alone, rests one who can truly give us all that we need, want, and desire.

"You should respond as I would respond." Each of us is different with different frames of reference and influences and therefore the other may not respond to the same situation as I do, and I should not assume they will do so. As we become more the new person we will find that our responses may be similar.

"Commitment is surrendering and obedience." To pledge to a particular course or us in the case of the new person requires action. That initial action is hearing, but the true action begins when the new person surrenders to God and obeys him. Once this happens, the new person never wants to let the commitment go away.

"Mary as model." Mary becomes cross-gender and a model to women and men of how to be the new person. The derivative of the logic of who she is and without sin brings in all the characteristics of the new person for everyone. She becomes the true model especially for the new person woman. She is the model of the "companion" that has been deceived by the evil one.

"Our sin is inspiration for others." We all sin and the sin itself must be reconciled with God, the Church and those we have hurt. However, it is often in the way we handle our sin that is so very important. It is the "witnessing to our sin" that shows us to be striving to be new persons. Do we immediately realize and admit to the sin when another is involved? Do we immediately realize and admit to the sin when we sin against ourselves and God? Remember, when we sin against another person or ourselves we have also sinned against God. How we react and how we remedy in a quick fashion is what is important. Those words and actions in remedy can be a witness that leads another to conversion!

"The heart is interpreted by the 'masters of suspicion.'" Our secularist society would like to intellectualize away sin and ignore it in the way Freud (psychologically), Marx (materialism), and Nietzsche (power) explained human behavior as if there was no God. But somehow our hearts prefer the truth that comes from a heart oriented to God over humanistic theories that have proved to be weak in explaining human behavior.

"Am I a person or a gender?" First, we are persons and secondly gender. Today's society would like for us to believe that we need to emphasize our gender above all else and egotistically promote it in a disordered way. God sees us as persons. We are all the same in His eyes and that is all that matters.

"Am I an authentic person?" This is a question that the new person must ask themselves continuously. Am I being truthful, honest, and transparent to the degree I can be or am I sometimes manipulative, evasive, and self-centered to the degree I do know myself or to the degree I do not know myself. Relationships and everything become easier when we are authentic.

"It is always possible for man to kill the word of God that is in him." Conversion is not a one-time deal in which we are justified for life no matter what we do. It is possible to be so self-centered that we destroy the redemption of Christ by deliberate free will actions that are sinful and which we have no remorse or petition for forgiveness from our Savior. There is no elect or non-elect. This makes God a liar. This is man's free will deliberately rejecting the love of God for us.

The Foundation

Reflect on: It seems that God is asking humanity to live inside of a cosmic humility, as God also does.

—Richard Rohr[2]

The underlying foundation, the underlying philosophy, of this book is based upon the belief that Jesus, understood only as God Incarnate, chose to radically change the world and to radically change the individual by coming to earth to save us from ourselves, reconcile us with the Omnipotent God, and provide an eternal home for those who would say "yes" to eternal life with Him. The changing of the individual, the changing of the world required Jesus to tell us and show us what He meant, and this is most vividly reflected in our understanding of the Beatitudes and the Sermon on the Mount. With the resurrection and the sharing of the faith by the Apostles and the early Church Fathers, followed by their works of evangelization and the addition of the Scriptures, the world began to move out of darkness into the light and the life of the Triune God.

This movement from darkness to light can be well seen in the movement away from the "dual consciousness" that had permeated the world view of man and existence into Christ's message and the underlying philosophy of "non-dual consciousness," establishing the true understanding of Jesus and His sayings, His teachings, His parables, and His actions, thus creating the basis for radically changing the world and individuals. This "new teaching" of Jesus continued to develop in the minds and hearts of man and the great Saints and affected society in a continued crescendo of God's plan for the world. And then, with the success of the evil one, with the Reformation and the Enlightenment, this progress in God's early kingdom building as a whole stopped. And there, it has lain with the exceptions of isolated individuals until very recently.

As you read this book, note that the radical transformation that Christ demands in the Beatitudes and the Sermon on the Mount, the new concept of "the new person," the actualization of the "new person woman" in her ordered place in society and the graces and trials of the new person's interaction with others are all based on a world that has returned to a world of non-dual consciousness. This new world is moving away, once again, from a dualistic world. Only in a non-dual world can we truly understand our Triune God's purpose for mankind and only with this foundation can we begin to, "love thy neighbor as ourselves," fulfilling all that Christ demands of us.

This non-dual consciousness is the underlying philosophy/theology that is necessary to understand the principles of this book as being real in concept and experience. This understanding of non-dual consciousness is heavily based on the work of Richard Rohr's and his understanding of non-dual consciousness.

Now, let us explore non-dual consciousness as it is used in this book. That will give us the "foundation" for beginning to understand the desires of Christ given to those who say, "Yes to God" to the challenge of free will and the acceptance of the Triune God, i.e., the "new person."

In generalizations, dualism—whether in philosophy, theology, or psychology—separates the good from the bad in exact distinction. Prior to Christianity, this was even seen in theology as the existence of two separate gods, one good and one evil with the corresponding human explanation as the spirit being good and matter or body or flesh being evil. The two could never be united into the one. Therefore, much of our world and its existence was considered evil, not good, and things we humans did are clearly either good or bad. We had dark, complete dark; and we had light, complete light. There was no in-between, no twilight. We therefore explained everything with certitude, a need for perfection, everything requiring resolution and answers, judgment, clear understanding of what was right and what was wrong, analysis, and critique. This dualistic consciousness permeated everything to include religion, society, politics, and relationships.

As we know, Judaism and then Islam embraced the monotheistic God opposed to dualism but, to a major degree, kept the black and whiteness as sin and righteousness, with Judaism adding to the original Ten Commandments all of the circumstances in which these commandments could occur to the tune of hundreds of laws. This later movement of dualism to the monotheistic God began to dissipate in explanation of all with the advent of Jesus and the development of Christianity.

How is that a single Triune God, Father, Son, and Holy Spirit could be? An only God but yet with three persons. Dualistic consciousness could never conceive that the Omnipotent God of the universe could bring all, good and evil, or combine matter, man with the spirit. But the Second Person of the Trinity is exactly that, Jesus Christ, 100 percent God and 100 percent man in the body of flesh with the spirit, the Holy Spirit, the Third Person of the Trinity dwelling not only in the Triune God but also dwelling in the body of each one of us as a result of Christ. How could God, a pure, sinless spirit to the dualist, become a wretched fleshed creature in order to save that wretched creature from damnation and elevate him to live in eternity with the Omnipotent God? Christianity was truly radical!

The only philosophical/theological environment Christianity can really exist in, in order to understand the teachings of Jesus, is not a dualistic world! It is a non-dualistic world, the world Christ came to transform us to from being dualistic people to an understanding of what it means to love the Lord your God with all your, mind, body, and heart and to love your neighbor as yourself. This can only be understood in a non-dualistic consciousness.

Non-dual consciousness is defined by Rohr as "a panoramic, receptive awareness whereby you take in all that the situation, the moment, the event offers without eliminating anything." Rohr also defines "contemplation" as the same thing as non-dual consciousness. As Rohr continues he says that we define "thinking" as, "our need to make distinctions and judgments…yet almost all thinking [as being]…compulsive and habitual." Non-dual consciousness means we have to work at knowing our compulsive and recurrent patterns of thinking of everything as being dualistically finite.

> *Non-Dual Consciousness is about receiving and being present to the moment and to the now exactly as it is, without judgment, without analysis, without critique, without your ego deciding whether you like it or whether you don't like it. It is a much more holistic knowing, where your mind, heart and soul and senses are open and receptive to the moment just as it is.…The non-dual, contemplative mind is a whole new mind!…[It allows you] to look at yourself and others calmly and compassionately because you are able to see things as they are in themselves and not from the viewpoint of how they affect you.* (R. Rohr)[3]

Do not misunderstand! We are not suggesting that making judgments, doing analysis, using critique is evil, incorrect, etc. This mode of approaching our physical and even our psychological world is not wrong. The problem is that these areas and more importantly in our interpersonal relationships with God, ourselves, and our fellow man cannot be looked at by a new person Christian in just a dualistic way! It requires also the expanding of the impulse to explain everything away in a dualistic fashion and realize that there is always a non-dualistic consciousness component and that is the part that allows us to think more like Christ and be more like Christ and to understand better all He had to say to us. The real problem is that since the Reformation and the Enlightenment we as a general statement have only thought the dualistic thought. This is not the world of the "new person." This does not lead to being a disciple. It leads to playing God yourself and constantly stroking your own ego; it leads to brinkmanship and zero-sum games—"I am right, you are wrong." The truth is that you may be partly right or not right at all and the other may be partly right or not right at all. You are not the judge; God is the judge. The new person lives in an interpersonal world of "charitable interpretation," not in a world of egotistical absolutes.

> *The lower level, "un-conscious" mind is always dualistic,*
> *which is judgmental and oppositional. It always divides*
> *the field of the moment and takes sides. Whatever is*
> *unfamiliar, or whatever it does not already understand or*

agree with, is judged as totally wrong. In contemplative practice, you are refusing to take sides. Contemplation goes beyond words (which naturally differentiate this from that) to experience (which has the potential to unify seeming contradictions). This requires a higher level of consciousness that we are calling non-dual consciousness. (R. Rohr)[4]

The basis of dualistic consciousness is ego, self-centeredness, and selfishness, a major theme of this book. Only by saying "yes" and journeying to become the new person do we realize we are called to not be dualistic but to move beyond into a new realm, which is the world as non-dual consciousness, which sees the meaning of Christianity and the Church in its purpose,

to not be a monitor and police society in regards to morals. Religion became all about morality instead of being a result and corollary of Divine Encounter. As such this was much more a search for control or righteousness than it was a search for truth, love, or God. It had to do with the ego's need for certitude, superiority, and order. Is this what Jesus came for? Jesus never said, 'You must be right,' or much less, 'You must be sure you are good and right'. Instead he said, 'You must love one another.' His agenda is about growing in faith, hope, and love while always knowing that 'God alone is good'." (R. Rohr)[5]

One has to work at moving their head forward out of our post-Christian mind-set of dualism only and move into the non-dual consciousness of the new person. "This does not come naturally. You have to work at it and develop practices whereby you recognize your compulsive and repetitive patterns." But then you truly begin to understand the radical transformation demanded by Christ in the Beatitudes and the Sermon on the Mount that molds you into a new being, then you begin to understand the parable of the woman caught in adultery and the other parables, our spouses and spiritual friends, and the other gender and incredibly ourselves!

> *God does not want us to be perfect, he wants us to have unity with Him.* (Origin unknown)

Transforming the "New Person"

The Foundation of All Hope

The Trinity and Mary

How We View the Triune God

Reflect on: *When I pray, to whom do I pray? When I say Lord, what do I mean?*

—Henri Nouwen[6]

Our view of the Triune God affects our ability to communicate with the Holy Trinity's three persons through prayer. By communicating with the Triune God, we mean listening for and to Him, verbal and mental communication with Him, as well as recognizing Him in all the ways the three persons communicate with us through nonverbal/non-mental means. Too often, we may acknowledge Him in the beauty of nature or want to confine Him only to times and spaces in our lives, institutions, and buildings, days of the week, and creeds in an effort to control Him and adapt Him to our lives. We forget that He is the one in control.

We may have a problem seeing God as Triune in nature. We may mainly see Him as the Father, or mainly as Jesus, or mainly as the Holy Spirit. The idea of three persons in one may be difficult for us to grasp and that may influence our ability to relate to Him and determine our communicative ability with Him.

How we as individuals view the Triune God greatly influences how we respond to Him in all conditions of our lives. Our view affects His relationship with us, our response in that relationship and how we interact with others in relationships. Our view may often be rooted in childhood and may remain stuck in the childhood's view. We may have not progressed in our view of God since childhood, or we may have made real progress on the path to a closer relationship. In any event, we were influenced and are influenced by what our parents taught us, what our faith leaders have said, what we observed in others, what we read, what was comfortable for us, and what was uncomfortable, what restrictions our faith placed on ourselves and others.

To us, God may be a God of benevolent love or a stern judge or something gray and unclear. Our belief in God may resemble the Catechism of our Catholic faith or the influences of other Christian communities or may even have been guided by the influences from the secular world. Our God may be a cafeteria tray with our own selections.

Our view of God greatly affects our ability to relate to Him in a personal and intimate way, which is necessary if we are to respond to the call of the Holy Spirit and be a new person and be on the journey. For example, how many believe that God loves them? How many more could say that they know that God loves them just the way they are? And how many would be able to say that they accept that God loves them the actual way they are? We suspect that many do not believe that God loves them the way they truthfully view themselves. Our ability to accept that God loves us completely, each and every one of us as His only Beloved is necessary for an intimate, personal relationship with God.

> *It is always possible for man to kill the word of God that is in him. By denying what the word is and what it means for him, he can, at any time participate actively in the death sentence spoken by Pilate. But he who kills the word kills himself. He does so who fails to keep alive the word that has been entrusted to him…If I do not want this, I kill the word. That has nothing to do with my attendance at sermons or my reading of Holy Scripture. It is a quality of the word in me that is determined by my "Yes" or "No" to God's Call.* (A. von Speyr)[7]

Despite potential influences, the view of God manifested in the Scriptures and the Church Fathers that best resonates with all Scripture and tradition is a Marian view of the Triune God. The Marian view of God is the Triune God, Creator of the universe, overwhelmingly love beyond our mortal understanding and eternal hope for our salvation. The God who became fully human with the DNA of Mary yet remained fully God. The God who suffered and died to allow His creatures through free will to be with Him for eternity.

The God who called His creation "good" and therefore made His creatures "good." The God who made us and therefore capable in the Catholic view of being, "Holy as our Father in heaven is Holy." We are called by Him to a continuous conversion throughout our lives to be "good," to be "holy," to be more than Luther's "snow on dung" as we respond to a more and more intimate relationship with all persons of the Triune divinity through continuous conversion.

God has plans for each of us that begins before our conception and never ends even in eternity. God sees each one of us as His only Beloved both on Earth and for eternity. God is continually actively present in our lives and participates fully in our human struggle; God committed to living in solidarity with us—to share our joys and pains, to defend and protect us. God continually pursues us. The Triune God that became the Word incarnate as Jesus Christ and who is completely inclusive in offering salvation to everyone who will believe in Him. Also through love He is willing to allow us to reject Him, His Son, and eternity through free will. God is with each one of us as the Holy Spirit and makes each of us a Temple of God.

God is so in love with us that He asked Mary, a beloved creature, to allow Him to enter her to be conceived from the Holy Spirit, becoming fully human yet being fully God, so that we, His creatures, could kill Him so that He, in turn, could save us from the sin of Adam and death and have us live with Him for eternity.

The Triune God is most interested in being in relationship with us, His creatures and wishes His love to flow through us to others in relationships as the Holy Spirit's love flowed through Mary to our Redeemer. And therefore, we are called in turn to acknowledge that our Triune God in flowing His divine love to mankind is indeed three persons as one because we as His creatures need all three in our lives to return us to Himself in the Garden. We are called in our response to this God's overwhelming love to give our lives completely to all three divine persons and receive the graces afforded to us.

As we acknowledge this view of the Trinity we all are called to enter upon a journey, to follow a path back to the Garden where we belong, to live in eternity with the Triune God in a way that we cannot even imagine on our best day. And to do so with Mary as our guide, the unique woman given to all mankind as the model to bring each one of us personally home.

The call to be on the journey is not a metaphor. It is a real call that each and every one of us receives. Through free will, we can choose to hear or not. That is up to us.

We do have to move beyond our egocentric nature and seek God to hear the call. We must hear the call and be willing to give up our selfish nature and turn our lives over to the Triune God. Everyone's call is different; everyone's journey is different because each of us is a unique Beloved to God, but all are called to only one right response that has only one conclusion. That call and conclusion is only to the truth. That truth is that there is a truth and only one, the Triune God and Jesus Christ as the Second Person, the incarnation of God. God does not ask us to go on other searches that go nowhere. There is only one path to the only one truth.

The plan for our salvation and return to the Garden in response to God's love and the invitation to go on the journey was always there in eternity and this overwhelming love for us by the Trinity was from eternity meant to bring each to the journey. The love for us manifested in the eternal plan, the journey, the path of the journey has one single mortal creation of God as our compass and guide, Mary.

Before we begin our discussion of the journey back to the Garden, we need to stop and understand who this guide is and why. Our precept later will be that God comes to the male through the woman as did Eve come to Adam because the woman is most like God of humanity. And God comes to the mortal woman and all of mankind through Mary, the new Eve who said "yes" to God in counter to Eve's "no" and became our guide.

"And what the evil one will do to keep us from this truth!"

> *Are we not also challenged and encouraged to look more deeply at the way God sees us—beloved, accepted, affirmed, and worthy of salvation?* (Henri Nouwen)[8]

> *Becoming the Beloved means letting the truth of our Belovedness become enfleshed in everything we think, say, or do.* (Henri Nouwen)[9]

Dear Trinity

> **Reflect on:** *We had no right as creatures, to know the mystery of God's intimate life. However, God has made it known to us, for He did not wish to leave us in our natural state, that of a simple creature, but willed to raise us to dignity of sons, of friends.*
>
> —Divine Intimacy[10]

I cannot deny that You have always been in my life and of great importance to me despite my actions toward You at any given time. Nor can I deny that I have always thought that You have taken care of me and that I am very thankful. I do believe in You intellectually and in my heart. And I believe in its entirety what the Catholic Church teaches.

You have bestowed on me many graces. If I take the time to look, I readily see Your graces in family, friends, and career. You have given me graces that allow me to begin to understand how you loved us in order to redeem us and understand the mortal scripting of our redemption in your sacred scripture and the gift to be able to want to share it with others. You have given me an understanding of Your Blessed Mother in my life and her role in salvation history once again in spite of all the odds against that happening. And possibly, the greatest grace You have given me is bringing me to Catholicism, the truth, with its rich understanding of things spiritual, again despite all the odds against it happening. You have even graced me with being less than perfect physically, maybe a blessing more than a cross/curse.

You have given me all this despite my being one of Your poorest disciples. And now, You are testing me in a very strange and unique way that can only have come from You. I know from the bottom of my heart more than I have known anything in my lifetime that this test is from You. I feel I am not able to fully realize the importance of Your gift.

Instead, I really fear that I will lose my salvation as a result of this gift or realize that I am not one of the "elect" at all. Maybe, I have just "wanted to be one," which means nothing unless You have selected me since I am not able to earn salvation on my own! Or maybe You have rejected me because I have failed to take advantage of all the graces and plans You had for me that I never could see. Maybe, Calvin is right since to me my life does not show the signs of the elect!

I seem to be weak. I easily give in to the evil one who knows me only too well. I literally hate myself for my failures, as You well know, and my inability to do what I know is right. I have no excuses to offer You as well again You know. My history seems to only show my inability to serve You with fidelity, and time is running out.

I cannot fail forever, and I cannot be okay with being a "C" student at this too! Yet I lack the confidence to be sure I can overcome my sin.

And You have now through Your grace brought me into this strange and unique situation that defies logic but which I continually confirm as being from You. You do it to test me? Or am I damned and You are using me to sanctify another! That would at least give purpose to my life and my damnation. Will the other endure and is the other really for another and not for me?

If I am not damned, then why am I not given the graces to overcome the sin? Why do You leave me to the evil one? Why am I left to do what all say can only be done with the help of the Trinity? I believe in the God of Nouwen (see Vocabulary), but I do not seem to be able to be faithful to You as one of His Beloveds. If I am one of Calvin's damned then I am just Your robot. I need to know which I am my God. If I am one of Your sheep, then, Shepherd, show me the way to overcome sin and realize the joy of this unique Trinitarian Communion You have placed me in. Please show me?

Remind me, dear Lord:

- I am, as each is, the Beloved of God.
- Sin may always be with me, and it probably is the same sin.
- This sin may be deeply rooted in my psyche.
- But God forgives me seventy times seven.
- Each of us hears You in a unique way.
- But my heart is with You, wanting to pursue You.

Lord, help me to persevere despite myself, leave the evil one's lies behind and strive not to so much to be perfect as to be Yours.

Bob

Dear Trinity

> **Reflect on:** *Create in me a clean heart O Lord and put a new and right spirit within me.*
>
> —Psalm 51:10, NABCE

> *He said to him, "You shall love the Lord, your God, with all you heart, with all your soul, and with all your mind. This is the greatest and the first commandment. The second is like it: You shall love your neighbor as yourself."*
>
> —Matthew 22:37–39, NABCE

Come, Holy Spirit, fill the hearts of Your faithful and kindle in them the fire of Your love. Send forth Your Spirit and they shall be created. And You shall renew the face of the earth. O, God, who, by the light of the Holy Spirit, did instruct the hearts of the faithful, grant that by the same Holy Spirit we may be truly wise and ever enjoy His consolations. Through Christ our Lord. Amen

All praise, glory, and honor are Yours now and forever. Amen. You have blessed my life beyond my comprehension and understanding. I am simply and forever grateful. I believe, my struggles, obstacles, and opportunities on the journey are no different than anyone else's who has accepted Your invitation to embark on a journey of faith with You. The most incredible aspect about Your invitation is that it is extended to everyone absolutely everyone who has existed and will exist. Bless You! I love You, and my greatest desire is to continue to know and love You as I learn how to surrender my entire being to You.

> *Father in heaven You have given me a **mind** to know You, a **will** to serve You and a **heart** to love You. Give me today the grace and strength to embrace Your Holy Will and fill my heart with Your Love that all my intentions and actions may be pleasing to You. Help me to be kind and forgiving towards my neighbor as You have been towards me. Amen.* (Laudate 10-8-14, Dan Schwager, DailyScripture.net)

Love, how do we define it? There are many ways to do so. We have individual ideas of love and community ideas of love, God's love is family love—between a man and woman and children and extending to our neighbors. This familial love extends to all our brothers and sisters, creating a family whose desire is to give and show God's love through our actions, words, and through that indescribable quality of the heart. The heart that is newly created over and over as we surrender to You. The heart that is designed to freely give

God's infinite love to those we encounter. Within this family, God is our Father and each person is a member, our brothers and sisters, our neighbors.

I am grateful that my individual desire and collective family desire is to become a disciple of Jesus. "Becoming a disciple of Jesus means accepting the invitation to belong to God's family, to live in conformity with His way of life" (CCC 2233).

Following Jesus, being in His family, is not the easiest path to walk. It is a walk, a journey, a marathon race that provides us with light and life. It is a lifetime journey, a journey of a lifetime giving each follower the time and space to ask, to seek, and to knock and allowing Jesus to create in us/me a new heart. Recreating my mind, will, and heart daily so that I may have the grace and strength to embrace His will in my life, so that I may love others and forgive others as You love and forgive me.

Lord, teach me how to cooperate with You, as You and I together clean my heart. My imagination turns to the task of "spring cleaning" around the house. The kitchen is generally thought of as the heart of the home, so let's start there with the food pantry. It holds many items behind its closed door. Items that are used daily—others occasionally, others rarely—and there are items that are forgotten, hidden, overlooked, but nonetheless still there. I ignore them and decide I will deal with them later, but still, the items take up precious space.

I normally don't ask You to clean out my pantry; honestly, I would prefer another to do it for me. I enjoy a cleaned-out pantry because it is clean and shiny and seems new, and it is devoid of the items that are expired, dried up, sticky, and that are no longer useful. If I want a clean pantry, I must do the work to clean it out; it takes my time and participation. To keep it that way, it takes discipline and constant monitoring. This discipline and monitoring can be tiring and frustrating especially when I am constantly on the go. It is easier to purchase the item I need, use it, throw it in the pantry, forget about it, buy another one just like it, use it, throw it in the pantry, close the door, open it, close it, and never truly take stock of what is in there.

And then I realize that same type of behavior is mimicked in many areas of my life. Including within my relationship with You. I imagine locking the door of my heart tightly behind the sternum and rib cage of my chest. Even to the point of desiring to hide the door from myself so I don't have to see it nor open the door to view its uncleanliness. I become afraid to expose myself to You. You tell me "do not be afraid." Then I remember asking/begging You to create a clean heart in me, it is a bold, courageous, and humble request because it is Your desire to do so. You love me beyond my imagination. I recall the book of Hosea; he will do anything to win back the heart of his adulteress wife Gomer! Anything—he loves her so much. The book of Hosea is an analogy of God's love for His people Israel, for me, for us. He wants me back. He wants us back—all of who we are, not just the pretty parts or the good parts or the parts I/we desire to show You, but everything, the good, the bad, and the ugly. Your love is my/our salvation and redemption. Thank You, my Love.

I ask You, my Love, that I may be receptive to the ways You desire to clean out my heart. In my imagination with You at my side, us holding hands I reach into my chest, pull my heart out, lay it down in front of us, open its door cautiously at first then fling it open, and together we look in. We dissect it, we move things around, and we look around even into the corners like I would in the pantry. I ask You, "What items are in there that need to be removed that are not of You?" Items that are used daily, occasionally, rarely, forgotten, hidden, overlooked, yet are still taking up precious space like embarrassment, jealousy, envy, gluttony, pride, self-centeredness, vanity, anxiety, lack of trust, prejudice, perfectionistic tendencies, lack of forgiveness, old wounds—what is expired, dried up, sticky, and simply worn out "baggage" that You desire I be rid of. That I desire to be rid of. I turn and look at You, Jesus, and then allow You to look, I know You know they are there. I so desire to cooperate with You and let You remove them from me. It is work, it is not easy, the directives are simple, and the work worthwhile. Our relationships are worth my effort to surrender to You. So that my heart reflects You. So You can fill me with what is of You. So I am free to serve You with the gifts You desire to be within me and given to those in my family and community

I encounter: love, patience, gentleness, kindness, self-control, knowledge, understanding, and so much more.

Thank You, Lord, for being with me every step of the way as I place my clean heart back within my chest. You are the new and right spirit within me. May I never stop responding to Your love regardless of the times I stumble, trip, and fall. May I not be afraid of You and return to You over and over and over. May I believe You more than I believe the evil one that can lead me from You. May I turn to You always trusting You and Your ways more than myself.

Create in me a clean heart O Lord and put a new and right spirit within me. (Ps 51:10, NABCE)

I love You, my God and my Love,
Sherri

God Calls the Meeting

"But We Are Already in Attendance"

Reflect on: *As soon as you turned to me again, you see I was beside you.*

—R. Wise[11]

God seeks us first and in free will we respond. Then we seek God as we move into the journey as new persons. He meets continuously with us, often with no words or thoughts. We are often not sure when and where the meeting is with Him, but we do desire to meet in a way that obsesses: creating a thirst, a yearning greater than that of the "deer searching for running streams" of the Psalms or a man for that certain woman. We think of times and spaces, we think of agendas and formats and protocols. He is without the burden of time and cares not about agendas or formats or protocols. So without these burdens, He meets us, "where we are."

What a hackneyed and abused expression that is, but what else says it better? For all of us on the journey whether it be our first step or our last step in that journey, we try to organize our lives so that we are "productive" to fulfill the expectations of others concerning us. God, the only thing that really matters could care less. He has no expectations of us other than to really try to love Him with all our heart, mind, and body and our neighbor as ourselves. He has no schedule or agenda or meeting place. He wants us all the time. If He has us all the time those organizing words are not needed. He is ready to meet us whenever and wherever. We just have to show up at our forced appointed time, the time and space forced by us, not Him.

Now there is nothing wrong with plans, schedules and agendas because we mortals need them. He does not, and we should never think for a moment that showing our love for Him is trying to force Him into our times and spaces. He has as much time as He wants and if He has something to say to us He will take all the time He wants whether we have scheduled it or not. He will continue His dialogue with us and our souls even after our meeting time if He sole chooses. We may even not realize the meeting is still in progress and He may use everything at His disposal to talk to and with us outside the times of our scheduled meeting. He may use nature, man-made things, others, such as friends or not, and even communicate with our souls and hearts with complete separation from our conscious.

So He meets us where we are in time and space, neither of which He needs. As is obvious from all this, God, our Triune God, meets us "where we are," which really means to us that He meets us at every single moment of our lives. So whatever the conditions of our new person lives are at that moment it is where we are. Each moment for us is often a variable in reality and not a point of a series of constants. We may be in a time of consolation or a time of desolation or coming into or out of one or the other. We may feel the presence of God or we may be in the midst of a spiritual desert.

What we can say as mortals is that we and God are not where we have been or where we will be. God knows all this and can do whatever He desires as Creator and the "Omnipotent One." We, however, are forced to live in the moment, the current, the present. God and us—i.e., "we" in our communion of master and disciple—meet each other in the "now." So God meets us not where our old sins are or were but in the now in their state of being already forgiven by God and maybe even forgotten or unknown by us. Nothing can be done about them because they are no more.

In our minds, we may have a deficit list of sins that haunt us and we can never make up for, but this, too, does not exist. In the mind of the only one that matters—our Triune God— they are gone, forgiven, forgotten. If they do not exist in His mind, then why do they exist in ours? God deals with us where we are in the "moment," the "now," and in the future since the moment and the now for us and our response to it can help determine the future, already known by God. This is the only place where anything can be consciously and truthfully done, the present. So yes, we can worry about the future and about the past, but they do not exist in the only space where we can do anything, the present, which is now.

If He deals with us in the present, i.e. loving, forgiving, helping us in the now, then this is the only place where we can actually deal with others. We can love the Lord our God with all our heart, mind, and soul in the present only, and love our fellow man as ourselves only in the present.

Therefore, if we must assign time for our understanding as mortals, each and every day is a new start for us in our relationship with the Triune God and our fellow human beings. There is no old baggage of sins and their deficit that we have to make up. Only those sins of the moment and the day must be forgiven, and they are. God is always there, and sins are always forgiven if forgiveness is asked for, because Jesus, God Incarnate, died for every one of them and has freed us from their guilt. Since God is always present, then that asking on our part and His forgiveness can be at any time. With tools given by God through man, we are allowed to "examen" our sins at least daily. We have the celebration of forgiveness, for the forgiveness given by God for these sins, and then, the celebration of the already forgiven by providing the ceremony of reinstatement in the community of the faithful through the Sacrament of Reconciliation. In the relatively short time of the present moment and the moments that make up a day, the sins against the Triune God and one's self and fellow man are forgiven, in the past, and therefore cease to exist. But we are aware of where we have been with God, and this is not forgotten because it builds in relationship with God as we move forward in our life with Him. That is why it is so important for the new person to be aware of interaction with the members of the Triune God as the conscious is of the Holy Spirit flowing from God and His Son.

It is in the solitude and the silence of the moment that we meet God causing the forgiveness, reconciliation, and cleansing needed to move into the next moment of human time. How true then are the Scriptures, "Do not let the Sun go down on your anger." If you do, you compromise your search for God and you ally with the evil one. God forgives in the moment, and He expects you to do the same of yourself and others so that there ceases to be a past, a history you can do nothing about.

This continuous belief of the constant presence of God and our constant interface with Him in all of His Trinitarian persons graces the new person with the communion fellowship that will be "all" in eternity. As new persons, we must be aware of our actions and communicate with our Triune God continuously, i.e., without ceasing. We must do this in a time/space of each day, if not less, so the past is over and forgiven and forgotten and we can move on as renewed new persons moving down the path of the journey.

Let's not confuse our relationship with God in this communication of continuance with our interaction with our neighbor. God is always there, our neighbor may not be, and we may not be able to make things right within the length of the mortal day. But we have the obligation to make the event or thought forgiven and reconciled and then history. Certainly, we recognize that men and women process things equally but differently. There is a natural possibility and legitimate lag time for many women to process feelings as opposed to men, who generally do so more quickly, but the new person woman has this continuous relationship with the Triune God, whereby emotional response time may be longer than a day, the new person woman will not allow the lag so much time as to create baggage within either party. This lag is only with her neighbor. There is no lag directly with her Triune God on her part.

The key element in the new person's continuous communication, continuous meeting with God, is grounded in the new person's view of God. This continuous communication cannot be until the new person's view of God has become one of the real God, a God of unconditional love who is always there, considers each one of us His only Beloved, is always forgiving and seeks us in a never-ceasing invitation to meet with Him. If the new person has this view of God, then the new person in all aspects of their life uses all the types of prayer to hear God speak to them either within their defined time or space or in God's other space of continuous meeting. The new person then can mirror this relationship of God and himself to another human being and thereby show a continuous state of unconditional love in the mirrored image of God.

Then, while in our earthly home, we begin to see God not so dimly as in our mortal mirror but more clearly in the mirror of the new person who is always seeking and searching to meet God in all of His different ways of communicating and thereby always knowing that the meeting never stops nor does His unconditional love always manifest in the moment with no baggage from the past and complete confidence in His future for us. We live in the moment, completely forgiven, blessed, and graced by God who is always meeting us where we are at any given moment!

> *The prayer continues to pray within me even when I am talking with others or concentrating on manual work. The prayer has become the active presence of God's Spirit guiding me through life.* (Henri Nouwen)[12]

Mary's Role in Salvation History

Reflect on: *Elizabeth praised Mary's faith above all her other virtues, not her virginity.*

—F. Suarez[13]

Is it not interesting that Mary, the principal antagonist of the evil one in this world is so maligned by so many outside of Catholic Christianity and even by many in the Church. As a Protestant, I just ignored her. "So what?" I said. "The virgin birth is just another miracle of God, end of story, nothing special about Mary." Mary's absolutely critical role in salvation history is sadly not well understood by many in her own Catholic community. Even many priests seem to only give her credit for saying "yes" to the angel on only her behalf without any good theological explanation beyond that and then only see her as the object of pious veneration with little to no understanding of her significance. She has been called by those outside of Catholicism an invention of the Church in the Middle Ages, as someone adored by Catholics in substitute of Jesus and described by feminists as a weak and meek woman model for Catholic women as a pacifier for those angry because they are not allowed to become priests.

These maligned views of Mary are lies by those who are either ignorant of the truth or are unwitting or deliberate helpers of the father of lies. Let's remember that in all of Christianity, the truth, which is the Catholic Church, teaches that Mary's role in salvation history is unique among all humans in eternity. Mary, next to Jesus, the incarnation of God in His 100 percent man nature and His 100 percent God nature is the most important human being in eternity. It is not Peter nor Paul nor David. It is a woman, Mary.

The Church teaches that Mary's actions are critical and never point to her. She always points to Jesus. She never points to herself. She is venerated but never adored.

Mary was destined from the beginning of time to fulfill the role of the failed Eve and to succeed as the new Eve, the new mother of all. She was destined by God to be the mother of all those redeemed by the blood of Christ, the Theotokos, the Mother of the Church and our mother. Most fundamentally, she did say "yes" but not just for herself as the God bearer. She said "yes" for all mankind for eternity to answer the question that only she could answer, to say "yes" to the Triune God and to allow the Holy Spirit to conceive God as man in her. Mary was the only person in all of eternity that could answer the free will question because she was full of grace and without sin. That meant that she was not egocentric, self-centered, and would not look just after her own interests. It meant that she was able to clearly and rationally say "yes" for all of us. She was able to answer without the many self-centered influences that we, as people capable of sin, would entertain.

Mary's role in salvation history does not end there. Mary is the "exercise" of Christianity. Mary makes Christianity real and concrete instead of a philosophy or abstraction or some ideal. Mary gives physical human birth to the incarnation of the Triune God who is human in every way that she is and yet completely divine.

She keeps Christianity from being dualistic, i.e. body/matter is incompatible with the soul/spirit, by incorporating into one human body a matter which is Mary, and the spirit of God, the Holy Spirit, and producing the perfect incarnation of mind/body/spirit/soul in the Christ. In her synthesis of mind, body, spirit, and soul, she becomes John Paul II's "theology of the body" as the Theotokos of God, Spouse of the Holy Spirit, Jesus' human birth mother, Joseph's human spouse, Mother of the Church, spiritual mother of all people, and the "created exemplar" of all human persons.

Given her unique vocation in eternity, as Catholics, we believe that Mary is the mother of the Church. We believe that she prays with us and for us, and she is our advocate with the Father through her Son.

In her role as our model for Christ's disciples, she helps us to understand the conversion required by us through her Son as she continues to be the protagonist of the evil one, the new Eve, by denouncing egocentric orientation, the route of all sin and the gateway for the evil one in our lives.

In these continuing roles, she, though a mother, a woman, and the new Eve, as our model, bridges the gaps that we create in relationships and shows us how to "love one another." No matter what the circumstances Mary's role through deduction from a sinless manner clearly leads us to the model for righteous behavior with the Triune God and God's creatures and between God's creatures. Mary then, as a mother, bridges the genders of man and woman truly becoming both genders in her characteristics.

Thus in Marian Spirituality a different mind-set than is typical is required to truly see the model that Mary is to all Christians moving us into the type of Trinity-driven relationships that we are suppose to have with others. These relationships allow us to be able to "love thy neighbor as thyself" and allow us to receive love from our neighbor. This reaches its most fervent degree of holiness in the cross-gender Trinitarian Communion relationships that have been so wounded by sin as to seemingly be beyond our options, but which we realize through grace as so important for acceptance of ourselves and which we are most vulnerable in misunderstanding God's will in our lives. The Trinitarian Communion is the Marian/Christian foundation of all human relationships with Mary as the model—God, me, you, with all sides of the triangle always connected as we will see in later discussion.

Mary's capacity for communion with God was immense. She could exist and act independently of all other creatures. (F. Suarez)[14]

Untouched by sin, original sin, and all other sin...two highest faculties that man possess, intelligence and will, united themselves in our Lady with their proper objects, Truth and Good. (F. Suarez)[15]

Discipleship: Transforming into the New Person

The New Person

Reflect on: *It is this fully integrated Christian personality, the "new person" who is able to establish and maintain communal relationships in the building up of the "new community."*

—Fr. J. Kentenich[16]

All are asked to respond to God's invitation and say "yes" as Mary did, a "yes" to His free invitation of salvation and eternal life. There are many reasons why so many do not positively respond. Sadly, as we have noted, many do not listen and do not hear the invitation because they are focused elsewhere. Many simply do not believe. Others exercise this free will to say "no" at the present time, and they say "no." All are on a journey that will ultimately bring them back to God for His blessing or His judgment.

But there are those who hear God's call, embrace His invitation, say "yes," and pursue Him back to the Garden. These are what we will call "new persons." They are "new" because Jesus in the Beatitudes and the Sermon on the Mount tells us not to just obey the Law of Moses but to be transformed, converted into "new" people and to "live it" in our minds and bodies and most importantly in our hearts. We are asked to "be holy" as "God is holy," to change our "stony hearts into fleshy hearts," to love God with all of our being, and to love our neighbors as ourselves. Only through a decision on our part to say "yes" to become the new person are we able to do this and then only when we allow help from the Holy Spirit.

This decision requires us to be a completely new person. This is a hard task, a task that goes against much of our God-given human nature, a task that is counter to our society, a task that may turn spouses, family, friends and others against us, but a task not commanded by a charismatic leader or by a philosophy of living or by a messianic personality, but by Jesus the Christ, the second person of the Triune God, the only God, who created us and has our eternal plan in His hands. Becoming the new person is not a suggestion, not a goal, not a noble idea. It is a direct command from Jesus if we wish to spend eternity with Him, in other words,

> *"This is my commandment that you love one another as I have loved you."* (John 15:12)

> *"You are my friends if you do what I command you… This I command you, to love one another."* (John 15:17)

> *"You therefore must be perfect as your heavenly Father is perfect."* (Matthew 5:48).

And from Paul,

> *"Do not be conformed to this world but be transformed by the renewal of your mind that you may prove what is the will of God, what is good and acceptable and perfect."* (Romans 12:2, RSVCE)

We have to desire Him, we have to pursue Him, we have to follow Him 24-7 in the pursuit of perfection. We do not have to arrive at perfection, but we have to in every minute of our life strive for perfection. In return, He will give us His grace, which is happiness beyond understanding in this life and in eternity.

> *Through this unique response to God the person in concrete history becomes the bearer of a mission—to respond to God as a new person. The person is mysteriously taken into the inner Trinitarian life of God and thus becomes a partner of the Trinity.* [Sarah, Abraham, Peter, Paul]. (Sr. M. Naumann)[17]

The new person's transformed mission is to cooperate with Christ and the Holy Spirit in the work of salvation. To do this, we have responded positively to God's call, we have willingly begun the journey back to the Garden down a path that leads us there, following Jesus Christ as His disciples and having Mary as our guide. We have agreed to be transformed, converted over the rest of our lives in the pursuit of moral perfection.

But what does it really mean to be the new person? What are our characteristics, what is expected of us as individuals, how do we be faithful disciples of Jesus, how do we experience solitude, community, and service and how do we get to the place where we can love our neighbor as ourselves? Our following discussion will help us to understand that what Jesus asks is "doable." He would not ask us to do something we cannot do. He will give us the graces to meet the challenge as we pursue being the new person in our personal lives. The outcome of events is determined, the end is determined, as we surrender to Him we will succeed hand-in-hand with the Holy Spirit.

Loving our neighbor requires a radical transformation in becoming new persons. We have to really accept ourselves first, which allows for "self-transcendence" and real communion with another, with the ultimate focus being "what one would want most for the other in God's divine plan." The new person knows that he has a false self and willfully does not cater to it. "He possesses so much of himself that he can share it with another." This requires a true transformation in the mind-set that supersedes thoughts, words, and actions. This is only possible with the help of the Holy Spirit.

> *The change in mind set becomes one of acute mental change through the action of the Holy Spirit. It is "real" but not "okay" to be in constant mental combat (prayer allows this heroic virtue) with love verses discipline, although discipline plays a part. As we will say again and again,*

"Success in the Christian life is measured with the 'rule of love'." (Fr. J. Kentenich)[18]

He has surrendered to God with the intent of obeying Him and placing his life into God's hands each day. He believes from the bottom of his heart that God will do what is best for him. He yearns for God with all his being. He fears God in a reverent fear and a continual "awe." He believes from the bottom of his heart that he can with submission to God, with the Holy Spirit's active participation and with Mary as a model, become the new person, the new person commanded by Jesus. He prays to become the integrated Christian personality as is Mary our model and to think, feel, and do as Mary. He believes above all that in humility he will become strong!

This surrender to the Trinity allows him to deal with others as children of God. He eliminates the physical differences of humans (gender, color, age, ethnicity, etc.) as important and sees himself and others as "made in the image of God" without qualification or reservation. He is able to transcend the difficulties of cross-gender relationships through heroic virtue. He sees all relationships as potentially nuptial, i.e. bringing forth spiritual fruit. He is self-giving to the point of making it hurt.

The new person is on the journey and is being transformed continually in evolution of thought/word/deed. He may not be graced with the interior and exterior discipline to be transformed instantly into the new person. Awareness of transformation and conversion will become apparent as the grace of the Holy Spirit is allowed to enter the heart through prayer, Bible study, and spiritual reading and that there is a new way of living and a perspective that is necessary to live a life of love. He will seek it and want to embrace it. Frustration may enter and the evil one may play with him, but the new person will strive to think and feel and do as Mary, the same thinking and feeling and doing that is the new person being honed into Christ.

We have just experienced how the new person looks at himself in his most important relationship, his relationship with the Trinity. Now we will discuss how this foundation of God-centric relationship is manifested in his personal characteristics. These personal characteristics allow him to interact with others as the new person in ordered relationships with others, and how he relates in community and how he reacts in deepening relationships with others.

With these new person characteristics in mind, we then will discuss Trinitarian Communions in general, in marriages and in the evolved ultimate new person relationship, the cross-gender Trinitarian Communion. We are now at "love thy neighbor as thyself" in its truest sense!

The new person with his understanding of his complete dependence on God will pursue a type of persona that combines his mind, his heart, and his gut into thought and actions that are open and reciprocal in giving of himself. He is a strong but ordered personality. He is an independent thinker and is neither rigidly enslaved to form nor arbitrary in being unattached. He combines the characteristics of the Triune God, autonomy and heteronomy in the right mix. He is inwardly free so that he can express outer freedom. He has the freedom of his heart so that he is free from all that is not divine.

In his thoughts and words, he is inspired. In his words and actions, he is joyful and brings joy to others.

He is ready and willing to make decisions and carry them out. He does them in love, not for himself, but for the other. The "rule of love" determines his success in life and nothing else.

As we said, this is not automatic. It is hard work; it is training with the Holy Spirit as our coach, working directly but also through others. This requires and employs real discipline and love to become the new person but discipline evolves more and more into love as the main component of the thoughts and actions of the new person (like training for a marathon race).

The new person in his individual characteristics is mimicking Christ and His Mother so he does not have the luxury of being in solitude. His environment is community. God seeks to unite human persons to Himself in an everlasting relationship community formed by the Church. He does not move away from others. He does not isolate himself in his quest for God. He is part of a social and collaborative union with others and the Triune God. He acknowledges not only his own legitimate needs but also his relationship with others and the Triune God. This is the molding of a "new person" in a new community with the characteristics of "openness and surrender [submission]," in the reciprocal personal giving of oneself. The bond of love is between the I and *You*. This new community is

> *a perfect community based on perfect personalities, both of which are born by the elemental fundamental power of love, the new person is a personality who is independent, inspired, inwardly responsive and inwardly free, who is joyful, ready to make decisions, who distances himself equally from rigid enslavement to form, and arbitrariness that results from being completely unattached.* (Fr. J. Kentenich)[19]

Even new persons who are discerning a vocation or a lay apostolate are being molded in the same way by the Holy Spirit. The tendency may be to withdraw from the community and go it alone with God in order to be "holy" but even with this focus on *Thou* the Holy Spirit demands community, not just solitude.

As we summarize Fr. Kentenich,

> *Put in a negative way, the meaning would be that self-centered people will never develop character or a sensitive*

conscience because they tend to equate their real needs with what they desire according to the criteria of the pleasure of the senses and other criteria, namely the desire for created goods without reference to what is reasonable. To explain: Like the sin of Adam and Eve, some people can love themselves in a disorderly way, undermining their true vocation and sense of values due to their living by the pleasures of the senses (as in lust or gluttony) or even the spirit (as in avarice). St. Thomas shows throughout his writings that the foundations for undermining the moral life reduce themselves to false self-love flowing from either avarice and pride or unreasonably turning to created things and thereby, as a consequence turning away from God.

By contrast, a true understanding of the moral life means that the human person is created to be social and in collaborative union with others, including God; following one's senses, on the other hand, looks to self as the exclusive or primary measure of happiness, allowing personal pleasure to override the needs of others. A truer perspective means human personas must take into account not only their own legitimate needs but also relationships with other persons, including the Triune God. (D. Calloway)[20]

The new person's deepening relationships with others as seen in friendships has enthusiasm, yes, even more like passion for the welfare of the other based upon his freedom to do otherwise! His passion is ordered and governed by reason. His passion:

- fosters strong relationships with images and affections that are acceptable as ordered and morally good,

- shows love of desire for interaction with another that must in some way contribute to one's self-being but not be an extension of self-domination,

- should always incline one toward "good,"

- means pleasure as part of any relationship,

- shows real pleasure as suffering to do something for a friend.

His existing friendships with those who are not new persons change into a different kind of relationship that will either through grace transform the other and the friendship into a new form or compromise it into something less than friendship on its way toward death. The new person is on the journey, and he will not compromise himself in his faith. This new person persona is not crammed down the throat of the other. The new person is not trying to change the other into his own image but help the Holy Spirit to be more able to possibly reach the other. The new person's actions and interest in the welfare of the other will be the strongest witness possible. The new person with his characteristics will show clarity, truth, honesty, love, and true friendship for the other through the focus that the other is a child of God like himself and worthy of salvation. There will be no ulterior motives, no deception, no manipulation, no abandonment, and no periods of ignoring the other on the part of the new person. The other will see and sense that something is different no matter the length of the friendship to date. The new person will do all he can and leave the rest to the Holy Spirit. There will be intense prayer for the friend that is focused on the welfare of the other with no benefits for the new person.

How the other reacts to all the transformation is the other's response to God as seen in the new person. And through free will the other may react to the new person in many different ways. A true miracle may happen in the other, the friendship may endure and grow orderly, or the friendship may slowly dissipate. But the new person has brought God to his friend, the best gift of love possible!

In friendships, between two new persons on the journey the enrichment of existing friendships moves the relationship closer. Not just one, but both seek the physical as well as the spiritual welfare of the other. The sequence is always spiritual first since interior spiritual transformation manifest itself in love for the other in all ways at all times. With God running their friendship, both surrender in their common bond in a Trinitarian Communion. Each looks to God with the new person characteristics and their friendship moves from acquaintance and friend to spiritual friendship. We are now holding hands and helping each other down the path of the journey to the Garden with Mary leading us both. This friendship is now eternal!

> *Do not conform yourselves to this age but be transformed by the renewal of your mind, that you may discern what is the will of God, what is good and pleasing and perfect.* (Romans 12:2)

> *The "new person" requires a changed mind-set and is impossible to achieve without the actions of the Holy Spirit.* (Bob/Sherri)

The New Person and Surrendering to God

A Desire of the Journey

Reflect on: No one can serve two masters; for either he will hate the one and love the other, or he will be devoted to the one and despise the other. You cannot serve God and mammon.

—Mathew 6:24, RSVCE

As we continue on the journey in response to God's call and that call becomes clearer and more accepted in an interior way as the new person we begin to realize that we are being led by the Holy Spirit to surrender to God. Our heart begins to yearn to surrender to God in a complete and total way and to be obedient to Him above all else. We begin to feel in our soul a hint of the utter grace and joy that the surrender will provide. "Surrender" leads to obedience and the willingness through free will to want to be obedient, providing the potential ability to be free from sin and willingly exercise that freedom to obey God in surrendering to Him. Thus, the fostering of the "right relationship with God" as we see in our model, the Blessed Mother. In its complete sense,

To surrender oneself is more than to devote oneself, more than to give oneself; it is even more than to abandon oneself to God. In a word, to surrender oneself is to die to everything and to self, to be no longer concerned with self except to keep it continually turned towards God. (St. Therese Couderc)[21]

To surrender oneself, is moreover, no longer to seek oneself in anything for the spiritual or the material, that is to say, no longer to seek one's own satisfaction, but solely the divine good pleasure. (St. Therese Couderc)[22]

It should be added that to surrender oneself is also to follow that spirit of detachment which holds to nothing; neither to persons nor to things; neither to time nor to place. It means to adhere to everything, to submit to everything. (St. Therese Couderc)[23]

This may not happen early in the journey and takes perseverance, fortitude, and spiritual and physical courage. We will have had to change to the point of being truly sincere in surrendering to God. It is not a matter of "wanting to surrender" or trying to "make it happen" or "wishing it." God has created the desire in our hearts for Him and nurtures its development if we are willing to get out of the way. When we truly surrender, we become indifferent to what others think about our transformation and we let these concerns go.

This surrender may not be quick and complete. It is usually a form of conversion that may even extend into eternity. But we desire it and we attempt in sincerity to achieve it above all else no matter where we are in our conversion. We have a deep desire to surrender! God does not seek the completeness of our work in process, but He does seek our desire and continued desire. We seek unity with the divine through surrender. We may still have many sins and challenges but our goal never moves from the desire for that unity.

This extraordinary and supernatural surrender is most closely spiritually and physically approximated in sexual intercourse of man and woman in the Trinitarian Communion of the marriage vocation. And emphatically, it is only possible in the context of a man and woman in a Trinitarian Communion of marriage when both are seeking God and are on the journey in response to God's clear call.

The woman, of course, better understands this extraordinary occurrence of surrender physically and mentally because of her ability to completely surrender to the male in sexual intercourse. Her complete sexual surrender to her husband is in true sincerity when she is being herself as a woman of God and not when she is faking or coalescing or manipulating. She is giving herself in freedom to him in an utterly and complete way.

Her surrender is extraordinary and supernatural in nature. She cannot come to surrender with her own notions and abiding in her own ideas. She has committed before God to surrender these in complete submission without reservation.

In a Trinitarian Communion, the man does not experience surrender in the sexual act, yet he does give himself in a total and supernatural way. Yet God comes to the male through the woman by her showing him the grace of surrendering completely, as God asks him to completely surrender to Him.

The man sees the woman not only surrendering to him in love making but in all areas of life. She surrenders to him in total belief that he will love her unconditionally and always do for her what is in her best interest. Her surrender will allow her to always willingly defer first to him any of his natural male responsibilities. Even when the male causes a fracture in the Trinitarian Communion marriage and veers from the journey, the woman will try to defer to him first those things that he should handle and only take those responsibilities on herself when he fails to do his duty.

As a new person, she will always try to keep the relationship with God intact even if the relationship is broken between the man and God and/or her and the man. In a valid Catholic marriage, she may be most likely not willing to dissolve the Trinitarian Communion through divorce even if the Trinitarian Communion seems to be destroyed with no real hope of recovery. She is well aware of how she has contributed to the destruction of the marriage.

Stuck as she may seem to be, she may have to pursue the journey, physically separated from her mate and emotionally meld with Trinitarian Communion friends to acquire the right relationships for her journey. She must then attempt do all she can to keep the line of the triangle between her and her husband intact in the way of "one being on the journey" and pursuing God. This requires her to forfeit her desire for a Trinitarian Communion marriage in a way foreign to her inclination to surrender.

In this situation, "she" must also enter into the suffering of Christ on the cross in her own way. She will have to look for spiritual companionship in the body of Christ as a whole and in individual relationships within the body of Christ. And of course, she must pray for the conversion of the spouse, knowing that her efforts may be to no avail.

The new person man has her, his spouse, as his example of the surrendering that he himself must give to God. He achieves this through complete mimicking the confidence in God that the woman shows in her confidence in her husband. A complete confidence that shows complete trust in God to take care of him and do what is best for him always. This only deepens the hunger and desire for God that the man in the Trinitarian Communion already feels—not unlike the sexual hunger he feels for the woman. The man shows his obedience in his response to God in his vocation to the woman, in his falling on God's mercy for his difficulties in moving down the path of the journey, in the confessional and in the obedience of the Eucharist.

This surrendering either for the man or the woman in lay vocations of any kind requires us to come before God in complete nakedness. There can be nothing between us and God either physically, emotionally, or spiritually. For the committing of a mortal sin is as to God in our personal relationship with Him as is adultery is in a marriage.

As we willingly surrender to God and become naked before Him to do His will, we become aware of a gratitude that surpasses understanding. It is a "thanksgiving" for our state, a state of peace in the love and trust of God that brings us closer to the understanding of our eternal heirship, a thanksgiving not unlike the Trinitarian Communion lover feels in thanksgiving for the unconditional love of the other. This thanksgiving is a realization of the divine graces that come with surrender. Our path's ground may continue to be rocky at times, but we feel in our souls that God's future for us is all that ever matters and gives us a feeling of freedom from our egocentric alternative. This is the result of the desire; this is desire for divine unity.

These graces received in thanksgiving that are so overwhelming moves us to a deep conversional feeling that "God is with us" and that although our journey leads to death and heaven it also provides the benefits of the heir ship of salvation in this world. We are allowed to feast on the graces of God that surpass all understanding and we do so in this life as well. With surrender and with willing obedience to God, we enjoy complete freedom in living the wonderful life given to those who are His disciples.

As to our personal place in eternity, we can only hope in God and God revealed through Scripture. Not one of us can be sure of how we really measure up in the eyes of God. We can hope only that His love for us, so great that He sacrificed His Son, His gift of free will to us and our response will give us eternal rest in His company.

We alone influence our personal relationship with God and His redeeming Son. We are told repeatedly in Scripture that the "gate is narrow" and few pass through. All are called without reservation, but so many refuse to give up their selfishness and surrender to Him.

When we think of surrendering, we always think of a loss of freedom in being ourselves and making our own choices. But the freedom we are relating to surrendering is a freedom from slavery to our self-centeredness and sin. We have the freedom to do God's will. That acquiescing can only come with a complete trust in God that He will always do what is best for us and bring us to the best version of ourselves that we can be on this earth and bring us to eternity with Him.

We accept God and the supernatural on faith and belief. This is verified in our lives in multiple of ways that are faith- and belief-oriented since most of us never see God or experience the supernatural physically and directly. However, through at least faith, we can understand our relationship with the Trinity through our soul and intellect to be the heritage of St. Thomas when Christ told him that more blessed than he was those who would never press their fingers into the hands and side of the "Crucified" but believed anyway.

So through faith, as if we had experienced the supernatural ourselves, we are transformed into a new understanding of freedom. This freedom to do God's will surpass our instinct to want to do our will. With this freedom of the new person, we now can in all aspects of our life "do God's will." And we now want to do God's will above all, even above our own will. We are then free to begin the transforming journey and move to loving God unconditionally, as He loves us unconditionally. We can now have the ability to love others unconditionally as we are loved unconditionally. This is the new psyche of the new person—total surrender to Him, the total acceptance of unconditional love from the Creator, and the willingness to give up things in our life that keep us from doing God's will and to do so without reservation, even to the point of giving up people or things that are really "use" for us or dependency for us and which it would seem our dependence on them is crucial to our existence as a functioning person. We now experience freedom as never before because we "trust" in the Triune God in a way not possible before, in a "supernatural way" because we know that God will take care of us no matter what.

As the new person, we will not reach perfection ever in discipleship, but we must try in desire and effort. We must try to surrender, we must try to obey, and we must try to do so willingly. And always understand that God never meant for us to walk alone; He is always our enabler—we can never do it without Him. In the end, we surrender to God having total faith that He will save us from our sins even if our "trying" does not reach perfection.

For others who are not new persons, who have not listened or who have rejected the heard "call," we can only hope and pray. We simply do not know nor do we have the right to speculate and to judge. That is the Triune God's domain alone. We only know that the gate to heaven is a narrow one, and it takes faith and works and all of God's graces, love, and forgiveness to make entry even remotely possible.

But there is also a narrow gate in this world, and "we can know" the results of deciding to go through or not go through that narrow gate. Free will is our ticket for the gate. The ticket has already been purchased for everyone by Christ. We just need to decide to use it or not. If we choose to use the ticket we have to surrender to God, leave our egocentric nature outside the gate, and be obedient to His will, with a willing and loving motivation. Once again, we need not to be perfect, but we must "want to be perfect" and strive to be each and every day. This gets our ticket punched, and we go through the gate with Christ. Going through the gate means we receive all the graces, happiness, and all the freedoms we have discussed—*and in this life*! Now life is fulfilling because we are pursuing the very reason we were put here to begin with—"for the glory of God"—for a surrender to our Creator for an eternity with the Triune God. Fear is gone, worry is put in its proper place, purpose is realized, and we are "new persons in Christ"!

If our love of self, our disordered view of freedom, our disobedience, runs our hearts and minds, then we are once more barred from the Gates of Eden. We have made ourselves too wide of self to fit through the narrow gate! We have selected ourselves out! We continue to pursue falsehood, false gods, our false self, lust and coveting, self-importance, and somehow we never feel quite right, we never feel happy, we are never satisfied. Is it the gate that is narrow, or are we the ones that are narrow? In reality, have we actively worked at keeping ourselves outside of the narrow gate?

> *God desires the least degree of obedience and submissiveness more than all those services you think of rendering him.* (St. John of the Cross)[24]

> *It is utterly false to oppose freedom and self-surrender, because self-surrender is a consequence of freedom.* (J. M. Escriva)[25]

> *God's love is a jealous love. He is not satisfied if we come to meet him with conditions.* (J. M. Escriva)[26]

Key Characteristics of the New Person

Obedience and the New Person

Reflect on: *So, by one man's disobedience many were made sinners, so by one man's obedience many will be made righteous.*

—Romans 5:19, RSVCE

Obedience follows from and is the visual (hidden or not hidden) manifestation of our surrender to God. It tests our degree of desire and truthfulness in our yearning to surrender to God. Surrendering is different from the intention to surrender. Intention leads and is a precondition of actually doing something, i.e. are the actual acts of surrendering within the context of free will (freedom). Christianity after all is a religion of discipleship where we have the freedom to believe to follow a man we believe to also be God. Our God-given freedom allows us to choose or choose not to believe. But if we believe this we are obligated to follow and obey. Jesus being God only ramps the stakes as we follow a single being of divinity and humanity. As surrendering, obedience is not a one-time moment of agreement to obey but a continuous opportunity with a willing heart to obey or not.

As a disciple, we are by definition to obey our master. We freely choose to obey. We choose to convert ourselves so that we hope to eventually be the "do whatever He tells you" imitator of our Blessed Mother, in right relationship to our master, our God, and being Him to all we meet.

This obedience to God that continually allows us to surrender to the will of God for us is not a reluctance based upon an if or then or fear proposition. It is based upon a freedom to love our master and do His will always. The willingness to obey is based upon a desire on our part for complete love for and trust in our Triune God. Only then, through this surrender, can we feel completely confident that God will take care of us always.

Is there a "rule of sin" for Christians? Do we only admit to our sin if it is a grievous sin? Do we not admit to the sin if it is not grievous? We are kidding ourselves, aren't we? Deliberate venial sin is never okay with our fellow man or our God. To think other is poor logic and dishonesty with our soul. We are supposed to love God. He knows everything; why think we can lie to Him? Obedience is not just avoiding mortal sin!

Since obedience provides us with a continual opportunity to surrender to the will of God through choosing to do His will over our will it is part of our conversion process that never ends. As with any other aspect of "being on the path of the journey," we will encounter obstacles and times of failure produced by ourselves or our submission to the evil one. The seeds God throws to us and those we sow may fall on rocky ground and our obedience may not reflect the degree of surrender of Mary's "do as He says." But a willingness to "work on" being obedient and doing so not with a sense of obligation but with love and a grateful heart shows we have never really left the path.

Obedience shows us how far we have come in surrendering our life to God and overcoming our egocentric focus.

> *Obedience, then, is a key virtue; if we obey God it is enough; everything else follows as a consequence. Moreover, obedience is nothing more than the fulfillment of the vocation proper to creatures, for every creature has been made to give glory to God; that is what constitutes his whole raison d'être, that is the purpose of his life on earth: that and nothing else, not even salvation, which is itself only a consequence. The first sin in the world was disobedience…It was through obedience, on the other hand, that reparation was made and hope could return to the heart of man, for it was through obedience that Christ saved us.* (F. Suarez)[27]

Obedience assumes the ability and willingness to listen to God so we can understand His will and be obedient to His will. To do this, we have to be in a state of surrender or trying to surrender. We have to be moving beyond our self-centeredness. We have to be open to however God chooses to communicate His will. We can move quickly down the path to listening by taking notes from our Blessed Mother and "do whatever her Son tells us (prayer, scripture, Mass, etc.), obey Him willingly, be ready to do anything, obey promptly, silently, fully, not only with our will but also with our intelligence, with our heart, putting our whole being into it—as she did, as He did.

> *Although he was a Son, he learned obedience through what he suffered; and being made perfect he became the source of eternal salvation to all who obey him.* (Hebrews 5:8–9)

> *What was demanded of her was truly superhuman grandeur, a limitless, absolute and blind belief in the word of God in relation to the incarnation and everything associated with it. This was a hugely great act of faith!* (F. Suarez)[28]

Change and Being on the Journey

Reflect on: *The authentic person will find in his inner depths indications of the presence and operation of the Holy Spirit.*

—T. Dubay[29]

The new person on the journey is implied change! There is nothing new here in the context of the new person. Change implies a stop and a start in behavior. All want to change, "but…I" I have these obstacles that are unique to me and that I have to overcome. I want to change, "but…"

Reality is that despite desire, "change" will be the reason some will not be on the journey. It is sort of like the parable of the seeds. The change can be the seed that falls on fertile ground of one engaged with the Holy Spirit, or it can fall and begin to happen but the demands of the world become more important than the journey and the change never happens. Just the "idea of change" in its reality when one has to can destroy the journey before the journey begins. Change is hard, and in the back of our minds, we ask ourselves whether we can ever really change in the manner required by our Savior and actually stick with it. We fear our shadow self that lies in wait.

Discomfort in our life often brings us to the journey or I should say "that God often brings us to the journey," using discomfort in our lives as the motivator. This discomfort before the journey usually results in a temporary state of comfort. We may even become complacent with the new status quo and loose some of the first momentum of the journey. However, once on the journey, a status quo is a feeling of being uncomfortable since we will never finish the journey while on this earth. For one on the journey, the change is often subtle revelation of our understanding of God's view, bringing us slowly more close to Him.

The initial euphoria of realizing we are on the journey evolves into a different type of effort that is necessary to remain with the initial enthusiasm but in a very different way requiring a different type of effort in prayer and in our relationships with the Church and those around us.

In the Trinitarian Communion relationships of marriage and non-marriage, we see changes in each new person happening over years. Does the enthusiasm of the first day's relationship continue always? Adrienne von Speyr would suggest that we should strive to maintain that day-one euphoria of marriage or conversion or non-marriage relationships. How do we do that? Is this challenge doable?

What matters is not the discomfort but how we respond to this discomfort as new persons on the journey. How do we respond to God's changing our lives and to those people who make changes to our lives, especially if they are change agents of the Holy Spirit? The change is indeed subtle but continuous, resulting in a change in attitude that results in a change in many practical experiences in our lives. We may not realize or appreciate these subtle changes. Hints come to us by what others say to us, which challenges our interior orientation. As noted, the change will not be 100 percent, but it will be significant to us if our interior allows us to look at our environment objectively.

One change that comes about very gradually is an evolution to what we might call "loving honesty." We must remind ourselves that to be on the journey requires us to act in a truthful manner in all walks of our lives, be that a walk with ourselves or a walk with others. Being on the journey means that we have to deal with reality, our own and others, where we and others are at and often reality hurts.

Loving honesty allows us to interact more truthfully with those we meet and particularly with those close to us. That includes our ability to admonish others if we truly love them, our neighbors. As Ezekiel and Paul well told us, this is expected of a Christian and expected of the Church. This is very difficult for most of us. We do not feel comfortable since we know all too well that we "cannot throw the first stone," since we can be as fragile as glass.

If we are on the journey and as we allow God to change us, we have a frame of reference that overcomes our fears and self-love to the extent that we are even able to more comfortably love our neighbor even to the point of helping them on their journey when ordered admonition is required. Ordered admonition being "doing things in a selfless environment with our love focused on the other." Therefore, with an ordered and self-less approach to admonition, we seek out the questions that make the other feel comfortable in discussing the circumstances and move with them, not ourselves, toward an understanding of how God asks us to resolve the problem.

Our Lord used parables to admonish, allowing the parable to convict the sinners to different degrees as was right for each of those listening. He admonished through invitation to the sinner to do what was right as opposed to just chastising and bringing to life the sin. He loved the sinner and hated the sin, which is the only court in which we can play as new persons.

Loving honesty starts in our heart and is a by-product of the journey. What makes loving honesty work, be it in a ordered relationship with any others in our lives or be it in an admonishing role, is the helpers that the Holy Spirit sends us along the way to remind us that when we love our neighbor that helper can be anyone!

> *Conversion is susceptible of degrees, and so therefore is the attainment of the divine mind.* (T. Dubay)[30]

> *The indwelling Lord leads us into all truth* (John 14:26; 16:13) *in diverse ways and degrees.* (T. Dubay)[31]

Adaptability as the New Person

Reflect on: For though I am free from all men, I have made myself a slave to all, that I might win the more…I have become all things to all men, that I might by all means save some.

—1 Corinthians 9:19–22, RSVCE

"Change" could be thought as a generalization with specific thoughts, words, actions, etc. being the actual change agents. "Adaptability" is also generalized in nature but closely related to the concept of change and specific change agents. Changing to the new person requires the right kind of adaptability to a whole host of environmental variables. Adaptability makes us aware through ordered comparison of how we are the same or different from the characteristics of the new person as well as how we are the same or different from others on the journey and from others in general. As new persons, we are to look at everything with the eyes of God.

What are the new person's characteristics of adaptability? The new person will have to adapt to a new way of thinking, a new way of looking at themselves, possibly a new view of the Triune God, a new way of looking at the Church in the world, a new way of viewing hope, a new way of interacting with others, a new way of continuing on the journey, and a new way of dealing with the things we meet along the way or perceive while on the journey. "Change as a concept" can be disruptive to many but "adapting as a result of change" can turn one's daily life on end.

Adaptability can be disordered or ordered. The assumption is that if we are talking about the new person, then adaptability should be ordered and coming from the Holy Spirit, i.e. adapting in a way that is acceptable to God. We show ourselves to be children of God and neighbors to our fellow men in a loving way. We are adapting to a life that is surrendering to God in obedience in a Marian way, i.e., in a selfless, right-relationship way. As with our Blessed Mother, we are adapting to God's rule of our lives, no longer asking Him to adapt to us.

One of the difficulties in adapting to our new life requires us to change both our spontaneity in response to others and our frame of reference or legacy of dealing with others. The deep internal factors affecting our spontaneity to others may not all be known to us, but many may be apparent. We react a certain way to our gender or the other gender, other races, those from other geographic areas and those in other social stations other than ours. These reactions when we meet another are subject to our control simply through our deferral of any reaction. Perception in spontaneity may prove to be completely wrong. Adapting means we deliberately forget our old spontaneity of initial response in favor of a more loving, less-guarded response. There is no room here for prejudice of any kind in the new person.

We also must be aware that we imitate ourselves. Our legacy of action in spontaneity may no longer be appropriate. We deal with all in the same way despite former habits and perceptions.

We adapt in an ordered way to different personalities, different mannerisms, material environmental factors such as heat, cold, water, food, time changes, routine changes, etc. This requires our orientation to shift at all times away from ourselves to others even in the briefest of spontaneous interactions. None of these factors should ever lead us to sin or near-sin. Adaptability requires us to give up some of our self to be with others in the new frame of mind.

And it is not just a matter of adapting to being a new person and adjusting. It is adjusting through adapting and liking it. God has us where we find ourselves for a reason. He is just training us to be adapting to new goals and expectations regarding today's situations and the next life.

Adaptation is a Marian Spirituality executive; through humility, we adapt to others without compromising an ordered view of ourselves, and we become strong in our relationships and in our ordered influence on others as did Mary.

Expectedly, at the heart of the adoption of adaptability is overcoming our self-centeredness, our false self, our disordered ego, and replacing these with a focus on the other, the exercised loving of the other, the loving of our neighbor. This allows the overwhelming flow of love from the Trinity to flow through us to the other creating harmony. We simply on a daily basis begin to see God in all others without real thought or personal strategy. It does not make us foolish or weak or naïve; it simply creates a union between two persons that allow us to really see the other person for what they are, perfected or flawed, but as they really are and then we can be God to them, we can be Jesus to them, we can bring our self-centeredness and give ourselves to them as a gift.

We seek the daily tranquility that is possible and that existed during the "quiet years in Nazareth" (a Marian theme) between Joseph and Mary, and man (Mary) and God (Jesus). This perfect model is our model for speculation and meditation on how our relationship with Christ can be as new persons and how we can be Christ in our daily lives.

As at Nazareth, that mutual existence (mutual adaptability) with God does not have to be continually a heroic virtue or a battle with ourselves and others wanting to not do God's will. It can be one of near continuous harmony. Given the grace of adaptability as a true change agent in our lives the new person should be able to better interact with God's plan for his/her life. And as that occurs the relationship with others, new persons or not becomes easier no matter the circumstances. The new person through adaptability creates a non-tense environment in all situations achieving even in the most difficult situations a greater since of harmony.

Mary was natural. Being natural is not so much in making great efforts to avoid attention, as in behaving as we are, doing what we should do in whatever situation we happen to be in even if that attracts attention; for it is not a matter of hiding or disguising anything, or of deceiving in order to avoid the limelight. (F. Suarez)[32]

To the Jews I became as a Jew, in order to win Jews; to those under the law I became as one under the law (though not being myself under the law) that I might win those under the law. To those outside the law I became as one outside the law—not being without law toward God but under the law of Christ—that I might win those outside the law. To the weak, I have become weak, that I might win the weak…. I do all for the sake of the gospel, that I may share in its blessings. (1 Cor. 9:20–23, NRSVCE)

Commitment and the New Person

Reflect on: Commit your way to the Lord; trust in him, and he will act.

—Psalm 37:5, RSVCE

Commitment is, "to pledge or assign to some particular course or use—a promise, an engagement, an undertaking." This implies that action takes place and that there is something "to do."

Until a certain point, those who have heard the call of God, the invitation to seek Him, have been moving from an invitation manifested by the Holy Spirit, to hearing the Holy Spirit in our hearts, to a conceptualization of the "new person," to an analysis of the "new person," to a movement toward action contained in our discussions of change, adaptability, pride, etc., to now a "pledge" to do specific action. In his heart as he initially responds to the call:

> *One who has answered God's call may have to live [what seems] a long time in dryness, in spiritual darkness… he must not lose certainty of being on the path indicated by*

the call. It is not possible for someone to answer God's call and for God not to hear his answer. (A. von Speyr)[33]

Catholic Christian commitment means "action" on our part, being the results of free will to pledge to God effort that will result in a greater closeness to God and a better love of neighbor. In our context, it is a "sacred pledge," a conscious effort needed, a monitoring of day-to-day actions. It is fostering a closer communion with God through the corporate activities of the Body of Christ through attendance or increased attendance at Mass, all types of prayer both public and private, Bible study and meditation, involvement in other sacramental and non-sacramental Church activities. The underlying commitment is the faith that we are on a journey ordered by God that we have freely accepted and that we will be on that journey and committed to that journey as long as we are on earth.

Commitment disciplines us while we evolve from discipline to love as the motivator of the new person. Eventually, this commitment will become more commonplace in our lives and require fewer struggles and less organization on our part.

Commitment needs to be a conscious plan to begin with. The commitment means to be faithful to the plan. It orients our life in all its facets and gives structure to the journey. However, commitment is not a solely human characteristic of the new person. The Holy Spirit is there all the time, making the commitment supernatural by making the exercise of the commitment not a burden but laced with a foundation of joy that gives us daily graces.

As a new person, what is the "commitment" to? What is the specific undertaking asked by God? What is the "action"? Yes, of course it is to do God's will. But how are we to know God's will? We have to admit to some knowledge of God's will for our lives given to us in Scripture and tradition. We can study this. But to do God's will are we asked to be "obedient" to God in doing the will of the Scriptures and tradition. Is this enough, to do what we know, to follow the Decalogue, the Beatitudes, the expressions of how to love one's neighbor in tradition or are we asked to do more? Are we asked to go with "what we have and are certain of," or are we asked to go further? Are we asked more correctly to "surrender" to God, i.e., to "surrender unconditionally" to God in order to do His will and in the process to learn what His will is even in the "not yet known" as well as in the "given." Is there a difference in obedience and surrender? What was Jesus really asking of the rich young man?

Even as new persons are we able to be obedient to God? Are we able to surrender to God unconditionally? As new persons we should guess, even early in our journey, that the answer is "no" in its most complete response if we are relying on just, "our God-given humanity." But with our humanity, we can strive toward and somewhat be obedient and with this plus the Triune God's Holy Spirit we begin to approach the possibility of a "surrender." Through the will and human effort, we begin to be obedient as we respond to our Triune God:

> *Without the strength and infallibility of the Word who became man for us, we would be unable to obey God. The Word makes us obedient. The Word shows us the divine will. The Word gives us the infallibility of faith, of the Christian way, of the way of mission, whatever form it may take.* (A. von Speyr)

Through obedience, we begin to understand that the will to obey brings us to surrendering to Him to do His will:

> *As von Speyr suggests we have to adapt ourselves to God, not God to us. We must give up control and let Him take us where He may over a life time of conversion as we slowly journey in prayer and action toward a change in our internal being through the fruits of prayer. We attempt to adapt perfectly to His divine will. To accomplish this we must be willing and have the attitude to strive toward the center of His will and not be inclined to veer off of center in our lives. Even our thoughts which are not sinful in nature but are maybe not oriented to God must leave us if they are not pursuing life internally and externally the accomplishment of His will in our lives. He will form us more expeditiously and more completely only if we are willing to stay in the center of the path of His will.*

Jesus's teachings are not based on human criteria so that humans may not be able to judge themselves but on criteria that must be discovered in that which God requires of us.

The new person will show commitment to obedience and surrendering to God in his life not by being without sin but dealing with it as concupiscence and a state of our fallen nature. It is how he deals with sin that matters. Mary teaches us how to avoid sin and how to forgive others for their sins, the Holy Spirit nurtures us on how to handle the sin that we are bound to commit whether saint or Saint.

Sin can never be "good" because even from just a hedonistic view of animal joy associated with the sin, it is fleeting at best with always the result being depressing. But if the cycle of sin, judgment, and redemption teaches me something then the redemption and even the judgment help me (grace despite myself) and I have maybe moved along the path. Maybe the message is that I am more vulnerable than I thought despite my assumed sanctity…i.e., I still need God as much as ever or even more than I am aware of.

We each are inclined to sin in some specific ways, i.e., we are more susceptible to certain sins giving the evil one a more easy way in. With hope, which we never leave our sins, will not make us give up or fail to work at the journey. We have time, and the journey will put us into many different positions. Somewhere we might fail, and there is no helping us to do better. It is our effort, the getting up that shows commitment to perseverance. Our attitude at this point will play a big role. If our attitude toward people or things we don't like is allowed to be used against us by the evil one, then we fall flat or stay in a period of spiritual desolation. As St. Ignatius of Loyola warns us, we should not be surprised if even after a period of good and long spiritual consolation, we fall flat on our face. God is trying to show us that we must be on our guard, a guard that does not have to be negative but can be a positive "on our guard."

The new person is committed to be enthusiastic, positive, committed during times of desolation, and to not be surprised if he sins but to move forward after sin—always with a sense of personal responsibility, the Sacrament of Reconciliation and the attitude to be the positive side of the new person and the journey.

We should never despair if we fall off the wagon into our particular sins despite our desires and our best efforts. Jesus died for our sins, every single one of them with no exceptions, and that allows us to always be constantly falling but never lying prone but getting up again to continue on the journey. The commitment is that we will remember that we remain the child of God, the Beloved, and that we will persevere in trying always!

The new person lives an unceasing personal commitment buoyed by "prayer as the executor." (More on this in a later discussion.) This unceasing commitment becomes his very self:

> *Regard faith as something living, as something that daily*
> *makes new demands upon our whole life. Day by day,*
> *God's love is bestowed on us anew so that we, too, can give*
> *it anew to God and neighbor.* (A von Speyr)

Our personal journey then becomes not unlike Dante's in Virgil's great work. As we move up the mountain from the depths of sin into the journey, which is purgatory, toward living a more holy life and becoming more intimate with God we move toward the world to come.

Along with our personal commitment as new persons come more formal opportunities that God may call us to be in special commitments to Him or to another.

> *One seeks a sign, some human evidence, forgetting that*
> *a vocation is not simply a natural fact but, rather, a*
> *supernatural reality.* (Bob/Sherri)

As vocations our commitments become focused and our life somewhat structured for us by the demands of the calling itself. The call by God to the priesthood or the religious life takes on a supernatural identity and a supernatural support that stands apart from the vocation of marriage or the demands of the lay single life as new persons. Here the personal journey of the new person intertwines with a very special supernatural grace to bring Christ to His flock through special mortals. The commitment is eternal and the grace is eternal. There are no other options when we are called so specifically by our God. We surrender, we obey!

The Trinitarian Communion forged in the Sacrament of Marriage is the life-long free will human commitment mirroring the commitment of Christ to the Church. As with the commitment of Christ to the Church, our commitment in marriage is until "death do us part." This vocation truly requires our best human effort of discernment of vocation as well as discernment of companion. We may make the mistake of thinking this is within the realm of our human God-given abilities. But it is not. More so than so many things in life we need God here in both the discernment and the choice or else we condemn ourselves to the results of our own sins of self-centeredness.

So commitment brings graces and graces bring happiness and all come directly from our Triune God. We just have to listen for the call, embrace the call, and bask in the graces of the commitment.

> *Is there actually good to come from the human standpoint and the spiritual life from sin? Does God expect us to sin despite our very best efforts? What sins did our Christ die for? Isn't there growth in spiritual life from the cycle of sin, judgment and redemption? What are we committing to do?* (Bob/Sherri)

In Dante's Divina Comedia Pilate is found crucified in the lower levels of Hell. Those who are thought worse of are those who do nothing. (Bob/Sherri)

We are asked to give ourselves completely to God, not the part that is convenient. (Bob/Sherri)

Ordered Comparison and the Sin of Pride

Reflect on: As God's chosen ones, holy and beloved, clothe yourselves with compassion, kindness, humility, meekness, and patience.

—Colossians 3:12, NRSVCE

Comparison is a natural and ordered part of the human existence. We all do it. It is done consciously and unconsciously. It is the human way for each one of us to determine where we are in our community of species. It helps us to see improvement or regression in many aspects of life as well as give us good insight in our survival against others of "our self" and others in our environment.

Comparison can be ordered or disordered. How we view ourselves and others and our environment determines whether our comparison orientation is ordered or disordered. This comparison view of our world will often determine how we interact in it therefore it can be an aid in our conversion to the new person or a hindrance.

For the new person ordered comparisons must be based on personal honesty. Honesty with ourselves about who we really are is essential. This is not just a matter of evaluation of our outward characteristics or a review of our lists of sins. But it is more of an attempt on our part to understand if we are able to make the evaluation, i.e. we may have, "conscious emotions" as noted by Keating that have been with us from childhood that obstruct our ability to look at ourselves with any degree of honesty. We don't have to be able to make a list of these initially, but we do have to have some understanding that there may be something there that inhibits our relationship with God and with others.

Why do I strive for communication with God but seem to have great problems doing it? Prayer is a means of communication with God. As with human communication, there are misunderstandings, struggles, frustrations, clarity problems, and love and joy that we encounter along the way. As we begin to be open and experiment with prayer, we begin to learn and be comfortable with our individualized invitation from God to be in communication with God, i.e., prayer. Through a life of disciplined prayer and experimentation we have a greater desire to open ourselves to the gift of contemplation.

The new person may not be completely successful in determining what these unconscious emotions may be. Over a period of time, we may, if we are honest, seek comparisons that allow us to still be on the journey and have some insight into what these conscious emotions may be. We then can pursue God in our spiritual life through comparison of our spiritual life with those of the Saints, with the characteristics of one on the journey, with Scripture, and with the Catechism's ordered spiritual behavior. In addition, we have our Lord Jesus Christ, His Blessed Mother and St. Joseph as the supreme examples for us of ordered comparison.

All these sources give the new person the information they need that is imperative for them to make a comparison with the characteristics of the "new person." This is ordered comparison and is spiritually healthy. Our only caveat is being sure that the sources of ordered comparison are from our Triune God, not our egocentric consciousness or the evil one. Comparison with the Church's teaching and our spiritual experience when we listen to God, must take place in order to verify the message is from God. Evaluation of success in spiritual matters requires the feeling that resources/abilities come from and are gifts from God and not necessarily of favoritism by God.

Comparison must be positive and evaluative for the new person instead of prideful in order to properly interact with self and others. Pride disorders comparison. Pride in a disordered way comes into play when, despite our outward mode of humility, we hide a heart that is prideful. We are always just a little jealous down deep inside of what others do and God's blessings for them even if their successes in spiritual life are not connected to our interests.

Even in positive ordered comparisons, the new person may slip into the sin of pride by perceiving that they must help others in their spiritual lives because they falsely assume that they are in a relationship with God that allows them to do so. This disordered perception of their spiritual relationship is deceiving.

Perceptions

Perception divides and honesty unites. Our perceptions may cause suppositions and actions that are based upon our view of another that seems clear to us but is totally incorrect. We must care enough to honestly know about others and not perceive them into hell in our minds. This is spontaneous disordered comparison at its worse. Even if our perceptions of the other pans out to be partly correct. This is pride.

The truth, reality, and honesty unite while perception divides! As new persons, we must never perceive until we have dialogued enough of the truth to do so. Then we can focus any ordered comparison onto the only objective—the love of others as we love ourselves.

As we are sure from God's messaging that we are making progress in our spiritual life, we can never ever forget that success means greater responsibility for us and greater responsibility to others—action for the welfare of others should always be the result! When we think we have arrived, we haven't.

Arrival in the theme of the new person happens when we are able to truly "wallow" in the success of others in spiritual and secular matters and ally a real thrill with their success! But knowing that we are on the journey really does bring a sense of peace that is different from the sense of pride, yet in a subtle way that is ordered and good. Comparison in order to help others, reverently and humbly, not pride fully is the new person remembering that our joy is always in the "other" if we are on the spiritual journey.

> *Each person is a Beloved Child of God and worthy for salvation in their own right in the eyes of God, the only eyes that really matter.* (H. Neuwen)[34]

The Dichotomy

In Becoming the New Person

> **Reflect on:** *A new heart I will give you, and a new spirit I will put within you; and I will take out of you the heart of stone and give you a heart of flesh. And I will put my spirit within you…*

—Ezekiel 36:26–27, RSVCE

Maybe I am trying to stretch the thought too far and enter the realm of rationalization for actions past taken but also maybe God over time transforms us from our previous way of dealing with issues, i.e. maybe "there is spiritual progress." Maybe that progress is not apparent to us. Maybe we missed God passing by.

Often our false self and persona may be to our liking and the way we see ourselves. If that persona is in our heads as being the proper approach to interaction and problem solving, then when our actions are inconsistent with that persona, we doubt our actions. We may not readily see that maybe a different tact of action is God speaking to us in a very profound way, and we are doing His will and not our own! It may be that we can only see ourselves in the light of the persona that makes us feel more comfortable and makes a better impression on others. It may have been with us a long time and inbred.

We may have liked to see things as more black and white in our heads because we fear that we really prefer the gray in our hearts. We have to live in blacks and whites, or we become victims of universalism, which is negated by an abundance of Scripture. God has given us blacks and whites because they are universal, and there is good and evil to contend with. If it were not so, then why free will and why have the evil one? There is also fear of not going the black and white way, the safe way, and the negative results that we are told will happen if we go gray.

Therefore, if my outward persona is to try to do what is right, i.e. what is white, then I will demand certain behavior, certain social situations, certain judgments, and certain punishments. However, the incongruence comes when that persona is not my heart, not what God has planted in my soul and is actually my applying my cherished norms to others and not to myself! The incongruence is from the gray heart trying to tell me that these universal norms of black and white, of right and wrong are applied by God and not applied by me. I am not capable to apply them to anyone else for every situation that appears because I have not been successful in applying them to myself first. I am only able to deal with God in my personal state of belovedness. Not being God I cannot evaluate or judge the state of others' belovedness relationship with God. God is able to take the gray and make it black and white, i.e. black and white, as He sees it without fuzz and without slander but with love and forgiveness.

So, so what? Well, when I act in my comfortable persona, I can be "strong" in the way we humans define it and properly judge others for failing to do the "obvious right." This allows me to be my persona and use my control and power over others to punish them by separating them from myself and from others. After all, the Ten Commandments from God Himself back me up. We have the right in many roles to righteously punish those in order to help them change their behavior. We may love them and want what is best for them, i.e. to be good people in my "right." I am quite capable as a male to deliberately and premeditatedly wield power over others. I am quite good at it. I am smart and know how to win "for the glory of God" and myself.

However, if this persona and my ability to wield it in all its facets is not the same as my soul, then am I being righteous, in the "right relationship with God"? Am I at odds with God's progressive spiritual work in my soul and in my life? Maybe I perceive my false self as my true self or maybe I feel that the real self, formed by God in my heart, is too weak for "my liking."

As the new person, what I fear and pray for at the same time is that my actions in dealing with others in very difficult situations such as drug use, violence, evil possession, deliberate sin, adultery, co-habitation and rejection have come not from a desired persona or false self but from the molding of my soul by God. God has sent Mary with her many gifts to help us understand that we are not the judge of all the Beloveds. The Holy Spirit is the one that brings the graces of Mary to our souls and hopefully our actions. Instead of being "strong" in the world's sense we are compassionate, loving, kind, welcoming, community building, inclusive, and very prayerful. Our actions though seemingly weak in these very difficult situations of sin really produce strength that is in the "right relationship with God." The outcome of the "strong actions" may have been a good course of action and lauded by our fellow men but may, as we know in the back of our minds, also have kept our ego and persona in good shape ending in disaster for others.

But with another, however, the Holy Spirit has brought us the spirituality of Mary to our hearts. Maybe we did not necessarily recognize it at the time. But our actions resulted in lives moving beyond drugs to faith in God and membership in the Church, to good relations with others both family and not, to the establishment of a Christian family, to a will and enthusiasm to live as God wants, to the defeat of the evil one in real battle, to a good home for an innocent child, and to a deepening in our own faith of God's perseverance in our own lives and His refining of our souls as we pray without ceasing. This is true strength and our real selves. This is the succumbing of the ego to Christ! Hail Mary!

The New Person and Daily Life Experiences

Skirmishes with the Enemy

> **Reflect on:** *Put on the armor of God so that you may be able to stand firm against the tactics of the devil. For our struggle is not with flesh and blood but with the principalities, with the powers, with the world rulers of this present darkness, with the evil spirits in the heavens. Therefore, put on the armor of God, that you may be able to resist on the evil day and having done everything, to hold your ground.*
>
> —Ephesians 6:11–13, NABCE

A new person on the path of the journey seeking the Triune God will be a prime target for the evil one. The new person is now subject to an entire world that prior to answering God's call, he may not have acknowledged. This is the supernatural world where a war is raging between God and Satan in a realm we do not see and can only poorly imagine. But it is a real world, and there is a war. We are engaged in the war, but most of us choose to not believe in it and we discount it as superstition. If we disallow this reality, then our lives will often have the effects of desolation in ourselves and in our relations with others, and we may not ever have a clue of what is really happening.

We are pawns in this war, and we are expected to choose sides. We are either consciously for the Triune God and followers of the Second Person, Jesus Christ, or we are consciously or unconsciously allied with the evil one. There are no fence sitters. The outcome of the war is never in doubt to the Christian, but the end is not yet and the war rages on.

Much of the war that is being fought on earth is within us. It is not psychological and cannot be explained by the sciences because it is beyond their realm of understanding. It is spiritual. As new persons, we are committed to obey God and our destiny is clear, but while we are on the path back to the Garden, we will have to fight many skirmishes with our age-old enemy, the evil one, the devil, the legacy of original sin who will pull us away from God and the path with the desires of the flesh, concupiscence, and the seven deadly sins. "He" will use images and our imagination and disorder these in our minds. "He" will disguise sin as goodness or as apparent pleasures to lure and hold us if possible. "He" will make our heart heavy while on the journey in relation to God; he will use hopelessness, darkness of the soul, move us to low and earthly thinking, tempt us with gratifications of the flesh, use our past failures to depress us, make us lazy, and give us a lack of confidence in ourselves and God.

As new persons, we defend ourselves in these skirmishes by first being aware that we are in the war and that skirmishes will occur and are part of our role as God's Beloved and servants. Our Triune God has given us weapons to use in these skirmishes. Our Baptism gives us the Holy Spirit, the power of Grace, the Son and the Father in Eucharist, influences that lead us to God and the holy angels with the power of God, as well as entry into His fortification against evil, the Church. Against the dark attacks of the evil one, our consolation comes in the "uplifting movement of the heart," inflamed with God's love for each of us as His only Beloved and forgiven. We have hope, faith, confidence, and interior joy that attract us to heavenly things and the things of salvation. This consolation quiets our soul from the battle with the enemy and gives us peace in the Creator and Lord.

We are speaking of skirmishes not necessarily major overt battles in the spiritual war going on in the cosmos. That means that these skirmishes are what might seem at times unimportant little exchanges. But do not be fooled if we do not engage at all or do not win the small skirmishes of life we will then lose the major battles in our lives and betray God in the process.

But as new persons in the reality of daily life, how do we know how to overcome the assaults by the evil one on our hearts and minds? How do we prepare for the skirmishes and how do we know which natural and supernatural weapons to use? How do we win the skirmishes for God as "soldiers of Christ"?

Most importantly, we turn to our Triune God in prayer and ensure that prayer is the "executor" in our life. This is the foundation of the new person.

With the gracious gifts that God bestowed on St. Ignatius of Loyola, we are given the additional insight into the nature of these skirmishes in order to understand the Holy Spirit's strategy and the strategy employed by the evil one. We learn the moves and countermoves of the evil one and the moves and countermoves the Holy Spirit gives us against him. We begin to train ourselves for our interior and exterior spiritual battles. And the battles will come! They will rage continuously.

St. Ignatius teaches us in "Discernment of Spirits" that we routinely have alternating periods of "spiritual consolation" and "spiritual desolation." Even sometimes they overlap as they move one to the other. The cycle rarely ever stops in the life of the new person. We must understand what consolation and desolation are, and we must be able to discern which period we are in at any given time and be able to discern when we are moving from one to another. Which period we are in and to which period we are moving gives us the strategy and tactics that we must employ to combat the evil one.

Spiritual consolation is a period of joy in the mind, heart, and soul. We experience an uplifting movement of the heart in our lives. We have an interior disposition of peace no matter what life might have for us that day. We are inflamed for

Christ, and we have an increase in hope, faith, and charity. We seek more heavenly things in thoughts, readings, attendance at Mass, we more objectively feel that we are God's Beloved, we feel His ever presence, and we feel forgiven. We also may receive nonspiritual consolation from the beauty of God in nature, through friends and even through the well-being we receive from activities like exercise.

Contrary to periods of spiritual consolation, periods of spiritual desolation provide us with main obstacles in our path while on the journey. We feel a heavy movement of the heart in our relationship with God. We feel hopelessness and a darkness of the soul. We feel our interest move to low and earthly thoughts and pursuits, and we tend toward the gratification of the flesh. We may be slothful and not tend to our responsibilities in life. We feel unloved during this period, by God and often by others, and ourselves. We feel separated from God, less beloved, and we doubt His ability to forgive us for sins since we view ourselves as wretched as we loathe ourselves and have no confidence in our ability to surrender to God and do His will. Our depression makes us feel physically tired and irritable.

There are also nonspiritual sources that affect us during this period of time. Depression may stem from a lack of sleep and rest giving us a foundation for gloominess. We may not even feel like praying during this period.

We must be aware that some nonspiritual desolation is normal and is not sourced from the evil one. Nor is this period of spiritual desolation a "dark night of the soul." It is as if an alternative cycle of thoughts very opposite of the period of spiritual consolation.

The problem arises when we do not understand that we do not move from one period of spiritual consolation or spiritual desolation automatically and without effort. The evil one will try to keep us in the period of spiritual desolation or false consolation where he has an advantage in winning the skirmish and can bog us down further by lengthening the time of the period of desolation. We want to win the skirmish in the period of desolation and move forward with haste on to the period of consolation where we have an advantage over the evil one.

St. Ignatius in his Discernment of Spirits teaches us the tactics that the evil one will use to try to defeat us in the skirmish. He also teaches us the tactics that we must employ to defeat the evil one.

During a period of spiritual desolation, the new person must employ tactics that thwart the tactics of the evil one. The first tactic is to continue everything you are currently doing in your spiritual consolation life. Never make a change during a spiritual desolation period. This is when change will be used by the evil one to subvert you. He will now have a change element on his side that he can possibly disorder. There should be absolutely no exceptions to this.

This is the time to especially seek the aid of nonspiritual elements such as sleep and exercise and make yourself tend to your temporal responsibilities. Concerning the spiritual this is when you do not miss Mass. Use the four tools: prayer, meditation, examination, and penance.

First, pray for God's help. Add to your prayer time and seek opportunities to pray.

Meditate on the truths of the faith. Draw from your own arsenal of spiritual weapons to use against the evil one, including favorite hymns, private revelation, pondering the life of Mary, and sacramentals. In meditation, remind yourself that you have been here in past periods of desolation and that God has always helped you come out into periods of consolation. See this as an opportunity to rely on God and draw closer to Him. He is always there to help and forgive. Ponder what God is trying to say to you during this period of desolation and what can you learn from this period. This discernment is the invitation from God.

In examination, try to work backward to understand how the period of desolation got started. What happened to bring it on? Can you do something associated with whatever brought it on to help you out of the period of desolation?

Use penance to counter the desolation. After the sacrament of confession do small and suitable penances that bring you away from your self-centeredness that the evil one so loves and brings you back to an orientation to others.

Above all, be patient and trust in God to help you out of this period of spiritual desolation. You may feel the heaviness of the desolation, but do not give up. The truth is that spiritual consolation will return. And God may have treasures in store for you when it does. Remember the past times that God brought you out of desolation into consolation.

You have the tools that the evil one fears. You have awareness that you are in a period of desolation, you understand what is happening, and you are taking action while being patient in order to counteract the desolation. Remember, "The cross on Friday led to Easter Sunday." As with salvation you cannot do works to get you out of this period—you have to do your part, but the Holy Spirit and all of heaven has to be there to guide and direct you through your executor of prayer.

"Spiritual desolation allows us to see spiritual consolation when it comes and remain humble about it." In spiritual consolation, our very soul is lifted up, and we experience joy and peace spiritually and in many other ways.

During this period of consolation is the time to prepare for the coming of the next period of spiritual desolation whenever that may happen. God never gives us spiritual desolation. We make it happen! Therefore, as new persons, we strive especially during this consolation period to train ourselves in the characteristics of the new person so we are ready to shut down, avoid, or minimize our movement into a period of spiritual desolation.

We do not let our self-centeredness get in the way of our relationship with God and our neighbors. If we stay focused on "the other" and the "Thou," we will be better suited to ward off the tactics of the evil one and not create actions that lead to a period of spiritual desolation.

In addition to tactics, there are a few important points that are in order in reference to periods of spiritual desolation and consolation.

- To repeat, spiritual desolation does not come from God. It comes from us and our sins.

- Why then does God allow us to go into spiritual desolation? God uses our own failures and sins to move us into spiritual desolation to train us to struggle against temptation, to be less self-centered and more neighbor-centered, and to show the faithfulness of God. This is the skirmish, the winnowing in the fire that makes us the new person.

- What causes spiritual desolation? We are usually slothful or tepid spiritually, we may be being tested through trial by God to help us learn and become better disciples, or to give us true recognition and understanding that all is a gift of God so we are not prideful and we grow in His love as new persons.

- The length of the periods of spiritual desolation and consolation cannot be predicted, but God is always there in the middle of it with us.

- The evil one will find and attack us at our weakest point in our spiritual life.

- The evil one is no stronger than a spoiled child. If you oppose him, he will flee with his expectations. We must stand firm from the beginning of the period of spiritual desolation, or it will be harder to defend against him when there are more temptations. When there are wrongful thoughts, "we must dash them against Christ with prayer."

- We must not go the journey alone through spiritual desolation and consolation. We must have someone or many to help us such as a spiritual director and/or a spiritual friend that can fight in the trenches with us when we need them. Remember, this is not what the evil one wants. "He" wants you to go it alone and hide your sins so that he can bring you down and weaken you. He wants you to keep secrets, particularly if those secrets hide sin or difficult personal situations. The Sacrament of Reconciliation and spiritual direction break the spiritual silence and wins the day against the enemy.

As we noted, it is not possible to predict the length of a period of spiritual desolation or consolation. One important aspect of these spiritual periods is that there is not a clear demarcation between the spiritual periods. One may flow into the other. You may be in a period of spiritual consolation and also without realizing it, be slipping into a period of spiritual desolation. You may be slipping from spiritual consolation to spiritual desolation, realize what is happening, and take action that with prayer it will lead you back to spiritual consolation. In any event, it takes diligence and continued spiritual awareness to progress in seeing these fluctuations in spirituality coming and going and to act accordingly. The more the new person allows prayer as our executor to manage lives and the more we strive at having the characteristics of the new person, the more we will be aware of the skirmishes of our spiritual life and the more we will defeat the evil one on the battle field of spiritual warfare.

> *The enemy will attack you as you experience conversion and do his best to inhibit your purification by using yourself against yourself through upset, sadness and other human emotions making it harder to pray and to stay on the path.* (Bob/Sherri)

> *To our own self be true as God sees us and has called us to be.* (Bob/Sherri)

The New Person's Daily Guide

- I want to do God's will in my life. I want to surrender to Him and be obedient.

- Be full of gratitude to God.

- Honor God throughout the day by being aware of His presence.

- I pray for help from the Holy Spirit to continually

  o think, feel, and do as Mary as a guide to daily life;
  o think that differences in others do not matter;
  o want what is best in the eyes of God for the other and self;
  o be self-giving to the point of making it hurt;
  o embrace the entire person in marriage. Never let courtship end. Love the whole spouse.

- With those close to me, do not be the following:
  o Pouty, bickering, petty, verbally abusive, unpleasant but be joyful, pliable, affectionate, forgiving, and amiable in resolving conflict.

- o   fight but discuss and listen.
- o   be a creator of a tense environment but instead work well with others.
- o   an ego driven person.
- o   "use" others.

- Know God comes to man through the woman and a woman's beauty is the acceptance of the graced role she has been given.

- Overcome my false self and personal deficits—physical, mental, circumstantial.

- Do physical and spiritual shape/training—exercise, eating, Mass, prayer, confession.

- Be real but be joyful and enthusiastic; remind yourself how good God has been to you.

- Do not compromise faith; judge with love.

- Keep diligent to ordered spontaneity.

- Maker ordered comparison.

- Be adaptable, pliable, compassionate, loving.

- Remember your commitments and keep them.

Note: This list is not meant to be exhaustive.

Influences Affecting

the New Person

Important Influences in the Life of the New Person

Reflect on: Therefore we must pay greater attention to what we have heard, so that we do not drift away from it.

—Hebrew 2:1, NRSVCE

As we evolve along our unique path to being new persons there are many pieces of pebbles, stones, boulders on our path to the Garden. These impediments ineffably slow us down, bog us down, run us off the path, and seem to confirm the lies of the evil one. These are personal and interpersonal issues that we have to deal with as new persons, i.e., in the way that Christ and Mary would deal with them. We must get them behind us and continue to move forward down the path of the journey.

These impediments often spring from "influences" in our lives that find us and challenge our new personhood. They are huddled around the most important characteristics of the new person, humility and the control of egocentric thoughts, words and actions. Our ability to love God above all else and to love our neighbor as ourselves is influenced by many factors that affect our mind and heart. We are influenced to various degrees in our ability to be less self-centered and to have the ability to love God, love our neighbor as ourselves and become Holy as we are required by Christ. These influencers may be major factors in allowing or denying God's grace in our lives. We are influenced in our ability to love ourselves in an ordered manner and therefore be able to love our neighbor as ourselves.

We are influenced by the following:

- our view of God and how we interact with a Tri-une God;
- our view of ourselves, i.e., our self-view and self-love;
- gender relations;
- our view of the Church from the parish to the Vatican;
- our view of and interaction with other Christian faith traditions and the secular world.

In the next few sections, we will discuss these influencers and the associated influences that they imply both as enablers and impediments to the commands to love and to be holy. Some will be major and others less so with each influence having the capacity to be either ordered or disordered.

> *What are the foundations of our influences that affect our listening and response on the journey as we seek God and ourselves as new persons? What keeps us from saying with clear heads and hearts,* **speak Lord, for your servant is listening?** (Bob/Sherri)

How Self-Love Affects Our Relations with Others

Reflect on: Do nothing from selfishness or conceit, but in humility count others better than yourselves. Let each of you look not only to your own interests, but also to the interests of others.

—Philippians 2:3–4, RSVCE

The "*greatest hurdle*" we have to overcome in seeking God is ourselves: "To thy own self be true and find truth or by thy own self be destroyed for eternity." Our self-view is often the domain of the evil one in his spiritual warfare with our souls and the Holy Spirit…his battlefield being our interior psyche and soul. There is no secular psychological analysis here. This is about our relationship with God and ourselves and real spiritual warfare. And this is about our vulnerability to one of our greatest human fears—"rejection," the evil one's infiltration of our psyche.

All else aside, if we are not narcissistic, we all experience rejection in some way at some time, and the memory of that rejection may never really leaves us. And as hard as we may try, we may never quite recover or heal from that wound.

Rejections come in so many different ways. Why do I not receive credit for what I do? Why must I always feed other's egos? Does anyone care except God? Does He even care? And then we experience the ultimate rejection of being ignored and as well as the always present components of loneliness rooted in rejection.

We all continually seek acceptance and affirmation from others and we often do not receive it in the manner in which we desire. And we are rejected by others sometimes just because they have a self-image that due to a frame-of-reference or schema does not allow them to be comfortable with us. We also place norms such as age, sex, etc. in the way of acceptance of others.

Often, fear of rejection and all of its corollaries is the underlying basis for our view of ourselves and is the justification for selfishness and self-centeredness. It affects our relationships with others but is misguided as a determinant of our behavior.

Self-centeredness leads to deception since we cannot live up to expectations. We deceive ourselves and others to protect ourselves.

We are influenced by so many factors in determining how we are to be accepted. But we do deal with and really prefer reality to deception, even well-intended unconscious and habitual deception. Deception is just another form of rejection since the truth is shunned for good or bad in favor of creating perception.

Perception is often wrong no matter how good our training and can never be really relied upon. How often in life do we receive reality from others and how often is it presented in a loving manner? Perception, a form of deception for the perceiver, is often used to circumvent the truth. Perception always divides and often draws unclear and false conclusions about others. Spontaneity, adaptability, commitment all enter into our perception of ourselves whether in the context of the new person or not. But honesty and truthfulness are reality and unites to overcome rejection.

Interactions, i.e. relationships, are more difficult if we are deceptive for any reason at all. Our new person demeanor while on the journey provides the reality of truth and honesty to others that we "are truly on the journey." Perception divides but the reality of truth, and honesty shows through to unite.

The televised fictional story of the serial killer Dexter is the ultimate example of deception—He knew who he was and deceived others by deliberately doing things that were deceptive to create an exterior that was not himself. We do the same in many ways to be accepted by others and to be who we think we should be to be accepted. We even deceive ourselves in our relationship with God, and in relation to ourselves and in relation to others. We deliberately bypass the reality of truth and honesty about ourselves.

And of course, so often, this leads to or becomes true crisis when rejection is by the other gender. Within close same gender and particularly between genders is where we find our ultimate personal rejections, often caused by our failure to agree with our own intuition about the other and ourselves. We succumb to enormous pressures from society to think differently in relationships even when our intuition tells us something differently. When this intuition is really the Holy Spirit speaking to us and we do not even know it, we may be on a true collision course to interpersonal disaster, particularly if we are dealing with cross-gender relationships. If we fail to bring the Holy Spirit into it we fail to bring reality and we continue to waller in egocentric piety and deception. The inward sin of non-acceptance then will manifest itself in ways of subtle outward evil toward others possibly couched in humor. Our canvas begins to paint our own portrait of ourselves as it did of Dorian Grey, showing a deceived and distorted view of ourselves.

As Christians seeking God on the journey, we may react in two very different ways. When we have not forgiven ourselves or we are unable to put rejection issues and failures (another form of rejection) behind us, we allow our interior feeling of frustration with ourselves to manifest itself in exterior extreme forms of piety, inadaptability, and comparison/judgment. This is further influenced by our failures, our short-comings and sins… especially those that we cannot seem to change even as they continue in our lives.

Our myopic view of ourselves we believe to be necessary for self-preservation and defense. We are helped along the path by past comments from parents, siblings (less so, due to natural rivalry), teachers, spouses, gender groups, and electronics. We feel that we must attempt to prove externally to ourselves and others that we are "well with God" and "well with ourselves" through the rejection of others as a result of rejection of ourselves.

However, in another reactive way, we easily seek to give up on ourselves, God or others as a way of avoiding an interior responsibility. We may become more egocentric and protective, becoming exteriorly liberal in our approach to our self-view and life, our fellow man, the Church, society, etc. We want no condemnation of the behavior of ourselves or others. We want no judgment. We become relative in our approach to life and our exterior prostrations may become either verbal and/or physical and are hostile toward the sacred. We become cynical and bitter by nature in dealing with all—all in an attempt to transfer our guilt/responsibility for our interior life away from ourselves. We question all to prove that we are "okay" ourselves.

And the evil one is so quick to throw in reality, "Can we really ever overcome our selfishness?" Besides, we are not Mary. But in the Beatitudes, Christ commands us to do exactly this! We know it is possible, and we are bold enough to ask "how"? How do we get beyond selfishness to be on the journey? How do we change the perception of others about us? How do we deal with our self-images when people we deal with are so self-centered themselves?

When and only when we begin to divest ourselves of an egocentric focus on our way to becoming the new person do we begin to also divest ourselves of the lies of the evil one about ourselves and begin to embrace who we are not in the context of our own psyche and those of relatives and others but in the face of God. If we can wrestle with and begin to believe that God loves us above all else, that we are His Beloved, that we must give up our selfish nature and surrender and obey Him in order to be happy, then we begin to be less concerned about the past and the present lies about ourselves.

If the new person is focused only on God and the welfare of others and surrenders to Him and wants to obey Him and relinquish control of their lives then the Holy Spirit will provide the supernatural transformation. And the person with all the negatives will have the negatives cease to exist over time or at least to diminish over time. During this journey over time happiness will replace selfishness. We are seen by others through this internal transformation leading to external transformation as being truly believed to care about others because we are seen by others to have truly moved beyond ourselves. We relate better, we are in better community, we are respected and respected because we have moved from "I" to "you" to "we." True Trinitarian Communion love slowly destroys the interior selfishness of denying one's self-worth.

Eventually we are so free of such a degree of selfishness that we see God's creative beauty in every individual. This is a discernment given to us by God as we experience Him through the other.

At the epitome of this grace we see true love for another without personal ego and selfishness with the possibility of transforming into true love for a "we" of the other gender either in marriage and/or in spiritual friendship. Thus love for God, by God is mirrored in human love that moves beyond ourselves. There may even be a "unique one" in which we see beauty through our unique eyes that involves the Holy Spirit in an ordered way with virtues as the core.

But the ordered ego is not gone as we become new persons. It is simply ordered in the way that the Holy Spirit has molded it. Our body is always a temple of God. Therefore we do have responsibility to maintain it as best we can until we are called home but we are not to do this in a disordered way. We must love ourselves in an ordered and healthy way. We must love our neighbors as temples of God themselves no matter who they are. We never possess God or another's body but we do love them as God's creations.

Thus victory over our greatest hurdle of ourselves lies in a God who sees us as a unique special Beloved and transforms us at our request into one who is oriented to God and the other with humility. Then and only then can true peace and acceptance of oneself be possible, only then do we begin to truly love ourselves and reject the lies of the evil one and only then do we find happiness in ourselves through others.

> *A healthy self-denial sensibly practiced and rightly motivated slowly lifts one out of his egoism, laziness, hedonistic inclinations. We are fitted to receive the clean light of the Spirit.* (T. Dubay)[35]

How Self-Love Affects Our Relations with Others

The Right Relationship with God

> **Reflect on:** *God is actively present…to be attuned to it and to allow God who is only love to be the source as well as the goal of all we think, say and do.*
>
> —H. Nouwen[36]

To be in the right relationship with God we have to understand and relate to a Triune God. Our view of the Trinity may be a reflection of how we view ourselves and our view of ourselves may vastly be affected by our view of the Father, Son, and Holy Spirit. Our view of ourselves and particularly our view of ourselves in relationship to the Trinity can affect our ability to relate to a God concept that has the ability for relationship. This relationship may greatly affect our journey back to the Garden.

Our deist secular society often negates the God of relationships. After all, if we have to have relationships with our Creator, we may have to be personally responsible to our Creator. If relationships are not possible between man and God, then why do we need a personal relationship with God Incarnate and His mother? We become unitarian, and we, in our spirit of fair humanism, become universalist.

But whether society acknowledges it or not, God is still the center of what is good and beautiful in society as it was in ancient and medieval times. Even today, we should be happy with what God has given us in the context of ourselves. As the new person, we are called to make the most of what we have in relation to God as our barometer and not society as our barometer. Remember as Catholics we believe that as in Scripture, we are created "very good" and through the new Adam and the new Eve we have been redeemed from the Fall. Despite rapid technology and the material upgrade of the human condition we in matters of divine and human relationships are no different from our ancestors for centuries. This means that we still can be "holy" as our Father in heaven is holy and through continual conversion become saints and disciples despite the humanist, relativists, and progressives. We can actually "love our neighbors as Christ has loved us."

The Church, teaching only the truth of our Christian Triune God for two thousand years, teaches that each one of us individually is the Beloved of God as if we were the only human being on earth. God Incarnate died for each one of us individually. God is always with us, trying to do all He can to bring us to eternity with Him. We are not only biologically unique; we are spiritually unique and just as our Blessed Mother's DNA ran through the veins of our Incarnate Creator so we are sons and daughters of God. The new dispensation is the true image of God in Jesus Christ, the one who Mary knew and loves. He is not, "a God of wrath" who is continually trying to separate us from Himself. We are neither a "depraved race" nor people that cannot hope to be more than "snow (Christ) on dung." We can be as our model, Mary, in the right relationship with God. But only if one chooses to hear the invitation and starts the journey.

On the journey we now have a God yearning for us to find Him as we yearn to find Him. Just as Mary daily dwelt with Jesus we daily accept God's presence with us no matter what. His Holy Spirit is our constant companion. He has always been there but now we know and may feel Him personally. Things of great importance yesterday are of less importance today. We now begin to see the beauty of God in our hearts and the potentiality to see the beauty of God in all others. One on the journey sees oneself as not a solitude unique piece of matter but sees oneself as always a communion of others in relationship to oneself and in relationship to our Triune God in a true Trinitarian Communion, a communion of relationships that always include God. This Trinitarian Communion then begins to slowly erode our interior selfishness by denial of our disordered self-worth by replacing it with a "Child of God," saved and eternal.

This unique Child of God is a unique temple of the Holy Spirit. God is always with us because He is always in us. As a new person we are to feel blessed with who we are in mind, body and spirit. Regardless of how we may appear to others we remain the Beloved of God. Does anything else matter?

As a new person we wonderfully take on the responsibility of acknowledging God's presence in us by honoring our beings. We must attempt to make this holy temple of God pure and undefiled through the power of the Holy Spirit motivating our efforts, adhering to our responsibilities to God and making holy our temple. We must be maintained but not in a disordered way. We must love our neighbors as true temples of God like ourselves in an ordered way that also must be maintained. We must never seek to possess God by trying to possess another or possess another's body, mind and soul but we must love them as unique Beloved creations of God and temples of the Holy Spirit.

God accepts us just as we are in reality and at all times. If we truly believe this then we do not have to deceive others. We will be accepted because God accepts us and that is all that really matters.

God never leaves us no matter what. He understands we will sin but He never abandons us and He always encourages us to continue on the journey to holiness. God never rejects. We reject God because we do not think we are worthy or capable of loving Him due to our disordered perspectives. We spend eternity with God who never rejects us and only a small percentage of that time with our fellow men who may reject us.

As the new person we are confident in relationships of all kinds that we have the capability to be Christ to them be they close enduring relationships or newly formed ones. We forget ourselves and turn our attention to the other as Mary forgot herself with her every gaze focused on Jesus. We move on the path of the journey to the acceptance of others, all others, with no exceptions as being fellow Beloveds of God, thus potentially walking toward right relationships.

Then we are able to see the grace of God's beauty individualized for us personally in God's vision of beauty…as given to us by God in an individualized person that transcends society's definition of beauty and moves into God's realm of beauty and truth. We truly experience Him in a very real way through another in a way that transcends beyond our self. The love of God for us is then starkly supernaturally mirrored in our love for the "other" even if that reality may not be really possible in this life.

As we begin to think and act as Mary in our pursuit of "right relationships," this supernatural mirroring is played out by seeing uniqueness in another that transcends and makes a unique beauty that does not have the characteristics of all. Our eyes see the uniqueness only of the other because a Trinitarian Communion is formed by the Holy Spirit with virtues wrapped in it that enhances the physical uniqueness of its core. We do not become preoccupied with what they think;

the uniqueness of the experience of the relationship comes from the Holy Spirit and is ours alone, i.e., a divine grace.

We become unique within our species. We become the counter culture in our search for divine beauty in others. We are reminded and assaulted daily how secular modern man views himself verses how the ancients viewed themselves with their responsibility being very different in the concept of beauty and good, of what attracts unique human relationships. Modern man as a humanist thinks he must improve God's creations or make them right. It is no longer the idea of "subduing or accepting nature in order to be able to live in it." We must constantly better oneself for this short time in eternity, for what end, because our only existence in this world is all that is important, i.e. acceptance in this world—not rejection. Ancient man was happy with the beauty of the art itself, never insinuating that one had to personally be the work of art personified and therefore be transformed into the perfect human being. Because God was the central good and beauty. God only was perfection. With humanism and relativism came the idea that we had to look like a god and be God. But the Holy Spirit acting in the new person sees the uniqueness of beauty of the special "other" as God defines it, the beauty that transcends and is made unique in the eyes of the person as a result of the Trinitarian Communion.

This is indeed grace. We have transcended our secular humanist culture on the journey, surrendered to God and been assured by the Holy Spirit we are on the path.

Thus, we see ourselves as not an artifact within a progressive culture but as the new counterculture leading man back to the Garden where he is meant to be. For we are a Beloved child of the only God who is always present, always forgiving, always helping our ability to think, see and do as Mary. We then reach a milestone on the journey's path that enables ordered confidence and self-worth.

Being unable to see ourselves in an ordered relationship with God, as did Mary, means an inward non-acceptance that may manifest itself in subtle ways that are outwardly evil, even often couched in humor. We have difficulty hearing the invitation to the journey and we may even reject the journey or become frustrated with the trip along the path. We through a misunderstanding of the nature of the Catholic Christian God become bitter. Despite whatever wealth and significance we may have in our secular life our spiritual life slowly paints our Portrait of Dorian Gray leading us to negate the reason for our very existence

But do not make the mistake that this is a Catholic opinion of God. There is Truth and as Catholics we know what it is. It shows in our Beloved beings in solitude, in our community, and in our service. We are Christians by our love, by our love. "They will know them by their fruits." We are believed to really care about others because we are seen by others as having really loved ourselves because we have moved "beyond ourselves." They intuitively know this. We do not have to tell them.

No truth can be found unless there is a search for meaning, recognition of human vulnerability and limitation, relationships with trusted spiritual friends, and openness to the disclosure of the transcendent mystery of God, before whom all questions cease. (Henri Nouwen)[37]

Becoming the Beloved means letting the truth of our Belovedness become enfleshed in everything we think, say and do. A long and painful process of appropriation or, better, incarnation. Prayer is required. (Henri Nouwen)[38]

The Influence of Church

"Only at Church"

Reflect on: There is but one Church in which men find salvation, just as outside the ark of Noah it was not possible for anyone to be saved.

—St. Thomas Aquinas[39]

There seems to be no formula of how to create a "good Catholic family" to insure that children continue in the faith when they become adults. Going to Mass each Sunday must be just part of it. If prayers and rosaries and other family activities are involved and possibly if sacramentals are used in the home then it may set a tone for future family life established by the child when they become an adult. In the interpersonal relationship as it develops between parent and child there may not be a basis for understanding how to pass on the faith. The explanation of the faith may not be understood either by the child or the parent. Even Catholic school does not seem to provide any guarantees. Church burn-out can also distort views of Church as kids become adults who have led the life but not personally understood the spiritual relationships that go with the life.

It seems so easy to drift away after Confirmation looking for more variety in worship verses the repeated cadence of the Mass which may seem boring. We balk at our lack of understanding and the tradition of two thousand years. Other individuals such as close friends, boy/girlfriends, spouses can often provide an alternative to the Church which is easier to follow. The perceived rigidity of the Church, moral exactitudes, and other alternatives in life other than Church can easily help us move away into a more relaxed non-Church going life style that makes us occasional attendees. Other faiths do not have the penalties associated with not attending that are part of our Catholic Church consciousness and part of our physical response to the demands of the Church. The belief surfaces from viewing those around us that believe in Jesus Christ as our Lord and Savior is sufficient into itself and can be obtained even without a church and certainly without the Church.

Church is experiential and has to be experienced on an individual basis motivated by the Holy Spirit. It has to supersede the building, the current pastor, the Magisterium, and become something to us other than these. This comes often in experiences that are mini conversions and often over a long period of time as the Holy Spirit works on us. Praise God if He gives us enough time to respond!

Seeds can be planted by Church, parents, schools and others but those seeds have to fall on our individual fertile ground that has been prepared by the Holy Spirit and ground that is willing to receive and nurture the seed. This is often exampled by a belief in God and even Jesus that is planted but lays dormant for a long time before becoming a sprout that can be tended. Then there may come an event that takes the mini conversions and moves them along toward a greater conversion that leads to a journey and commitment to being a disciple of Christ and not just an observer. If we allow it the Holy Spirit will provide the opportunity and direction but this takes listening and most of us do not listen at all very well. We are good at putting obstacles in the way of the Holy Spirit and the evil one is so good at helping us understand that we do not have the ability, the resolve, the dedication to become children of God and Church.

If we are from a tradition that is not Church we often wander in the desert with God like the Israelites did. We could see the Promised Land but we are blinded to it because of personal self-centeredness that does not allow us to go directly to the Church. We wander and many of us wander forever until the time has run out. We cannot see the Master calling us on the journey home. Sometimes we do not know enough to even consider the road to the Church as an alternative. Even if we have come from the Church to begin with we do not see the road to it to be the only real road to an intimate relationship with Christ. The evil one provides us with so many wonderful stops along the way to waste our time and so many back roads that lead us nowhere. We know in the depths of our heart that there is a true road but we just cannot find it even when it is right at the next turn in our road.

If we listen, if God's graces are given, and if we are willing to receive the seed, then the Holy Spirit puts us on the journey and we never want to get off of it. Conversion is never a one big sign and stopping place of the journey. Conversion is always, "until we see Him as we were meant to see Him," and we are physically dead.

Some are even sought out by the Holy Spirit in more direct ways. Here I am speaking of those not in ecclesial religious vocations. Regardless of our vocation, God, often through others plants more seeds even if we are already on the journey. He takes all of our foibles, our experiences, especially our failures because they help us have humility, particularly our failures with others, our secret addictions and adds these to our inward burning love of Him deep in our heart and makes us an even newer person to serve Him. We then know a new form of obsession, an obsession directed at Him which drives us in ways that secular position, power and fame can never satisfy. We do things that we are uniquely gifted to do and we do them in Church because Church is where He really lives, i.e. in the Tabernacle and in the Monstrance.

He gives us a desire to improve and want to become worthy but in a spiritual sense and in improvement and worthiness as He defines it. We begin to realize that the basis for His call is to become humble before Him and humble in our relationship to our fellow man, and that through this humility comes strength, a strength that surpasses any physical or mental prowess, a strength that makes us Sons of God and defines our vocation to others in the Church.

It is impossible to take the right road or even to know it exists, it is impossible to be graced with our vocation from God, it is impossible to become the new person, to let the seed grow into the tree and it is impossible to become strong beyond our dreams outside of the Church. The Church is the only ground that is fertile, the only ground that provides the nourishment needed, the only ground that lets us grow for eternity and the only ground that was meant to return us to the Garden of Eden where we were meant to be eternally in the right relationship with God and with our advocate and true mentor our Blessed Mary. Other ground, no matter how appealing can never do this; it can only keep us from the Garden by delaying or destroying our journey all together. That is why Mary is often left out of our journey if we seek other roads and other ground other than the Church. The evil one knows all too well that she is the enabler, the clarity leading to the right way, of showing us what sin is and how we have to avoid it to be on the journey and take the right road. She is our compass that if used always points us to Christ, i.e. Church.

When we come to terms with Church we move beyond the physical to the spiritual and to the humility not only in the supernatural Eucharist but in our own right relationship with God, our humility toward ourselves and our neighbors. We become detectable by others intuitively as having the Holy Spirit. We don't have to tell anyone that we are trying to be holy. They sense it. They know it. They want to embrace it.

They may even want it. Then we begin to have the tools to be Christ to others. We are now at a different juncture traversing the path on the journey leading to eternity. We now have the ability to do more. Before we could do nothing without the Holy Spirit leading us by every step. Now through grace we lead others, not without the Holy Spirit, but through greater grace than before, able to be strong far beyond our expectations. We become supernatural. We experience in an even greater way the supernatural as Church.

As the new person we no longer obsess about our dignity as a response to others who might wish to do us harm, we are no longer preoccupied with what others may misunderstand. We know who we are in relationship to God and that righteousness helps us deal with those situations and with others that previously would have compromised us. Our humility helps us to try to love instead of judging, to understand instead of being wounded, to help instead of going on the attack. They instinctively know, and despite their sin, they know we have something they want and this is the true source of their frustration. They have entertained the evil one and are oblivious to his presence—his presence in church. Our parrying is always our truthfulness and honesty, our love for Christ, and our spiritual Mother who continues to defeat him—always in Church.

We cannot get to Christ in solitude. We must have the Church. As Catholics we believe that only through His Church are we able to be "one with Him" as is in the

Eucharist and therefore able to come closer to doing His will in our/His eyes. He said, "Eat my body and drink my blood." Many in other Christian traditions can only "want to be closer to Christ" and seek greater closeness in trying to be a "good Christian." But this is a mortal effort and worthy but is not becoming one with Him in the Eucharist which is a supernatural event.

Only when we truly understand the Eucharist through the grace of the Holy Spirit do we see it as the ultimate expression of the convergence of the Divine and the earthly and the ultimate response to the command of Christ. Here, we become true "sons of God." Then, and only then, do we transcend from being "good people" to being Church, Christ on earth.

Church and the sacraments are Heaven come down to earth. As one on the journey we must acknowledge that we are there to worship the Triune, the only God, who has given us His Church. Therefore, we should never be "outside" of what is worthy of God, including "outside" the Catholic Church founded by Jesus Christ! But all Christians are part of the Roman Catholic Church whether they are in communion with the Pope or not. There is only one Church, the Roman Catholic Church and we are united with other Christians whether they acknowledge it or not. Christians are saved only through Jesus Christ and the Church He founded.

The call of the Lord to those on the journey puts our entire life in requisition, and one of the things that belong to life is activity. The believer, the new person, lives in responsibility! Everything the new person does must be an answer to the call of the Lord. We are the properties of the Lord; we are His witnesses with humility and gentleness, truth, strength and might in a secular world! As Ephesians 4:8 says, "Ascending on high He has taken captivity captive, giving gifts to men"—this is His Church with Himself in His complete body, blood, soul, and divinity of the Eucharist.

Then there becomes a different view of "Church" in our daily lives when we acknowledge and then are able to try to live "in one with Him"—to take the Eucharist in our hearts out the doors of the Church. Without this we are just a bunch of "do gooders" and moralists and one does not have to be a Christian to be one of these. As Catholics we are not spectators to Christianity, nor fans. We are on the team and willing to go to the games as did the Saints and martyrs if God should require!

> *Just as God's will is creation and is called "the world," so his intention is the salvation of men, and it is called "the Church.* (CCC)[40]

> *All who have been justified by faith in Baptism are incorporated into Christ; they therefore have a right to be called Christians, and with good reason are accepted as brothers in the Lord by the children of the Catholic Church.* (CCC)[41]

The Church as a Marian Church

Reflect on: The traits of our Blessed Mother of God become the traits of the new persons whose repose lies in the Church with the traits of Christ, the Church transformed by Christ through Mary.

—F. Saurez[42]

"The Society of Mary (a Catholic religious congregation focused on Mary and her spirituality) exists not because of the early Marists' concern for Mary or because of their concern about people's devotion to her, but because of her devotion to God's people.

A Church that is Marian is what we would expect it to be as the home of the new persons. Mary is the Mother of the Church today and will continue to be. A Marian Church would reflect Mary in thought, word and deed as the model of the new persons who make up and will continue to make up the Body of Christ. This has nothing to do with woman's role in the Church and everything to do with the Church, women and men, as Christ on earth and how this is manifested to those who are not.

The characteristics of the new persons are the character-istics of the Church. These have always been the characteris-tics of the Catholic Church but now with a new application to the way the faith is to be exercised in the world by the new persons. There have always been new persons in Christ's Church. However, now through God's continued revela-tion of the "new person woman" as the meant companion of the man we now see the new companionship of man and woman actually taking place. This is not a new Church in hierarchy, nor theology, nor purpose, but a church that has an altered clientele to serve, in the new man and new woman in companionship.

What was initially Marian Spirituality now moves to a greater extent into mainstream Catholicism's thinking as we pursue the will of the Son through the presence of His Mother. We see this most dramatically in our daily lives.

As Mary as our model for the new person we embrace that model individually in our relationships with other new persons and others and as a piece of the mosaic of its corporate calculus, the Body of Christ. So that the characteristics of the individual new person also become more the characteristics of that body.

That means that the Marian charism of being, "hidden and unknown in this world" and being, "Mary in today's world," are manifested in a counterintuitive way to their surface meaning. All new persons are in the Marian terms of adoption, "chosen by God and Mary as a special grace," to be the new persons, to be in companionship in and out of the gender; called to be different, called to in a sense, "make the whole world Marian."

So what does it mean for the new persons to seize these counterintuitive three Marian dictums as individuals and Church? It is to be where Mary always is pointing—to Christ, God Incarnate.

To be "hidden and unknown in the world" is to not be self-centered the root of all sin, but surrendered to Christ in obedience but with the "other's" welfare always as the priority and with giving and not taking as the action. As we have seen in the discussion of the new person the humility of the new persons creates authenticity in one's self and in their relationships with others in and out of their gender. They are beneath the radar of selfishness and make good things happen without fanfare. The result is that we become better witnesses, bringing more to Christ and giving hope to a modernized, secularized world that is without hope.

Secondly, by just being the new persons we by default become Mary in today's world. She, herself is active today in the world and by extension we share in her activity. She naturally is our model; we are striving for the "right relationship" with her Son through her model of the "right relationship" with the Trinity.

Thirdly, we begin to make, "the whole world Marian," especially, as we offer the broken world the true nature and purpose of God's creation, the man and the woman in companionship with submission to God with the only purpose being eternity with Him. Then we see Mary righting the evil of the Reformation fallout by defeating the evil one and restoring all Christians to "one." And as the helpers of Mary we, as new persons, help fulfill her role in salvation history to bring all back to her Son and his Church.

So what does this "Mary-influenced Church" look like? As with Mary the Marian Church is to be all "inclusive" with no exceptions. Mary's role is to bring everyone to her Son! This means all the saints and the sinners, all Christians, all Muslims, all secularists, etc. through words and actions, through making life meaningful and eternity available to all.

The Marian Church is "open" to all no matter their history or degree of sin. The bars are never on the doors. The Church spills out to all in the community from its doors as they stay open to allow our Lord's call to go out to everyone. Nothing is exclusive. We are not about politics or power or wealth. We are about openness in addressing the social, political, personal, spiritual problems, hopes, dreams in an open manner.

With "inclusive" and with "openness" goes justice. We give God the justice that He deserves and we give men and women the justice they deserve so that all may hear our Lord's call to the journey. We are non-judgmental but we are ordered in judgment. This does not mean we compromise or not catechize sound dogma. It means we bar none from its saving grace and reconciliation with our God, and we leave the final judging of sin to God.

The Marian Church "meets people where they are." Married, divorced, lapsed Catholic, abortionist, convict, poor, rich, Protestant or Jew or Muslim, man, woman, or child we will provide for their spiritual education in the truth, in the gentle, loving way that Jesus and His Mother met all those in Nazareth.

> *The general aim of the Society [as phrased in the Constitution of the Society of Mary] is to contribute in the best possible way, both by its prayers and its efforts, to the conversion of sinners and the perseverance of the just, and to gather, so to speak, all the members of Christ, whatever their age, sex or standing, under the protection of the blessed Mary Immaculate, Mother of God; and to revive their faith and piety and nourish them with the doctrine of the Roman Church, so that, at the end of time as the beginning, all of the faithful may with God's help be one heart and mind in the bosom of the Roman Church and that all, walking worthily before God and under Mary's guidance, may attain eternal life.* (Constitution, Society of Mary)[43]

The Marian Church is merciful and we are its "instruments of mercy." We are an extension of the Divine Mercy of Jesus Christ, the hands of mercy to all who need it in the world. We live the mercy for others!

The Marian Church is a, "stranger to greed." We glorify God with as much grandeur as our individual Parish needs allow. But we seek to glorify the "temples within us" with our spiritual means. As individuals and as a Parish we do not seek vanity or rankings or sophistication or any disordered comparison with other Parishes, other denominations or any other part of society. We do well what we do but what we do is a product of all those characteristics above of the Marian Church. We serve all others with Christ instead of serving ourselves. As members of the Body of Christ we individually know at what point our income and its use becomes "greed." We then provide the surplus to others to help them on their road to salvation always knowing that, "there but for the grace of God go you and I."

Above all, we and our Church are humble, the most important human characteristic of Mary and our Lord. We embrace the Marian spiritual idea of, "when we are humble, we are strong." Mary is a very strong woman. She is not weak. Her and our humility attracts others. They see no reason to keep their guard up. They believe because we are authentic, we lack harmful agendas. Through our inclusiveness, our openness, our just nature and our mercy we draw those who we could never approach before. This makes the new persons able to empathize with the other and foster relationships that mitigate confrontation and develop alliances with all others.

And with humility comes simplicity. Life and relationships become simple. Simple does not imply boredom or lack of motivation. Simple means the wonderful simplicity of pleasing God and doing His will only. The simplicity is in the way we live our lives which reflects this God focus in our ordered relationships with others. We have what we need and we help others in material and in spiritual matters. We avoid positions of honor and prestige because our honor and prestige is just whatever it is that God has asked us to do. The self-centered focus becomes the God focused. We deal with others in simplicity of truthfulness, honesty, clarity and transparency. Life becomes less complicated and others become more dear to us, ending in a sense of personal happiness.

We take this simplicity into the Body of Christ. The others sense that the Church is focused on them, their relationship with Christ and their salvation. The transparency is overwhelmingly welcoming. The institution, with all of its heritage, simply adds another dimension of love.

So the Marian-influenced Church providing the home for the new persons in a new age of companionship simply keeps all that exists intact and reaches out in a slightly different way in orientation to bring the world to Christ, i.e., to make the whole world Marian. That Church:

- Keeps the all important and authenticity of the hierarchy but with less emphasis on the offices and more on the function of those who are vocational to being the shepherds of the flock;

- The shepherding is lay-oriented since the object of the ecclesia is the laity. The hierarchy and Mary as the "mother of the faithful." The purpose is one of enablement, enablement for the laity to become new persons in a church that with our Mother as the model moves toward a world where all relationships are ordered;

- An emphasis by the Church on the "Nazareth years," i.e. our everyday playing out of the Gospel message in our daily lives as new persons, not just in theory but in real practice.

- To bring the culture of death and apostasy from slavery to a Christ-centered culture portrayed in the lives of the new persons in Christ.

Mary as the bearer of the Church's hope in answer to a crisis of faith understood as the beginning of the end times. (Pope Francis)[44]

If not a single hair falls from our head unless it is the will of the Father in heaven, we must not think that this happened by chance. Yes, indeed, for this is an age of indifference, unbelief, an age of crime, of false learning... (J. Snijders, SM)[45]

The New Person in Gender Relationships

Reflect on: *Be subject to one another out of reverence for Christ.*

—Ephesians 5:21, NRSVCE

We have reviewed the new person as woman or man, their characteristics and how they interact with others whether they are new persons or not. Much of what we have said characterizes these relationships in general whether the "other" is woman or man. However, when the relationship is between the genders there is a uniqueness in these relationships that leads to complexity. Human actions transcend gender. Each gender has the same actions but they are manifested in different ways. Gender majorly gets in the way of interaction and separates humanity due to frames of reference and other experienced and imagined issues. History and our own lives bear this out in profound ways.

We move from the general new person relationships to the cross gender relationships beginning with the man.

But I say to you that everyone who looks at a woman lustfully has already committed adultery with her in his heart. (Matthew 5:28, RSVCE)

For the new person man our most difficult answer to Jesus' "appeal to the heart" in the Beatitudes is in dealing with the other gender. We must have the "new heart" as the new person. We must have respect for the whole woman whether she is a new person woman or not. She is our equal in the eyes of God. We must embrace the entire woman in any gender relationship for she too is a Child of God and our companion.

"But I say to you that everyone who looks at a woman lustfully has already committed adultery with her in his heart." Jesus is very clear; there is no other interpretation but that lust in any fashion toward a woman be in or out of marriage is a mortal sin no matter how we disguise it. Then, we are not treating a woman as an equal or a Child of God. We must not see her as a sexual thing to be used and lusted after. This is the greatest problem for any man, new person or not. God made us passionate in an incredible way to pursue the woman sexually but in an ordered, not disordered way. Only a new person man will be able to understand this true meaning because it takes the male's commitment, discipline and the supernatural help of the Holy Spirit to conquer this. He can never do it alone!

In spontaneity he must be the new person in every encounter with a woman. He must understand that the price of self-control reaches more deeply and maturely in spontaneity and rediscover the "spiritual beauty" of the body. He must understand his own exterior and interior acts, having the ability to obey a correct conscience and be the true master of his own impulses while doing all of this consistently. He must desire in his heart the "fullness of her humanity," i.e., the mutual relationship of the woman.

He must not "lust only" in his heart in marriage or lust at all in other cross-gender new person relationships. He may acknowledge her attractiveness and beauty but not cross over into lust. He must realize the nuptial meaning of the body in the spiritual power and state of mastery that is the mastery of the lust in the flesh. He must allow Christian ethos and Eros to work together for what is true, good and beautiful, i.e., in his heart he must allow the erotic and ethical to meet!

Being the new person is not easy but being the new person male almost challenges our belief that the "new person" is possible. Our secular society, media and often women in general constantly challenge our ability to handle our male sexuality in an ordered way. Relativism at its best says we can do whatever we want as long as we don't harm another, with the definition of "harm" being individually defined. As new person men the demands of our Catholic Christian faith makes us clearly the counter culture and asks us to be transformed into beings quite different from other men.

The following discussion, "*Transforming the Male to the New Person*" explores the person man in cross-gender relationships. The following discussion from *Woman, A Gift from God* explores the new person woman in her divine role in relationships and particularly in the "companion" role with the male. In later discussions, we see how the new person man and woman in Trinitarian Communions enjoy the ultimate relationships in marriage and in spiritual friendship.

> *Body and Gender are an eternal gift from God and we must be happy with it and recognize our uniqueness, understanding that God made everything, "Good."* (Bob/Sherri)

Woman, A Gift from God

"It is not good for the man to be alone."

Reflect on: *If a woman understands Mary's role in salvation history then the straps of the curse are broken and she can participate with Mary in being the New Eve.*

—Bob/Sherri

So the Lord God caused a deep sleep to fall upon the man, and while he slept took one of his ribs and closed up its place with flesh; and the rib which the Lord God had taken from the man he made into a woman and brought her to the man. (Genesis. 2:21, RSVCE)

Then the man said, "This at last is bone of my bones and flesh of my flesh; she shall be call Woman, because she was taken out of Man." (Genesis. 2:23, RSVCE)

And Adam said: The woman, whom thou gavest me to be my companion… (Genesis. 3:12, CPDV)

"The man called his wife Eve, because she became the mother of all living." (Genesis. 3:20, RSVCE)

God brought woman to the man so woman could bring Man back to God.

God knew that in the Garden and eventually away from the Garden the man could choose to disobey; the free will which emanates from complete unrestricted love. God's eternal plan of unconditional and overwhelming love for man seen in the Garden in the single relationship of the Creator/creature and His plan for salvation outside the Garden provides the eventual redemption of man through God's Triune nature—God the Creator, Son the Redeemer, and the Holy Spirit, the Counselor—and Mary, the unique human.

Despite his failure in the Garden God never abandoned man for even a moment and provided him with a piece of His Divine help even while he was in the Garden. He provided Eve! She, as created companion for man also fails God. But it is Adam's free will in response to Eve by acquiescing to her temptation that allows both to fail. Both are subject to the curse for they are companions.

> *The harmony in which they[Adam and Eve] had found themselves, thanks to original justice, is now destroyed: the control of the soul's spiritual faculties over the body is shattered; the union of man and woman becomes subject to tensions, their relations henceforth marked by lust and domination. Harmony with creation is broken: visible creation has become alien and hostile to man. Because of man, creation is now subject to its bondage*

> *to decay. Finally, the consequence explicitly foretold*
> *for this disobedience will come true: man will return to*
> *the ground, for out of it he was taken. Death makes its*
> *entrance into human history.* (CCC)[46]

Jesus and Mary will be the true companions and will redeem man and woman in God's time through God's economy of salvation!

The woman is, "flesh of his flesh and bone of his bone," fully human, fully as he, but yet different. She is his companion, his helper, not his equal in strength and might, not him in head or heart. He is God's creation, his first born. But, she is his companion, ordered by God to bring him back to the Garden. She has no guarantee that she will come back with him. She also has to run the gauntlet of the world, fight the stigma of her first mother's failure and be the one most susceptible to the evil one.

But unlike the man the woman has more of the characteristics of God. She, in *her ordered state* of naturalness, being who she is and who she was meant to be, is God's most beautiful physical creation, exceeding the flowers and the choral and the most beautiful array of the heavens. And she is all this beauty as a gift from God to the man and to the world. In her ordered state, she is loving in a way that surpasses the man, surrendering, nurturing, sacrificial, preserver of life. In essence, she has the human characteristics of a creator of humans who loves the human creature. She is of course susceptible to the evil one because she represents a threat to the evil one.

She is the counter to the man in his need to dominate, lust, control, destroy, and kill, the qualities needed to subdue and control the environment. She, as mother and lover, is the very essence of what the man wants to be but is inhibited by his nature and tasks from being. In his ordered state he protects life or destroys it but he is not life, she is and he is never complete without her. She is the companion given to him by God who makes him whole. That is why he is so immensely drawn to her with all of his body, mind, heart and soul. His might becomes dwarfed and defeated by her and he would gladly give his life for her.

Woman was created to reveal to man something of God's love and life in a human way. She was supposed to fulfill in her ordered state of naturalness man's wishes, to quell his yearnings, and modify his behavior, to give full weight to his human existence by being human with him, coming from him and knowing him from the beginning. This is what she was meant to be; this is her natural occupation.

––––––––––––––

The problem is that the woman has never been able to reclaim what is her true occupation, her role defined by God as the companion of the man in an ordered way. Her ordered state is one of a particular nature, characteristics, roles, responsibilities and purpose meant for her by God.

Her state since Eden has always been one of disorder. The root cause of this disorder is her view of the Triune God that created her. Once out of the Garden she ceased to believe all that Eve knew about God but chose to disobey. Her view of God conflicts with God's true nature as well as His intention for His beautiful work, manifesting itself in her sexual relationship to the male.

Thus, woman has been preoccupied with the wrong divine occupation of her purpose since the Garden. From that perspective much of what she does negotiates, bends, compromises her nature to be accepted by the male. In a male dominated mindset everything she does is focused on her acceptance by the male, i.e. in what is a subservient role no matter the time or place in history. Even in her rejection of male contenders for her sexual and other favors, where she is in control, she is obsessed with him, controlled and subservient to him.

In the centuries of "might makes right" the woman acquiesced in a subservient role for her and her children's physical safety. Most of her motivations and actions in the end were for her own and her children's well-being with less devoted concern for a husband or a male figure. Her devotion for the male was always in the context of acquiring the male as protector and provider for her and her children. This disorder of divine occupation on the part of the woman has been humanity until the most recent time of history and has resulted in a distortion of God's plan, rather than creating more of a war of the sexes than a cooperation of the sexes.

But the Triune God in His economy reveals Himself to us as He feels we are able to understand and apply. Thus with the recent Popes of His Church and others inspired by the Holy Spirit He has begun a revelation to us of His divine plan for the future of saved humanity.

For those of us who reject modern relativism in favor of the absolutes of natural law and natural theology we see God revealing to us the foundations for our better understanding of His plan regarding male and female humanity. Technology has lessened the "might makes right" approach to interpersonal behavior, particularly in relationships between the sexes. We can now begin to see the equality of the different but common natures of the man and his companion. In essence, God is revealing to us what is not necessarily new roles but ordered roles and how to live them out. Relativism and modernism will pass away as untenable in defining and controlling anything and will commit intellectual suicide. When everything is relative nothing moves from the relative to the real; all arguments never end in a solution and nothing is accomplished. Alternatively, God's plan in natural philosophy will with great struggle become more and more apparent for the welfare of all humanity.

In the context of man and his companion this new divine revelation has nothing to do with our current and previous ideas of women as equals under the law: in jobs, in pay standards, in intellectual ability, ad infinity. What relativism and modernism becomes is just a "thrashing" about in endless illogic with no solutions to anything being the solution. These are humanistic concerns that can be engendered intellectually by modernistic philosophical means. In the end they do not really change behaviors between men and women and result in no further advancement in our understanding of woman's role as man's companion.

For those who instead choose God and natural law, God is revealing to us at this most wonderful time in eternity a return to the essence of the Garden. In our actual lives as new persons it is an intermediate step as we move back to the Garden through death. So the word companion truly becomes the key operative word divinely defined and lived out by both sexes in the way God's plan originally envisioned.

A companion is one of a pair of things that complements or matches each other, with which entails authentic, honest, open and true sharing of self with one another. Companionship started in the Garden between the Creator and the creature. God showed his complete love for man as true love itself. Adam was in the right relationship (righteous relationship) with God in the Garden. He loved the Creator in return and believed completely that God loved him in an overwhelming supernatural display of love. He never conceived that God's love would not take complete care of him.

In the Garden there was no opportunity for man to choose God and nowhere for Adam to express to another the love he received from God. This solitude of Adam was not God's design as we see in Genesis 2:18. He was meant to have a companion, a complement, "flesh of my flesh" yet different. God's complete divine plan for man was for man to live in community, a Trinitarian Communion of Adam and God and .... Eve brings the community and most importantly the Trinitarian Communion to Adam giving him the ability to show God's love to another human. Adam had the complete responsibility for the animals but needed like-companionship not possible with the animals. So God comes to Adam through Eve who is a complete "him." Eve makes this happen and brings to Adam, as woman, the ability to love another beyond the characteristics of the male, i.e., she possesses the human love characteristics of God, ordered characteristics that should exclude her from the worst sins such as homicide. All of mankind's expectations of the conduct of the woman are magnified due to these God-like qualities given to her. Even with the woman's disordered view of God and love, even when she does not know that what she is saying, doing or being is disordered, the woman is thought of as loving, kind, moral, etc. We are all horrified when she does not act accordingly. When she actually in the worst of her sins kills humans in any fashion we are dumb-founded as we are horrified when she betrays as did her mother Eve. We expect her to be the moral human, the good person for God has given her many of his traits, and the ability to produce life and nurture that life through love: God>>>Eve>>>Adam, the Trinitarian Communion of God, woman and man.

Therefore, ordered woman was to be the equivalent of God's love in human form for all mankind as shown in her love for the male as his companion. Woman's arrival creates human love. In the Garden their hyper-mutual magnetism for one another creates an indescribable union of oneness that edifies their differences in a physical and mystical union of body, mind and spirit not comprehensible on this side of Eden. Thus, woman brings God's love to man as "love between two humans," something the male can now grasp and understand as mirroring the unconditional love of God for him. In the divine plan God's gift transforms the man into having the ability to love the woman in an extraordinary but subsidiary form of his love for God. Man now sees love through the woman in an intimate way only possible between a human man and a human woman.

God's love for mankind has to be fully revealed to Adam and mankind, and Eve (woman) is the only one that can do it in and out of the Garden. That is why she "is" and "is" for eternity.

When Adam fails in his obedient love of God and "fails," his companion Eve also "fails" with him and fails in her occupation. Eve's seduction by the evil one, Eve's sin against Adam, is her unique part of the curse inbuilt and passed down to posterity. Her failure to save her companion from sin in the Garden creates the curse of the poor self-image that she passes down to her sisters. The curse of the poor self-image, i.e., "I am not capable of bringing God to the male and the human race," follows woman out of the Garden and into history. The evil one uses the poor self-image to help her deny that God is with her, that she is His Beloved, that she is worthy of Him and her salvation. This disordered view of God embraces her and mankind's view of her throughout history.

Therefore, her betrayal of God and Adam or should we say her failure to do God's will and save Adam from himself, means she no longer brings God to Adam and mankind. Her real purpose for existence is well buried by her, the male and the evil one. She becomes subservient to the male in all aspects of life because he is stronger and able to physically master the natural environment and her. She is continually reminded of her betrayal in this subservience and she sees it in the pains of child birth and other physical limitations of her sexual and physical nature.

Her physical role as human in reproduction supersedes her other role of godliness, and disorders her true role in the eyes of mankind. If she had lived "ordered" as a by-product of the Trinitarian Communion she would have ordered all of mankind and minimized the tragedies that exist in too many cross gender relationships.

Again, even in her disordered view of God and love she is aware enough of her difference from the male and her unique way of interacting with him to know despite appearing to be subservient she has power over him. As her occupation even if she is not realizing it, God has given her the tools to make her the gift of God to mankind which can be used in an ordered way or a disordered way, i.e. good or evil. God's ultimate creative beauty given to the woman combined with her sexual draw has enormous power over the male. The Bible is littered with stories of this power used with free will for good or evil.

Countering the male qualities as his companion the woman naturally brings the joy of romance and love to the male. Man is seduced into performing them. Incapable of the feeling without her as the prize he is unable to help himself since there is nothing more risky, painful and joyous than the pursuit of a woman. The male wants to love and possess and there is nothing more disastrous than her rejection of one he truly loves.

God could have arranged for reproduction for his unique human animal external to the man/woman's sexual union. But He did not. Only through the exercise of her unique gifts and God-like qualities of love and nurturing could she insure the survival of the species and the love bonding to the next generation that only she as woman can convey.

And she will use her own power to protect her children, protect her home and protect her monogamy even to death! Instinctively she knows that this is part of what God intended for her as man's companion despite her disordered view of God and love!

In an ordered state of the new persons relationships of women and men there is no longer a hierarchy. But in the intended companionship created by God the man, Adam, precedes the woman, Eve, who completes the man and is needed to save him. Eve is made by God for man as his companion. God gives Adam the role of protector of the "purity" of the woman and she is given the role of the "purity of the companionship." This does not imply a hierarchical relationship for forever but it was justified in the "might makes right" era of human history if not in our post era of God's revelation through technological innovation.

In the "might makes right" era, the man, through physical prowess, needed to subdue the world. He exercised this physical power in the physical protection and care of the woman and by default exercised a leadership role in the process.

In our post "might makes right" era the companionship relationship of the new persons means that the man, as a part of a companionship, exercises a leadership role of the companionship by continuing to exercise his basic instinct of protection of the woman and leadership among equals in the companionship, the relationship being mutual and not hierarchical. The woman willingly takes a helper and follower role that allows leadership by the man in a non-hierarchical manner as the companions are seen as a group with individual role relationships that complement each other and makes the companionship a synthesis of the two into the "one."

The woman therefore in her willingness to take on a surrendering role as exemplified in her completely surrendering to the man in sexual intercourse is able to surrender to the man in degrees as a helper and follower in the, "among equals," companionship context with no feeling of subordination.

In the companionship role the new woman represents and has the role of "purity" that requires protection by the new man. "Purity" as defined in the new person companionship includes more than sexual purity and is defined as the protection of the purity of the whole woman, her body, mind, heart and soul. This is the whole woman the man loves completely and wholly in the physical as well as the spiritual sense. The love of the man flows into this complete woman in a way that in eternity hints of the purity of the love that flows between the Three Persons of the Trinity.

This is seen in human sexual purity as it mimics the divine love that God has for man and can only exist in the relationship of marriage, a Trinitarian Communion marriage. The man is called by God to maintain her purity by providing her with his total love in which he loves all of her, body, mind, and spirit as he completely loves and gives himself totally to her in sexual intercourse.

In the protection of her purity by the new person man the idea of protection has transcended the "might makes right" idea that protected her as if she were property, subordinated to the man in an hierarchical dependence of "use" with elements of slavery and subject to being transferred as property to other men through divorce or subjection to physical abandonment or emotional/spiritual abandonment within marriage.

In the protection of her purity by the new person man the idea of protection transcends into a complete love of "all of her" and seeing her as the companion with the characteristics of God that allow them to blend into "one" in anticipation of eternity.

He must not go outside of marriage sexually in any form or fashion or he violates "her" purity and therefore he fails in his primeval responsibility to protect her. Whatever damage he has done to himself through sin he has now violated her in purity through adultery. And he has violated his innateness as a man by not protecting her. He has reversed her role and confirmed the disordered role of the "other woman" into a "use" and a property instead of creating a complete "rib of my rib." He has reversed himself into a slaver, a user instead of a protector. He has destroyed the role that makes him the leader among equals in companionship. If he has been with many women he has only repeatedly destroyed his own manhood, deviating from his leadership and protective reason for being.

If she sexually violates her purity through sexual relations with another man outside of her Trinitarian Communion marriage she not only negates her own purity but rejects the innateness of the man as her protector and violates the "manhood" God meant him to be. If her legacy is one of multiple men sexually acquired through society's expectations of dating she has become a "slave" and allowed herself to be "owned." She has already surrendered her purity in dating and may well not be able to completely surrender herself to the man God meant for her; the new man the new woman was meant for in companionship. She then, at best, is gravely wounded as if she had been raped and violated in abuse.

If the Trinitarian Communion of marriage is violated by either the new person man or the new person woman member the whole companionship is then destroyed by substituting the ordered role relationships of each sex that make up the common companionship of love with "use" and therefore destroying all purity and protection, the God-given roles of each member of the companionship. Now, what was once a synthesis of equal roles forming an oneness of companionship is now a hierarchical structure of "use" engendered not inside but outside of the Trinitarian Communion of marriage? Each then jockey for a disordered hierarchy of dominance or submission in relationship to one another.

Outside of new persons relationships this hierarchical relationship of men and women is seen continuously in the post era of technological innovation and is still the "might makes right" hierarchical relationships between men and women and not the companionship relationships intended by God for the post era of technological innovation.

We must be certain that we understand that the companionship relationship of women and men consists of new persons. If one in the marriage is not a new person then the purity aspect or the protection aspect goes out the window. If the male is not a new person he is not "protecting" the purity of the woman which is innate and a God demanded responsibility. There can be no companionship, only hierarchical relationship when the new person characteristics are missing. To abdicate God given responsibilities in loving the whole woman on the part of the man or surrendering of the whole woman on the part of the woman, then commitment to the complete love element in the relationship is not purity and is not protection. We are not defining terms in a secular dictionary. We are defining terms in God's dictionary! This is why a non-new person relationship of one of the parties can never be a Trinitarian Communion marriage. The new person must seriously through prayer and guidance determine if they are doing God's will, because in essence they are only "using the other."

Since the grace of the Trinity through the Holy Spirit comes to each person in God's time many respond to God at a later point in life and become new persons with a legacy other than that of the new person. As we are given the new sight through grace we may have compromised our innate male role of protector of her purity or compromised the purity of the companionship if we are female. Falling on our knees we ask for cleansing and renewal through the ever forgiving Christ and the reconciliation of His body on earth, the Church. Then, as Paul we pick ourselves up from the ground and we live new as the new person in the wonderful joy of grace given in the immeasurable flow of love from the

Trinity. With grace the purity of the woman and the purity of the companionship will be restored to our psyches and souls allowing us to move forward, no longer as slaves or slavers but lovers—as God meant for us to be!

The woman and God are now with the man at every stage of life. As a baby he separates from his mother's Garden womb where he resides with God in the state of the grace of the Garden. With birth, both man and woman begin their own version of the Fall as they move away from their mother through age and development as they move toward greater self-centeredness and therefore sin. They have begun their own journey which is meant to be a journey back to the Garden. But they, as Adam or Eve must through free will choose to respond to God's call to return. They may not choose to respond. They may seek to do their will instead of choosing happiness by doing God's will. They may choose to return. They may choose and discover the Son, the Redeemer, and then His Mother as model to lead them.

"And Then along Comes Mary"

Although, she does not come along, she has been there for eternity in the economy of God's plan for mankind's redemption. She is in her unique position as the human tabernacle of the God Man and most likely the one closest to understanding God's ordered plan for the woman and mankind. She is the Mother of the God Man, of the one that gives mankind the chance to overcome death and go back to the Garden. She is the one pointing to her Son, the Redeemer. She is the model for the woman. She is the one that will lead the woman out of disorder into order. She is the one who makes the woman the companion she was always meant to be. She is the one that brings the woman fully in line with the woman's divine gifts.

With Mary, Mary's crucial role in salvation history is coupled with woman's role in salvation history as the companion of man. Mary in a state of free will without spiritual coercion says "yes" for all of mankind for eternity. With free will she responds to God's invitation to ask her to bare the Incarnate Word, God with us, Jesus. She with her unique gift of freedom from original sin and any sin is the only human in eternity who can say "yes" to the salvation for all mankind with complete freedom.

Jesus is born fully human and fully God and mankind begins their salvation through Jesus. God's economy of salvation for man begins to lead mankind back to the Garden. It is not possible without Mary, the woman, the woman who understands completely God's intent for the creation of woman. She is Christ's companion, His helper, the mediatrix. She is the New Eve, the one who will not fail! Eve forfeited her entitlement to the Spirit and could only be a physical mother. Mary becomes the spiritual Mother because she subordinates even her body to the demands of the Holy Spirit.

The Holy Spirit as the spouse of Mary and Christ in the Beatitudes and the Sermon on the Mount transforms woman through Mary into the New Eve. Woman becomes the "New Woman" in Christ and a sister of the New Eve.

The Immaculate Conception and the Annunciation remove the curse of Eve. Woman is freed from guilt and the curse because she is reconciled to God by Mary, the New Eve, and once again has the ability to bring God to mankind. Mary is unique in all eternity in her role and therefore as her sister the woman's role is elevated. Woman's new role moves back to the Garden and becomes what Eve was not—the love of God in the world. With Mary as her model the woman begins to discover, when allowed and when willing, her true natural order. Mary brings God to man as Jesus, another man. Woman brings God to man once more as Eve was supposed to do. The Trinitarian Communion of Eve/God/Adam is re-established in Mary. The Earthly Trinitarian Communion of God/Man/Woman is re-established back as it was in the Garden.

However, woman's age old advisory, her seducer, the one with lies that she so eagerly sins to believe, the evil one, stalks Eve's posterity relentlessly. The evil one has always used the first woman as the means to discredit all women. He has been masterful and successful in making particularly womankind and mankind in general think that she is guilty and has betrayed all of humanity. She believes what the evil one so wants her to believe, that she is worthless, unable to be a companion to the man.

For most women they do not understand that the curse ended with the entrance of Mary. They are still stuck in the bog of the failed Eve and still believe all that the evil one wants them to believe about themselves. He continues to seduce them. But, gradually the new person woman's role is beginning to be revealed as more repel the lies of the evil one and understand the truth about Mary's role in salvation history.

Radical feminism is the new tree and serpent of today's "earthly garden" and is the true work of the evil one. It denies Mary's and all women's role in salvation and the redemption of the world for Christ. It denies the ordered role of woman as the companion of man. There are no societal equality issues here. Woman is the equal of man. But a woman is not a man. She is different. She complements. She does not replace. Issues such as equality of pay, etc. are used as placebos on the part of the evil one and those who would try to deny God's plan. These societal equality issues all happen for women through God's justice. This is not about these issues. It is about bringing the love of God to the male and mankind as a whole and using the characteristics of woman to be the "companion" created by God. It is about them becoming one ordered "human" as a result of their companionship.

That is why the woman is so easily compromised in the eyes of the male. He relies on God and woman to bring him back to the Garden. When she fails he intuitively knows that he also has failed. That is why modern feminism is so disastrous to the natural order of things and the anti-Marian positions of so many Catholic women hide their spiritual purpose in life. It is now with the freedom from the curse that we are in a position to "go back to the Garden" as well as begin the Garden while on earth. The evil one will fight this with his tool of radical feminism all the way.

According to God's plan technological innovation has provided woman with the physical means to overcome her environment and her reproductive task in an ordered way. The result is "time" allowing her to take different parts in her new role as the "new woman." The evil one will try to move women away from discovering the true natural order meant by God by moving her false guilt into modernism and the relativism of our secular society. Secularism will deny that the curse ever happened and claim that it is not real and will deny that Mary was necessary. Secular society will claim that the woman's feeling of inferiority stems from societal mores, comments of parents and others, and male infrastructures using pseudo-psychology to give the allure of scientific fact in an effort to move the woman away from God's plan—to deny Mary, Jesus and the reality of spiritual warfare here and in heaven.

Many women will through free will choose to keep and believe the tenants of the curse masked in relativism instead of believing they are sisters of the New Eve, Mary, and God's

Beloved and are the conduit of God to the world. As the woman becomes the new person she becomes like Mary, the new Eve in her being mediator of God's grace to men. Eve alienated herself from the image that God had for her. But the image remained in God and was now free for Mary. And by adoption free from Mary for the new woman. Man is no longer here to protect the weaker woman. There is no weaker woman. The new woman is here to complete the Trinitarian Communion between God, a woman and a man and bring man to salvation. She civilizes the male by using the part of her that came from him that he does not have. A man is influenced by a woman of the new person in such a way that he could communicate with God through her perhaps in those moments more intensively than he could without her. He experiences from the new person woman the experience of "mediated grace" from God that Mary and her new person woman give.

The new person woman to the man is concrete, i.e. real. Mary has been preconfigured as types in the Old Testament and then made concrete in Mary in the New Testament. These women are types of Mary in their "being" unlike their male counterparts in the Old Testament who are all mission oriented. This being type of Mary then is transmitted to the new person woman. This in turn is connected to the fact that the woman is more hidden than the man and that the man must experience in the woman the concreteness of their mutual relationship. In today's world the more spiritual a new person man's mission, the more concrete and embodied must be what happens to the new person woman.

To the Son of God His mother is not the "idea of His Mother." For Him His Mother is the most concrete reality. The concrete Mary is absolutely necessary for the whole of Christianity and absolutely necessary for explaining, grasping, and apprehending Christianity. Therefore, she is not made up. She is, was, and will be a reality. The unveiling of Mary in the Old Testament, viewed as an abstract instead of concreteness, makes her become only spiritual and sublimate. This gives the Church today an artificial embodiment. Mary in the Old Testament and New Testament is the spirit embodied in the flesh. She is "concrete" to be viewed by the new woman.

What this means to the new person seeking God is that Mary is not some theoretical role in a philosophy but a real main person in the real world and the spiritual world. Both worlds are real and Mary is really in both of them. Mary, then, is the "Exercise of Christianity." Mary makes Christianity real and concrete instead of a philosophy or abstraction or ideal. She keeps Christianity from being dualistic, i.e. body/matter and soul/spirit being incompatible. Mary, then, is the "created exemplar" of all human persons. She makes us as new persons real! She makes the new person male and female real!

Bound up in this image and task of the new person is Mary as model for all but in a unique way for women. She is the image of the integrated Christian personality, the fully redeemed person in Christ who is in union with Christ and is the "most perfect resemblance of Christ"—the Catholic image of the human person, the new human person, the transformed new woman who is ordered.

Mary is the truly free person. Mary as the truly free person is the "new person" in Christ. She is the expression of God's dictum to love God and love our neighbors as ourselves. Not in the trite sense of the phrase but in the full expression of God's dwelling in us. A dictum that goes beyond outward actions and plenitudes and excels supernaturally our regular natures having us become "new persons." Everywhere in the New Testament, more than fasting, alms giving, more than self-denial and living in poverty we are required to "have new hearts to replace the stony heart," to become a new person in Christ, to have a new frame of mind and "new being worthy" of fellowship with God. Mary is our model!

In this perspective Mary begins to emerge more completely as we move into the new mind change as the "many" verses the "one."

So who is the new person woman? How does she become what God created her to be? How does she fulfill the reason for her creation and become the ordered companion of the male and bring him to God? How does she move from disordered to ordered?

It takes a lot of hard work internally and externally, disciplining herself away from old patterns to new patterns thus orienting herself toward God. She first falls on her knees to ask God to help her be what she was meant to be. This is where we all start, on our knees in humility before our Creator! She no longer must be physically and mentally subservient to the male, or subservient to the dictatorship of the radical feminist. She no longer has to be obsessed with the relativists view of what she should look like, what she should say and what she should not say. Deriving her "being" from God and directly reasoning her role of companion she now can cooperate with God in striving to free herself from sin and be what she was meant to be, God's Beloved Daughter. A greater look at her companion will help put it in focus.

Her companion is man. Her existence is to be his companion. Her model for the new woman is Mary. This means first of all that she does not have to be "man." God has given her all the graces she needs as an ordered woman to fulfill her role.

"Ordered" first means that she must have the ordered view of the Triune God. Everything starts here where everything fell apart. She must understand that the Trinity is the eternal flow of love between its three persons that flows down to mankind. God is always with us, always trying to help us get to eternity. This God of pure love, compassion, forgiving, and perfection will always do what is best for the individual. He only requires our surrender of our will to Him, our obedience. He in turn will make us the happiest and the "best versions of ourselves" possible in this world and in eternity with Him.

Mary obeyed completely without qualification. Mary was born without sin and was free from sin, and could see this in a way we must struggle to see. She had perfectly clear vision in order to have a capacity for an immense communion with God. The new woman tries always to surrender to God, obey Him and completely give herself over to Him.

Ordered means she is proud to be a woman and is proud to have the task of bringing God to the male. She uses all of her graces to do so and God in turn makes her a happy woman. She is a being of relationships! She is a being that makes the male and her children whole. She brings God to them! She is the link between God and mankind.

All she has to do is have complete faith in God to do well by her and to use all her graces He has bestowed on her to do good to others. These will be all she needs. Her beauty, her overwhelming ability to love, her gentleness, nurturing spirit, her ability to conceive and produce life, her ability to interface with children in all development stages, her ability to forgive and her willingness to sacrifice. Summarized, her ability brings the characteristics of the Triune God in a human way to other humans. She brings a bit of the supernatural to all she meets. This is Mary. This is her sister, the new woman.

The new woman in her natural ordered self will be a natural draw to the new person male and she will be in a position of respect and honor beyond the wildest dreams of this century's woman. She will, as Mary did, say "yes" to God in free will, in complete freedom, in the complete right relationship with God as she says "yes" to being man's companion in humanity.

She will then use her gifts to forge humble relationships with all she meets. She will deliberately loose her egocentric focus to love purely on all those she meets. Her interaction with her intimate male companion and her spiritual friendship companions will show her in her surest way to humility which is her whole truthfulness and her ruthless sincerity. Spontaneity to others becomes ordered.

These human characteristics produce relationships that with her divine characteristics and her natural beauty forge almost fanatical loyalty from the male in all types of friendships. In her it fosters a supernatural virtue in relationship with God that mimic's Mary's righteous relationship and creates the indispensable foundation for her interior spiritual growth. This in turns allows the Trinity to do great things in her. This is Mary. This is her sister, the new woman.

The new woman no longer is subordinate to the male and no longer spends her time trying to foster subordination. She is just a natural woman, humble, truthful and sincere. These do not make her weak and easy prey but this makes her a strong individual free from sin, able to have the right relationship with God, and with her fellow man of either sex. She experiences serenity knowing that God will always take care of her and bring her home.

Each person has a function given by God to find their reason and purpose for existence. A new woman who is ordered understands her vocation as companion which allows her to listen to God in making her other vocational decisions.

She is now the true companion. The entity that now can be a companion to produce a whole, the whole meant by God and the whole that is able to bring God to the earth, to subdue it spiritually for God.

She is the new woman because she in free will has chosen to be so. She is the sister of Mary. Did Mary undergo supernatural coercion? Does the new woman undergo supernatural coercion to realize her natural ordered self? The concept of freedom is exactly understood when we realize that freedom is not independence. The Immaculate Conception of Mary and the absence of all sin in her united her supernaturally to God from the moment of her creation, linked her to the Creator and bound her closely and firmly to the Being who was absolutely free. This is the root of Mary's sovereign decision, because we are free in the exact proportion to our capacity for loving the beings and the things on which we are dependent. This is Mary. This is her sister, the new woman.

The new woman, as Mary, understands that she does not have to be in solitude to be the new person. She, as Mary, welcomes and seeks community and the opportunity to witness. Mary did not have a "public life" but she was always in complete community. She is not afraid of failing in community. She no longer considers herself inferior or superior in the context of others. She is always "the equal."

She always is humble and trying to understand the other and assist the other toward salvation. She is not afraid of her fellow man or woman. She loves them as she loves herself without disordered egocentrism in spontaneity and as an acquaintance, a friend or family member.

She seeks out those who she can call a friend. She seeks friendships where each is focused on the welfare of the other as was Mary. She seeks the companionship Mary sought in Elizabeth. Someone, a friend, you are so in tune with that you can reveal your inner most thoughts in freedom and without fear. She does not care of their gender because the new woman is no longer the subservient one but the equal one in all community. This is Mary, this is her sister, the new woman.

God gave Mary poverty because He loved her so much. "If God loved her so much why was she surrounded with poverty? Poverty is the best thing because God loved Jesus and Mary and gave them the "best thing." "Poverty freed Mary from a disordered attachment to "things." As her sister the new woman enjoys the freedom to, "give up voluntarily one's dominion over things." She is free whether financially rich or poor or in-between to know that her things are simply on loan to her and have utility only as she uses them for the welfare of her family, her friends and first of all God. She is detached so that she can be first of all be in step with God's vocation for her embracing a poverty in spirit, not in step and embracing a commercial culture. This is Mary, this is her sister, the new woman.

As mentioned earlier Mary is both a child of this world and a child of the supernatural. The new woman through her supernatural outlook puts her in contact with God and the supernatural world. She acquires an interior life which allows her to advance more deeply in her interior life. Christ brings meaning to her and the more meaningful the world is the more depth she discovers in people and events. She sees what Suarez so well displays in the chess analogy, "We are pawns in a chess game. When we forget we are pawns we have a human outlook [on things]. All the things that cause problems, impatience, and depression, behind these are something that gives them a definite purpose (Eccl. 3:1–8). Supernatural outlook leads to serenity and hope to those who love God. Supernatural outlook is simply living our faith every day in the most insignificant details of our existence." This is Mary. This is her sister, the new woman.

"Mary was natural. She was not so much in making great efforts to avoid attention, as in behaving as we are, doing what we should do in whatever situation we happen to be even if that attracts attention; for it is not a matter of hiding or disguising anything, or of deceiving in order to avoid the limelight. [Her], "greatness and sanctity consists not in what one does but in how one does it. [She was] faithful over little things. If you have contempt of little things you are lukewarm. No great spiritual or material catastrophe comes from nothing. Sanctity is union with God, and union with God consists in doing His will always and in everything." This is Mary. This is her sister, the new woman.

Mary pondered. This other aspect of her interior life was the source for all else that came from her and was her. She was the only human who in her "right relationship with God" was "righteous." She had no problem conversing with God in an unceasing way. And therefore her silence [in Scriptures and tradition] is often very revealing and can be thunderously elegant. Contemplative prayer in a way that we yearn for, she naturally achieved. God spoke, and she could naturally listen in a contemplative state that required no words. She was righteous. She pondered.

The new woman is asked to do the same. To seek God in prayer, to listen to God, to do God's will. She must strive for this. If she has enveloped into her being the characteristics of Mary and the new woman we have portrayed then God will give her the grace. This is Mary. This is her sister, the new woman.

Then, through Mary the new woman, the Catholic Christian woman, the ordered companion of man has begun through the revelation of the Triune God in our time to begin to take her equal place in humanity and become the New Eve as mirrored in her sister and our Mother, Mary, Mother of God!

> *She [Eve] could also influence Adam in such a way that he could communicate with God through her, perhaps in those moments more intensively than he could without her.* (A. von Speyr)[47]

Eve had been the mother of the living because she transmitted sin and atonement, belief and unbelief, in a muddled chaos and became the mother of both Cain and Abel. Mary, in contrast becomes progenitrix by entering into order. (A. von Speyr)

Transforming the Male into the New Person

Reflect on: God has ordained us to be companions, male and female. We are hand-in-hand as we move back to the Garden as new persons.

—Bob/Sherri

The new person man requires a true and complex transformation through conversion in order to be the companion of the new person woman. This should be no surprise to most of us since the conversion to the new person requires a radical transformation into itself. We are now asked to be Christ, to mimic his mother Mary who mimics Him.

What then does this mean for the new person male? It means he has to change, and keep the characteristics of Jesus, becoming a man that embodies these characteristics continuously in their daily lives. If the new person male places God at the center of his life then he, with free will, is surrendering to Him and asking Him to take over his life through the Holy Spirit and therefore places a desire within him to be obedient to God. His relationship with God becomes clear and a daily learning experience.

But what does this mean for the man's relationship with other fellow men and women? We must look to Jesus and how He, as a man, interfaced with others as our example of "loving our neighbor as our self." If we look at the human relations characteristics of Jesus we can at least say that He was loving, forgiving, merciful, compassionate, empathetic and humble, yet also a strong leader, comfortable in His role, confident, uncompromising, a protector, a good listener, and sacrificial. In fact did He not take these first nurturing characteristics and make them, though seemingly weak, into characteristics of strength, witnessing these God-given human characteristics in His Mother Mary?

What is to say that a man who has these Jesus characteristics and who is particularly humble is not a very strong man? These seemingly weaker characteristics really make him able to understand friend and foe better and help him to arrive at understanding and solutions that transcend the usual male reactions to ideas/events and thereby provide better solutions.

Secondly, and most often avoided in acknowledgement, are the characteristics that men naturally have that are not exemplified by Jesus. These negative characteristics are part of all men and are so often their undoing as well as being major impediments on our journey back to the Garden. These are characteristics that are not of the new person man, yet are part of his maleness and a part that he must learn to overcome and which represent the greatest challenges to him. These are the male characteristics of egocentric behavior, violence, sexual lust and sexual fixation, jealousy, aggressive behavior, having possessive, domineering and controlling behavior, extreme competitiveness, a hierarchical, superior, opinionated, and manipulative approach to society and relationships and a materialistic interpretation of life. These lead to serious sin, injustice, and an orientation more in support of the evil one than Christ. Yet, all men, meaning those not on the journey and those on the journey, have to deal with these innate characteristics and overcome them. The key is that those new person males have the Holy Spirit to help them. Those other males do not.

These characteristics can only be overcome with God's help. The male can only be the companion of the female sent by God if he overcomes the very characteristics that God gave him in order to "subdue the Earth." These God-given characteristics no longer dominate the new person man's life except in very extreme situations where he is needed to protect life and family. The new person male, as the new person female, is called by God to move "beyond themselves" and to work out new answers to questions requiring these original male characteristics. He not only has the Holy Spirit to help him but he has the new person woman, his companion, to help him transform these negative characteristics. God did not leave the new person male alone and a victim to his own male devices.

The problem for the new person male arises when he interacts with non-new persons, and women who are struggling to possibly be the new person female. If they can see Mary as their model of the new woman, then they will readily note her characteristics in her relations with her fellow men and women as being loving, comfortable in her role as a woman, ordered in her self-love, forgiving, merciful, compassionate, nurturing, and empathetic. She is surrendering, a follower, and a good listener. She is pious, obedient, protective, sacrificial, humble, a servicer, and helper. She mimics her Jesus with the additional qualities of a woman.

The woman who is not a new person woman and the woman struggling to be a new person very often have the characteristics left by Eve and accentuated by the lie of the evil one and the legacy of history. She has an inferiority complex, is uncomfortable with her role as woman. She is submissive, a gossiper showing her poor self-image, a manipulator. She is controlling, a seductress, egocentric, jealous, surrendering, and has an extreme disordered focus on male responses to all she does.

These are not the characteristics of the new person female and these are not the characteristics that God gave her in order to be the companion of man. These characteristics are often played out by the woman in response to the male's attitude, words and actions in interpersonal relationships and in her response to the interaction of men and women in society in general. The woman has learned that she can use her negative characteristics to get what she wants out of the male and to establish and maintain a disordered egocentric life. When the man who is not a new person deals with women who have these characteristics his views of his domination are confirmed. When the new person man is dealing with women with these negative characteristics he is unable to establish Trinitarian Communions at any level and he will avoid them if possible and they may cause boulders in the path of his journey. He must love her as a fellow Child of God realizing that she is disordered and must address her relationship with God before he can create any true friendship.

The new person man is asked to surrender to God and do His will. He is asked to pray for help from the Holy Spirit to transform him. Additionally, he must consciously transform himself into having the following characteristics:

- He must mimic the relationship characteristics of Jesus.

- He must be humble. Humility makes him powerful in the eyes of man and God. He begins to see others as children of God no matter who they may be.

- He must become a good listener in order to respond properly to God and others.

- He must be a benevolent leader in a dominant but ordered way. He must think always of how his words and actions affect others and never willingly do anything to commit sin.

- He must believe in the reality of spiritual warfare in heaven and understand that his heart, mind and soul are involved in this conflict here on earth. He must never inadvertently do the work of the enemy.

- He must strive to love his fellow man no matter who he is.

- He must be a protector of his biological family, friends and the marginalized and show it in his words and actions.

- He must be willing to sacrifice for God and others even if it means death.

- He must be compassionate to all.

- He must be nurturing by helping those in his life understand him and allow himself to receive information about others to help him better relate to and help women, children, and others that he comes in contact with.

- He must have an ordered self-love, i.e. a healthy ordered ego, ordered in the view of God.

- He must have an ordered sexuality in thought, word, and deed.

- He must believe that women are equal and that they are meant by God to be a male's companion and bring God to him as well as help him return to the Garden.

- He must work incessantly to temper his male's disordered characteristics in his life with the help of the woman, his companion.

- He must be aware that the evil one will try to use his woman companion to tempt him to sin overtly or covertly. She has such a potential influence on him that the evil one may use her to foster sin in him without her being aware of it nor culpable in it.

- He must always cherish all women and particularly the new woman as a true gift from God and acknowledge and accept her Godly characteristics and her divine mission seeing her as God's Grace!

To help him through the difficult task of becoming the new person male the new person woman must assist the male in tempering or modifying his male disordered characteristics with her characteristics and qualities that are more like God. This makes her the companion she was meant to be and for which she was created. The new woman's role as companion to the male is:

- She must strive to become the new person woman and all it entails on a personal basis.

- She must think of herself as an equal and a companion of the male, yet different from the male.

- If she engages in the negative characteristics that are contrary to the new person woman then she will create a schism and not unity between herself and the male in any relationship and will damage or destroy the companionship. She must not

  o consider herself inferior to the male and act inferior;
  o be submissive as though she was one of lesser value;
  o deliberately manipulate the male to get her way;
  o be totally obsessed with a male's response to her everything and allow this myopic focus to direct her life;
  o use sex to seduce the male to get her way. Sex should be sacred to her;
  o discourage but help to modify the male's disordered characteristics;
  o allow the evil one to use her consciously or unconsciously to foster sin in the man;
  o engage in deliberate actions that would in a disordered way create anger, jealousy, etc. in the actions of an ordered male.

- The new person woman is graced with the new person male as a true companion in Christ who shares with her this life and eternity to come. He protects her, cherishes her, loves her with a passion beyond understanding in this life and gives her the dignity in this world of the fulfillment of her creation.

Given that God has meant for men and women to be companions and equals with different characteristics given to us we contemplate whether God has also meant the new person to be in a hierarchical relationship with one another. Was God's intention from creation for the female in any way to be subordinate to the male? Is this the ordered, the natural state of affairs that God intended?

The issue begs. Should the new person woman acquiesce to the male and seek his approval on certain things? To attempt to answer, what are the reasons she might do this?

She might wish to receive another view from the male in order to be better informed in making a decision. This is not being subordinate.

Having the Godly characteristics she has she might want the decision to be made by the male in order that the decision not hurt in any way another. She may desire the confirmation of the male that the decision will not cause harm. This is a deferral of responsibility or maybe just additional input in a decision making process, not a submission.

Are there certain decisions that she does not want to make and would prefer that her companion make these decisions? Is she being subordinate or is she concerned about what her "herd" might think about a decision that she might make that might not be popular with them. Is she avoiding the decision making process? As a new person woman this does not work well in her companion role.

If we are to mimic Jesus and Mary and take on the new characteristics of the new person man and woman do we care about hierarchy? Maybe in the new person relationships it is the individual personality that dictates any hierarchy; one that is worked out between the two equal children of God as they journey on their paths back to the Garden. Only God is "hierarchy" in that Garden!

The new person man must understand that as Christ transforms him to the new person those close to him and maybe particularly his spouse may not appreciate this "new person." Her view of him and men in general may have been molded by her frame of reference of men who do not have nor try to exhibit the characteristics of the new person man. She may feel more comfortable with her image of a male. Even if this legacy image of hers has resulted in being seen as inferior, being a use object and even being abused in different ways she may find it more comfortable and easier to deal with as a woman. Conversely, she may respond in an aggressive manner righting the perceived disorder. In short, this new person is no longer the person she knew and/or married and she may have trouble adjusting or may not be able to adjust at all.

She may also feel inadequate in relationship to him if she is not on the journey herself and see his transformation as just another way of distancing their relationship. The man can only pray for her and always react to her as a new person man. But the best of effort may not make any difference in their relationship. Each has free will to respond to the Holy Spirit or not. There is no guarantee that the other will be open to the Holy Spirit and be transformed themselves. The new person man and new person woman may be caught in a relationship that is at odds with the intensity of their new faith and be functionally tied in a relationship of use with aspects of slavery.

If this is the case in the new person man's relationship it is often the case when the new person woman is confronted by those close to her who are not on the journey. In these situations the Holy Spirit is not asking us to compromise our conversion in any way. Nor does the Holy Spirit often allow us to end the relationship. Yes, we are to pray continuously and fervently for the other but we also have been given the grace to reach out to other new persons in ordered spiritual friendships of both genders in order to fill the holes in our lives.

Thus, we inherit as new persons, relationships in life that are commitments born in years when we were not putting God at the front of our lives and before we heard the Holy Spirit call and we said "yes" to responding as new persons. Yet, in our legacy commitments the Holy Spirit will give us gifts to compensate for the committed relationships we desire but cannot have. But, these gifts are given through the Holy Spirit and are given in "God's time," not ours. These gifts may be a more spiritual life which brings vitality to our faith and helps us to endure problems in relationships, or in discernment of service for Christ or in Spiritual Friendships.

The transformation of the male into the new person and true companion of the female brings happiness to him. He is at last fulfilling the role he was meant to have from the beginning of time with the true manly characteristics he was meant to have but for the Fall. And, best of all, he is a true companion of the woman as they in true companionship live out God's will for mankind.

> *He must know what is the sign of lust in the natural attraction of man.* (John Paul II)[48]

> *Few people hate their mothers but many hate their fathers?* (Bob/Sherri)

The New Person and Gender Relations

Seeking the Lighthouse in the Fog

Reflect on: He who says he is in the light and hates his brother is in the darkness still. He who abides in the light, and in it there is no cause for stumbling.

—1 John 2:9

In both a spiritual and a natural way the image of a lighthouse invokes a feeling of direction, a sense of knowing, a subsidence of fear, a way of avoiding a danger. In a fog when we are not sure where the lighthouse may be our only hope is in finding safe harbor and avoiding danger.

The "fog part" may be easy to relate to sometimes when we as new persons are interfacing with the other gender in the Trinitarian Communion of Marriage or in Spiritual Friendships. In these close relationships we may find ourselves at times in a "fog of not knowing" in dealing with the other. Despite our best efforts in trying to be new persons we often feel tension with the other and not understand why. It does not seem to be something overt and distinguishable as much as something that is subtle under the surface, hard to see, hard to acknowledge as if it were millions of particles of fog that make it difficult to see and relate to the other clearly in the relationship.

Could it be that despite our best efforts and their best efforts in being new persons and trying to exhibit heroic effort in our relationship, there are unknowingly to us hidden underneath in the fog subtle activities in thoughts, words and actions that create havoc. Are these possibly gender particles of fog that we are not conscious of? Are they maybe different particles for each sex and is the fog so thick that we don't even realize they are there?

How can we discern in the fog these so that as new persons we can avoid them? Or can we avoid them at all? And what are they anyway? What are you talking about? What are these gender elements in the fog that potentially create hurt, tension and animosity between the two?

They exist and are different for women and men. They are rocks in the shoals that are personal in nature and invoke profound emotion in the other. If we are aware of these rocks we can steer our own actions away from the rocks minimizing any damage to the other as well as understand where the other's rocks are and what they do to us.

The man can inadvertently embed dangerous rocks into interpersonal communications with the woman creating a fog of disruption between them. The man may not know he has done so and is ill equipped to understand how the woman will process these communications anyway.

The woman processes certain interpersonal relationship information in a different way than the man. Because she processes differently she may appear to the man and often to society in general to be weird or strange or a slave to monthly physical events in her life. It is joked that she is inherently emotional, irrational, moody, etc. But she is simply acting in her more God-like ways. Her God given nature of processing emotion and feelings is not the same way as the male.

That is why she (women in general) may say to the man that something, "makes her feel uncomfortable" without being able to explain what "uncomfortable means or how "uncomfortable feels." The man (men in general) in response moves to have her explain in detail and in all of its facets what she means when she says she "feels uncomfortable" with something. He wants to fix her "being uncomfortable" right then and there, i.e. being in his role as protector, defender and fixer. He is not trying to control her or dominate her. He loves her!

She may react by saying that she has no idea why she feels "uncomfortable" let alone what she means by "uncomfortable." Her feeling is that she does not have to be "fixed" at that moment nor understand the "uncomfortable" feeling at that moment.

That usually is not good enough for the man. He wants to fix her now in a loving way of course. She cannot give the explanation necessary to fix the problem in his view so he racks another one up to her "being a woman," i.e. in a nice way you make "no sense" and have no idea what you are doing. He often dismisses her! He turns his beam in the mutual lighthouse off!

This may without a real conscious thought awaken an embedded reaction on her part as she thinks or unconsciously assumes to herself that he is trying to be a demeaning, dominating, controlling, leader without her authorization to do so! How he invokes these emotions can be very subtle in words and nonverbal ways. She may be unconcerned if she makes sense or not. At some level she feels it and her feeling cannot be denied. Subtly without even being aware of it he has committed an atrocity, "He has dismissed her." At some level she is now ignored, she may feel worthless, she senses failure as his companion and she is considered not worthy to him as a person. This can be as devastating to her as an angry outburst of words and actions on his part and intentionally she does not recognize that anything has transpired within her. But she feels it within her and these minor and subtle actions may well foster insecurity, a sense of failure and resentment deep inside.

Due to experience the woman may react to this type of scenario by catering to the man's potential reaction whenever she can in a false way which means she deliberately does not tell him about what she is thinking or feeling and therefore communication is not established and lacks spontaneity. She moves her time to the kids and her herd. She has shut the beam of the lighthouse off.

What has really happened in this situation is that the woman simply processed the occurrence in her God-given way. She drew upon some or all of her femininity to love in many ways. She feels, loves, has emotions of all kinds, evaluates, she interjects, has compassion, and maybe tears as she evaluates. And all this takes time! And all this takes time!

And if she is not intimidated into keeping it all bottled up in her she may get back to him in a few hours or days of *"pondering"* with more information. She may want to "fix" and or understand or she may not but it will be processed and done by herself on her own time. And she may not ever understand her emotion of being "uncomfortable." She may be concerned and unaware interiorly. God has given her the ability to love and understand by emotions and the heart as well as logic and maybe understand at a different or deeper level of understanding through her "emotions" than logic.

As a woman with our perspective that she has characteristics more like God than the man her focus as psychology tells us is on relationships where her male counterpart is focused on problem solving first, often discarding the relationship aspects of a situation. It is hard to get away from the idea that God also is focused on relationships. Maybe, just maybe, that problems are solved better and more permanently through focusing on relationships first and then the solving of the more concrete aspects of the problem. Now, if you are one of our ancestors and a bear is trying to eat you then maybe you need to solve the problem with your sword first before you work on your relationship with the bear. However, most of us new persons in our post-technological age don't have to be worried about bears most of the time. We do, in fact, have the ability to tackle problems through relationships first and then take the relationship aspect and its results into the problem solving. Also, maybe so many problems, especially involving men, women, families and communities of various kinds are more about relationships than anything else.

So, the new person man's ordered nature in reference to the woman should be one of love shown through protecting, leading, providing, fixing with patience as the normal expectation. The new person man must be keenly aware that in no way should it be even implied in words and actions that the nurturing emotional qualities of the woman are in any way disordered or inferior. They come from God providing special insight to make us as companions in His image. We must give her the freedom to process in her own time and in her own emotional way no matter if it is strangely different from our own and the man must allow her to be herself. Together they navigate the journey as new persons eliciting an ordered way of being.

Oddly, if the truth be more prominent, man is not so far from the woman as we might think in emotion and in emotional processing. Men have deep emotions that when triggered are possibly even deeper than the woman's and when they are negative in some way may evoke a very negative, maybe even an acute negative emotion at some level of his psyche. Men just may not acknowledge it on the conscious level and may not realize what is happening on any level. If they do become aware of the pain of the emotion in some way they are reluctant to share it with anyone. Men have their own particles in the fog that are not known by them or their feminine partners.

The woman may invoke in the man an emotion, usually a negative one without intention or knowledge that she has done so. Women do this through subtle words, emotions and non-verbal ways without real knowledge of its existence or thought as to what they are doing.

Unfortunately, women execute an acute emotional response from the man in three ways: a revelation of "priorities in her life" and where the man fits into those priorities, an "emasculating of the man" and an attack on his masculinity, and the showing of a "lack of compassion" for the man on her part. Her words and/or actions may not be deliberate and may be more with neither person overtly aware that something has happened.

For example, the woman through actions/words will make it subtly known that he is not a priority to her. Herself, her children, her other relatives, her herd, her career or other males are at a higher priority level to her than "the man" in her life. Even her dress may reflect a degree of "not caring" that does not go unnoticed. She will claim if questioned that her lack of priority for him is not true but that is because she may not realize that she really feels that way. Her words and actions, no matter how subtle, speak loudly to him. Her actions may come in the form of dismissing him in favor of another option in regular daily life or ignoring him altogether in favor of something or someone else. She has a misplaced "focus" on relationships. She has forgotten her role and her God-like characteristics and she does not ever recognize it.

The hint at priority may continually be on the superficial level but when it subtly moves into the bedroom real damage is done to the relationship.

In the second subtle way she may unknowingly, and unknowingly here is probably the true essence, emasculate the man through her subtle words/actions verbal and non-verbal, not consciously and deliberately pointed at him in her mind. She may do this through subtly taking his jobs or responsibilities away from him for the sake of expediency or self-centeredness on her part. She may just assume that he does not want to be part of an event that in an ordered way he would be a participant and not be left out. She may especially do this when she is with members of her herd or family when he is present. She acts as if she alone has secret knowledge about him that she has to share in order to maintain her status in a group. She may think that she will always be believed in her circles.

In the third subtle way of subtly she may appear to have little or no compassion for him in a situation and may say so in a subtle way or leave with him the feeling that he should just "suck it up." This may be her response to his lack of compassion on his part at various times. Or as may be more occurring she may just ignore his situation. She may show great compassion for her children, relatives, etc. but with age and a deterioration in communication she may leave any compassion for him at the door.

In each of these three ways she is subtly saying to him, "I ignore you," "I can do better without you," "you are really not needed," "you are a non-person." This is the greatest rejection one can bestow on another. This is a truly sadistic way to destroy the male individual and the opportunity for companionship in the relationship. Possibly, she would never overtly do these things or all of these things more concretely in private or public. The damage is no different and neither may be aware that it is happening.

Wow! So if there are not already enough barriers between women and men in the full scene of consciousness now we have barriers at a level we don't even recognize exists that may be doing incremental harm!

From a spiritual perspective these subtle communications on the part of the man or woman create emotion on the part of the other that often will lead them into despair and even sin. This can be especially the case with the man. His nature to "bottle emotions up" to appear to be the leader, provider, protector on the outside may lead to being a target for the evil one on the inside and may sorely test the nature of his relationship with God. Her subtle action may be the catalyst that leads him to temptation and eventually to major sin.

With men the sexual component can never be dismissed. God made man this way but he expects the man to control it. Since in marriage she represents the sexual partner component in his life the temptation is often to move his increasing moodiness and depression to sin. He may seek priority, masculinity and compassion with another woman or through pornography and self-gratification. Either sin will greatly harm his relationship with the woman and often drastically affect his marriage. He may see his spouse as no longer necessary and the pain of dealing with her too great. He has no one to open up to and may pull away from the family in many different ways.

To the woman the reaction to the subtle negative communication of the man may be less sexually oriented in direction but the effect on the relationship can be devastating. She will begin to draw away from him if he continues the king/slave relationship. She will pull back into her children, her herd, her family, her job. The biting at the man will not cease on her part and may even intensify as she feels emotionally abandoned. If he is not acutely verbally and physically abusive she will not seek a divorce but the couple will become boarders in the same house instead of intimate companions in a family. She may even seek asylum with another male through divorce if she cannot live without male companionship.

The effects on the relationships due to subtle actions, verbal and non-verbal negative communications may seem extreme and certainly we are not implying that these subtle actions can destroy a relationship on their own. However, they can play a greater negative part in interpersonal relations between women and men than may be realized; the problem being they are stealth in nature and often we are not aware they even happen.

So, assuming that this information is reliable or even partially reliable, how does the new person deal with this? How does the new person defend themselves from this?

As in anything awareness has to take place first. Whether you can look at your relationship with the other and see these subtle bombs going off is neither here nor there. Being aware and anticipating that they can potentially exist means we must constantly be aware that they could exist in our relationship and make very sure they are expunged from the relationship if they are there and if they are not make sure they do not appear.

The real key for the new person is to make sure that your actions, verbal and non-verbal communications to the other do not lead them to sin! Period. This is the new person's responsibility—to not lead another to sin.

The lighthouse that gets us all through the fog and into harbor is the light of Christ. The new person is that light and their handling of these situations creates the light for others eventually leading us back to Christ, our true lighthouse that is always there for us and can always be seen from any point in our sea.

These situations of subtlety, which are always negative in nature is where the new person in a Trinitarian Communion of marriage or in a Spiritual Friendship must be vigilant in being the new person. If we are moving beyond ourselves and being more aware of ourselves and the new position of the other no matter who they are, then we should be in a state of awareness that allows us to see these subtle communications as we give them or receive them. In this effort of understanding the other we also must remind ourselves that we each process thoughts and especially emotions differently and therefore we should not assume the other will react in the same manner or timeframe as we do. If the subtle negative communications are destroyed at the source of them, our hearts, they will never become the seeds of the evil one and they will not grow actions and words that lead others to sin.

It really is all about the new person as a work in-process on the path on the journey, surrendering to God and trying to be the new person with all the characteristics we talk about in this book. If we are striving to achieve this as best we can understanding that we must always ask the Holy Spirit to help us and that we will not reach perfection on this side of the Garden, then we will be more aware of what we are doing and saying verbally and non-verbally. As always our greatest task before us and the continued source of temptation from the evil one is our self-centeredness. This truly requires us to move beyond ourselves to make sure we are not the instigator. Conversely if we are the receiver then we need to not allow the damage. In both situations our responsibility is to not allow its visibility in our relationships so that it leads to sin. As receivers we must try to forgive the other and try to understand what circumstances in that moment engendered that response from them. Likewise we cannot allow our moods or other circumstances to allow us to lash out at the other in such a manner. With both we must immediately get with the other and through honesty, truthfulness and transparency reconcile the problem with personal pride or self-centeredness. Remember, we and God are all about relationships! Remember, to the new person there is not a human winner and a loser! God is the only winner and we are the catalyst for making it so!

We must protect our marriages from the evil one who works in big and more so in small ways to unhinge them from God. In our Spiritual Friendships we must be acutely aware that the same phenomenon can happen and make sure it does not or is reconciled if it does occur. Even though sex should not be a major factor because of the celibate component in the Spiritual Friendship everything else in the marriage relationship can be mirrored in the Spiritual Friendship.

In this way even our most subtle communications obey God and lead to the exercise of, "loving our neighbor as ourselves."

> *No man has ever seen God; if we love one another, God abides in us and his love is perfected in us."* (1 John 4:12)

Do not speak evil against one another brethren. He that speaks evil against brother or judges his brother, speaks evil against the law and judges the law....There is one law giver and judge..." (James 4:11, 12)

Interfacing With Other Christian Traditions and the Secularized World

> *Reflect on: Proclaim the word; be persistent whether it is convenient or inconvenient; convince, reprimand, encourage through all patience and teaching. For the time will come when people will not tolerate sound doctrine but, following their own desires and insatiable curiosity will accumulate teachers and will stop listening to the truth and will be diverted to myths.*
>
> —2 Timothy 4:1–3, NAB

Almost daily, the new person may encounter a wide spectrum of ideas and influences that result from a shrinking interdependent technological world. Many of these ideas and influences do not stem from Catholic Christian tradition or Christian tradition at all but come from an increasingly secularized and non-Christian society.

Even when these influences come from other Christian traditions they may be disguised as a "one size fits all" mentality and theirs is the "one size." Since the Catholic Church and its dogma is the Church founded by Jesus and His Apostles and has endured for over two thousand years the Church usually finds itself being assaulted by those who have already compromised their Christian faith or don't choose to answer to any faith at all.

The new person's response is not a fear of being influenced by his fellow Christian's heretical views but does feel challenged as to how to admonish with love.

> *And the Lord's servant must not be quarrelsome but kindly to everyone, an apt teacher, patient, correcting opponents with gentleness. God may perhaps grant that they will repent and come to know the truth, and that they may escape from the snare of the devil, having been held captive by him to do his will.* (2 Timothy. 2:24–26, RSVCE)

Admonishing with love requires all the ordered interpersonal new person skills the Holy Spirit is trying to teach. It seems strange that the new person would have to admonish other Christians to believe the truths brought to us by Jesus Himself, and His Apostles, the Holy Spirit and in the writings of the early Church Fathers. Yet, that is our task as new persons. To return our and His beloved Christian sisters and brothers to the Truth and to the unity that the evil one has destroyed through schism.

We want their salvation. There is no argument or fight to win. There is no ego. The only victor in our view has to be our Triune God in a zero-sum game that He wins completely.

The new person as initiator or as responder to our fellow Christians must first deal with and expect prejudice from our fellow Christian's spontaneity. They may react in this manner, first because those who oppose the Catholic tradition are often misinformed. In general they have not reached a faith understanding of these matters through inquiry into what Catholics believe, nor read the Catechism of the Catholic Church (CCC), but have been proselytized into believing what has been told to them by others. Sadly, they may have been incorrectly informed by their faith leaders who have often come by their attitudes in the same uneducated manner.

As we deal with them in spontaneity no matter what their demeanor our spontaneity is that of the new person— we are to give love and respect. Our witness in spontaneity is what is really important. If we show respect and love and try to understand/feel what they are saying we have been Mary even if they display in their words and actions disorder or confusion or even blasphemy. Therefore, as in all spontaneity, we are to not profile nor rush to judgment in assuming who they are. However, our apostolate is to be the enabler of the Holy Spirit through better understanding who they are and what they think. Then we can see them better as being a fellow Child of God, without reservation and then begin to help them to understand the truth about the Truth. Showing love for them up front in spontaneity will begin to defeat the evil one as authentic love always does.

Then with the Holy Spirit speaking through us, remembering that as a new person we have surrendered to God and the "use" is ordered "use" in this case and He being the one who "uses" us, we begin to unfold the truth in an inquisitive format as we ask them to reveal to themselves the truths that the Holy Spirit has for them. Again the instruction in the faith to them is not an argument, nor a lecture, nor a personal condemnation of them personally or their position, but a revelation of the truth in a loving and respectful manner. And understanding that their discernment of the truth is in God's time and not in a moment of our verbal brilliance. In this manner we find the divide between us may be more of a brook than a canyon.

Whether this happens in spontaneity or over a period of time is immaterial since we are only the conveyer of God's truth and not the origin. We are simply to affirm our faith as opposed to condemning their faith. Whether the outcome can be seen or not is of no importance at all. It is never so much what is said if we speak the "truth," as the way we say it. It is the "way we say it" and our love for the other (our neighbor) that is all we are responsible for. The Holy Spirit has already been in the conversation before it even began and He will finish it for us.

And by the way, the issue that resulted from the spontaneity or further moments with them, is it truly important? It may be. It may be vitally important for the spiritual welfare of the other. However, maybe not also. It begs the question, "Are we the only representatives of our Triune God on earth? Are there elements of God's truth outside the Catholic Church? The Catechism says there are but the Catechism also says that we have within our Church, "the fullness of the truth." Then, do we have prudence or do we have zeal when we are talking the faith with other Christians? As new Christians we are not at odds with all of what other Christians think and believe about the elements of the faith. If we are going to help correct a misconception we need to pick what the Holy Spirit would pick, not what we discern as a topic in which we have a fighting, but loving chance. We have to continuously remind ourselves as new persons whose will we are doing. The role of the new person in these situations is not to be on the defensive or on the offense but to affirm our Catholic faith as opposed to condemning their faith. Just the Truth is all that is required.

Some of the true differences between Catholics and other Christians may help bring into focus several areas that are obvious and some that are not so obvious as well as areas not so obvious that directly affect the obvious ones. One of these is the nature and role of the clergy. Through specific New Testament Scripture we see two thousand years of apostolic succession from Peter who was specifically given along with his successors the keys to the kingdom by Christ Himself. Therefore, the successors of Peter have the full supernatural nature of the role embedded in the sacrament of Holy Orders. While the clergy of our non-Catholic Christian brothers and sisters are shepherds leading men and women to Christ and then shepherding them as Christ's own, they have no power to perform in a supernatural manner. They can baptize, perform marriage ceremonies and bury the dead since these with the exception of marriage in the Catholic Church do not require ordained persons to perform some type of a public rite.

These shepherds of non-Catholic Christian flocks do not have the supernatural authority to change bread and wine into the body, blood, soul and Divinity of Our Lord Jesus Christ in the Eucharist, they have no healing power to forgive sins, ordain the vocation of marriage for couples, exorcise the allies of the evil one, or ordain the successors of Peter. However, the Catholic clergy has the power given by Christ through Peter to "bind and loose" for Him what is on earth and has the power to administer the sacraments. You cannot administer the sacraments if you do not have the supernatural power and priest do, and non-Catholic Christian clergy do not. Therefore sacraments are not possible in non-Catholic Christian denominations and therefore they "do not believe in the sacraments" other than Baptism.

The supernatural powers of God bestowed by Jesus on Peter and his successors are resident only in the Church that Jesus left us and who is "He" on earth until He comes again. This is also the resident of the only "full truth" of the Gospel. As stated in the Catechism (CCC) the responsibility of the Church is to maintain the public revelation which is the dogma of the Church and this is done through those designated by the Holy Spirit, the Popes, working through Christ's Church to hand down from generation to generation the only Truth. Without this affirmation of what the Truth is the evil one has, is, and will distort the Truth and compromise those outside of the Truth.

Therefore, as new persons we are all called as part of our natural vocation/apostolate to help bring to our non-Catholic brethren the supernatural power residing in the Church in any way possible. This difference between us is significant. At best we can strive for some cooperation and the realization between us that we both believe what has always been true and believed by both, "Jesus Christ is our personal savior." No effort on our part to make this happen is insignificant.

Our Triune God asks one thing of us if we want to receive His graces and spend eternity with Him. We must surrender to Him and obey Him. This really means that through surrender of our self-centeredness we surrender our lives to Him and leave Him in control. This is obedience. As Catholics we are asked to be obedient to the Triune God. This simply means that we are obedient to Him in our physical and spiritual lives and we continually look for His guidance in our lives through prayer. We are obedient to Him not only in prayer, but we are obedient to the teachings and the Magisterium of His Church. Finally, we are obedient to Him in taking our individual relationship with Him out into the community as service to our neighbors. The differentiator here is we do not rely on our own interpretation of what this is because we know that the evil one may be speaking to us instead of the Holy Spirit and we are blaspheming God to assume we are not sinners and cannot be subject to error when interpreting.

As we believe in obedience to God and His Church as Catholics we believe that there is a "Truth" and that "Truth" is Jesus Christ and its fullness is found in His Church. There are not many truths. There is one Truth. That Truth is not open to just individual interpretation but is also guided by the Holy Spirit and the teachings of the Church. We are not open to the creation of new dogma so that we can qualify away our sins and not take on the responsibility for the consequences of those sins. We don't make up new dogma because we don't like the priest's homily or we want to commit sins against God's natural law and we need altered dogma to make it "okay."

As new persons interfacing with non-Catholic Christians we are asked by the Holy Spirit to be prepared to witness to others the fullness of the "Truth" through an understanding of our Bible and our Catechism. We are asked to embrace completely our vocation/apostolate as lay people living in the world. We do not abdicate this responsibility to priests and religious. We take it on as a responsibility to Christ resulting from our Baptism and Confirmation. So therefore we must prepare ourselves to explain our "Truth" in simple language without vagueness, without tepidity, knowing if our comments come from Scripture or Tradition and why. We do not have to become Biblical scholars or memorize verses from scripture but we do have to know what and why something became dogma!

Christian catechesis, John Paul II reminds us, must be systematic, not improvised but programmed to reach a precise goal; it must deal with essentials, without any claim to tackle all disputed questions or to transform itself into theological research or scientific exegesis; it must nevertheless be sufficiently complete, not stopping short at the initial proclamation of the Christian mystery such as we have in the **kerygma***; it must be an integral Christian initiation, open to all the other factors of Christian life.* (John Paul II)[49]

Prayer must be an integral part of this preparation and the execution of the witnessing opportunity. We must pray daily and specifically for the Holy Spirit to help us if we have the opportunity to witness to another. That prayer must include a petition for His divine help in engaging in a loving way each and every time. Love alone has brought many to reconciliation with the Church. And we must pray in our minds as we realize that we are entering into a witnessing conversation for the Holy Spirit to speak through us, not making us rely on our own intellect. We must remember, the third participant in any of these conversations is God and the only potential winner in any contentious discussion among fellow Christians has to be God.

The "new person mindset" in its interpersonal relationships has as its foundation, humility. As we have said before, it's not about "I," it's about "thou's" and "Thou." This is a major general differentiation between ourselves and our separated Christian brethren and particularly our secular society. As Catholics we believe what Jesus said in Scripture, "Whoever does not carry the cross and follow me cannot be my disciple."

Jesus does not guarantee that we will not suffer in this life. Yet, many of our non-Catholic Christian brethren think of suffering in the Old Testament view of suffering as an estrangement in some way of the individual from God. As Catholics we believe that our "suffering with Christ" brings us closer to the Triune God, not an estrangement.

Humility is tied up in this since in our Catholic view suffering brings us closer to God through humility. We realize through suffering of any kind that we are truly dependent on God for everything. We also realize that sin often causes suffering whether we are the source or someone else is. Sin is not a bad word to a Catholic. It is just a real word. We can no longer run on pride, ego and self-centeredness to do anything and everything because often the cause of the suffering is beyond our control. Our only recourse is to, "give it up to God." We don't confuse the journey, the path and suffering with the material success of ourselves or the mega-churches we attend or with a life full of human blessings. As Catholic new persons our only goal is to surrender to God, turn our lives over to Him, do His will and be the new person wherever He wants us. The dichotomy between Protestant and Catholic new person's thinking is their emphasis on the "I" doing everything with all the human success metrics attached and our emphasis on "Him" doing everything through our complete surrender. As new persons He is the only one we have to please and His only metric is how much we love Him and our neighbor. One is an obvious "push" to be righteous in one's own eyes and the eyes of others who make up the fractured separated while the other is a submission of the soul to its creator in humility. Admittedly, all are for the Lord our God but one with a distinct possibility of opening one's self up to the pridefulness that comes from the evil one.

As Christ has taught and as Henri Nouwen points out so poignantly in his *Spiritual Direction* that Christ always moved from personal isolated prayer with the Father to the community of His disciples and followers and then out to serve the community as a whole. Therefore, in our Christian communities we are asked to follow our Savior in His example and how we do this is starkly different between our Catholic communities and our non-Catholic communities. In the Catholic Church the presence of the Triune God is prominent drawing His people closer to Him in a "house of worship."

In contrast when the Christian enters a Catholic Church of any kind God is physically present in the elements of the Eucharist in the Tabernacle and if exposed in the Monstrance. Within the structure not only is housed our Triune God Himself but the consecrated humans in the reality of Priests and Bishops who have been given the vocation by the Holy Spirit to exercise the supernatural power that is able to turn the bread and wine into the body and blood of Christ, forgive us for our sins as persona Christi and reconcile us with God, to baptize us and confirm us into the "body of Christ," to marry us into a "one flesh" union and vocation till death do us part, to provide spiritual healing and possibly physical healing to our body and soul, and to send us off to eternity with God through burial.

The entire inside structure of the Catholic Church is the worship of God through all of our senses in celebration of our creation by God. We are surrounded by figures of our Christian "hall of fame," our Saints, who we venerate and honor for their surrender to God often as martyrs and always providing the community with models for "living Christ." And then to be blessed with the whole church, the Church Militant, the Church Suffering, and the Church Triumphant mystically there at the consecration in the Eucharist completing along with those in attendance the "Church Eternal."

So, one Christian tradition creates a communion of those here and now for fellowship and service. The other tradition creates a community, a communion, of fellowship and service for worship with those eternal and with the supernatural graces of the Triune God both here and now and in eternity—all for "worship."

The New Person Interfacing with Secular Society

Most new persons, especially lay people, are called to live in all three states of being as did Christ: solitude, community and service. Christ calls all Christians to spread the Gospel to everyone. There are no exceptions. There is nothing exclusive about Christianity on this side of the eternal. Nor is there anything exclusive about our role individually as Christians. We are to spread the Gospel. If we are not doing this we are not doing God's will, Period.

The new person must pray in solitude for the "conversion of sinners and the perseverance of the faithful," i.e. all of us and especially for those who do not believe in God and more specifically the Triune God with specific acceptance of the Second Person, Jesus Christ as their personal Savior. This is our daily general prayer that becomes specific as the Holy Spirit brings those into our lives that He is asking us to help in their conversion.

Prayer is the "executor" of the new person and is always paramount in our relations with God. Prayer is the foundation of all exercising of the faith as we deal with others in all three states of being. Prayer represents the foundation of any evangelism on our part.

First, as Catholics we believe that no one believes in God in any form, and certainly does not believe in a Triune God, and certainly no one comes to Christ and salvation through our own personal efforts alone. In fact, not through "our" efforts at all. God has instilled in the depths of every human heart the desire to believe in Him and we must work hard at removing that desire from ourselves if we choose to not believe. The soul, no matter how damaged or how hidden we may try to make it with our intellect, still wishes communication with God and will look for any small burst of a beam of His light to rekindle communication with Him.

Secondly, as new persons trying to surrender to God and put Him in control of our lives we have realized that we are simply conduits that God uses to bring Himself to others. As new persons we must in freedom allow our Triune God to use all conduits to reach others and these conduits can be almost as numerous as the stars in the sky since God reaches out to each person in a unique and special way using all aspects of human thought and activity to add to His flock. Given this, as new persons, we must be open to God to ask us to be these conduits in many different ways. This requires not only trying to listen to God through prayer but also being intellectually open to all the different ways that God may call us to evangelize. To begin to hear God's will for our words and actions for others we need to go to prayer specifically for purposes of understanding what God is asking us to do in areas of evangelization and who we are to evangelize to. As God speaks His directions may come to us in many different verbal and non-verbal ways from hearing His word directly to words and examples of others, through readings, through moments in His creation and through daily life. He will give us the opportunities and the situations to witness for Him in all of our human ways. We just have to remember that we must obey Him and not shy away from the opportunities.

We participate in our corporate or community evangelizing to our secular culture by meeting it directly. Here we engage in prayer for our secular neighbors as the community of the Church. Here we work in the community of our Church to meet people where they are as the body of Christ providing the bastion of truth and making our community a Marian community that excludes no one and invites all. Here we follow the teachings of the Church providing support to the outside by being who we are without compromise. This offers them a real solution for problems created by the unhealthy secular culture and gives them the opportunity for direction in life.

The new person is specifically called to two things we often would like to individually shy away from and leave to others. But we cannot do so. We individually must be evangelists. Secondly, we have to individually take care of the poor. Neither of these are just done by check for we must be faced with a direct and personal evangelistic challenge and we must see to the poor directly; not through agencies or groups but directly. There are enough poor to go around and usually they are closer than we think.

We go out beyond the Church into the community at large with each one of us as vocation/apostles working as one or in groups of many meeting the secular culture head-on, not in a "spirit of condemnation" but in a "spirit of love." We are actively offering a real alternative to a relativist society that can show the individual no way to go.

As new person Catholics we usually try to witness to those we come in contact with on a routine basis and we do not do this overtly. We wait for the opportunity to make comments and more importantly through our Catholic faith we provide witness in how we act in our lives. We do not try to force our witness on anyone but we should never hesitate to give the Holy Spirit all the opportunities we possibly can. When we are engaged in interfacing with the secular culture as activity teams, or civic or social or service groups we witness by the way we conduct ourselves. Showing our lives of "works" sourced in faith without compromise but steeped in love for our neighbor creates new souls for Christ and His Church one-by-one.

As we interface with our secular, actually neo-pagan world, we are confronted with not only people who have never considered God but who have looked at Christianity and the Church(s) and decided "no." This is not the pagan world that Paul confronted. It is a world that in general has known Christianity and rejected it. It is a culture that has in many instances taken Christian values and even Christian morality and taken Christ out of it. It is a culture that believes in humanism and an impersonal Unitarian type God that "created" but stays out of His creation. Where there is spirituality at all it is more of a Hindu or Buddhist introspective personal religion—far from Christianity's belief that God actually became man. Miracles now or then do not represent Divine intervention but man's lack of sufficient human knowledge.

This neo-pagan world may focus more on the "moment" than in the future and eternity. They do not take sin seriously even though they may acknowledge that the results of sin are burdening. They are not looking for salvation because they feel that their sin will not be of any matter in eternity.

> *But he thinks the way to have peace is not to have the weight lifted but to learn not to take it seriously. Hearing Christ's promise of forgiveness, he thinks, 'All those guilty Christians!' Having chosen to view the freest people as the most burdened, he naturally views the most burdened as the freest. 'Everyone has done things he regrets. Everyone lies. Get over it!* (J. Budziszewski)[50]

The other piece of the neo-pagan secular world we interact with as new persons is the phenomenon that there are now people who have never heard the Gospel even though they live in the midst of the modern technical communicative culture! There may even be those who are multi-generational in a lack of knowledge of the Gospel and Jesus!

So how does the new person fulfill his role of evangelization to those who have rejected Christianity and those who have never really heard or understood the basic elements of the Gospel message? How does the new person actually interface let alone evangelize with this neo-pagan world that is very large and may even be living next door?

As new persons the first thing we have to remember in interfacing with the secular culture is that our actions (witness) speak loudest. Therefore, all of our characteristics of new persons come into play so that we are acting often "differently" than our neo-pagan neighbors. We have to remember that many in the secular culture have moral standards that mimic Christian, even Catholic moral standards. But they are not. They may look alike but you will find at some point in time they abruptly no longer look like our moral standards because at the end of every moral effort of the neo-pagan is himself and self-centeredness that will show through at some point.

What truly impacts the neo-pagan is that we as Catholic new persons are doing whatever we do in a way that we are showing love to our neighbor, showing true joy, forgetting ourselves, and giving all the credit to our Triune God. There is no abrupt stop where we turn to self-centeredness. They are now being confronted with a Marian view of love that transcends sin and this is something that never crosses the secularist's thinking.

Need we be reminded that this cannot be words or actions of reprimanding or criticizing or condemnation? Accusations of sin will get you nowhere. They don't believe in sin. "Only love," as St. John said so often, as an aged but wise man, is what is needed. We love them and show that love in the ways of the characteristics of the new person. We do it in an authentic manner that is natural. We never sacrifice our sanctity or our dogma but we do it with love and above all we are consistent. And every moment we can we tell them where it is coming from. Not in trite phrases that sound memorized and made-up but in normal words that lead the other to feel that it is just a natural part of us. And oh, by the way, it is!

This way of approaching them will not jolt them into conversion in one fell swoop. It will take time and that is always defined as God's time. It may be that just the memory of the encounter over time makes them stop and think. But the actions on our part, whatever they were, may haunt them because there is something there that they do not have and they may not be able to just put it completely out of their minds.

The characteristics of the new person in dealing with the secularist culture will maybe be profound to the hearer but the other witness that makes such an impression on non-Catholics is to be able to defend your new person actions that come from the new person characteristics. The first of these is always the ability to transfer to the other in simple words that the Triune God loves them and what that means to them through what it has meant to you. The second is that this God is the only entity that they have to answer to and He is infinitely forgiving to those who just try to love and obey Him.

The third is to instill that this is not a matter of a variety of opinions on the subject but is the only truth. And that truth is that we are called to do what is the real barrier to Christianity for the neo-pagans and secularist Christians. This is giving up control to God and in trusting Him. Saying "no" to our culture's manic obsession with freedom as defined as, "doing whatever I want to do, when I want to do it," is a big and hard pill to swallow even though it cures the illness. This neo-pagan obsession with freedom has resulted in excuses for selfish and harmful behavior to ourselves and others okayed in the name of relativism. The secularist does not realize that we were made by God to want to surrender to Him and do His will. And that God has given us freedom to say no to Him but with the warning label in the form of the conscience that tells us that if we do not surrender to Him we have a greater probability of unhappiness. We, through free will have decided to be someone else and to do something other than what we were meant to do and be.

When the secularist or the neo-pagan interacts with a new person who is personally loving, forgiving, adaptable, empathetic, non-judgmental, yet strong in belief they see that the idea of loving thy neighbor as thyself is apparently actually doable and they can feel it. Some may actually wonder if being less self-centered and more loving of the other would make them happy people. Through our words and actions we want them to join us as happy people. If done in authenticity and sincerity of love for the other we have done our job for our Triune God and it is now up to the Holy Spirit to take over.

> *God willing, the new evangelization will happen, but let us not imagine that this time will be like the first time.* (J. Budziszewski)[51]

> *As for you, always be sober, endure suffering, do the work of an evangelist, carry out your ministry fully.* (2 Timothy 4:5)

Summary of the Transformation

In Summary, the New Person: Characteristics and Roles

The following are characteristics of Jesus and Mary in human-to-human relationships:

Characteristics of Jesus as Man:	Characteristics of Mary
Loving	Loving
Leader	Follower
Forgiving	Forgiving
Merciful	Merciful
Surrendering	Surrendering
Confident	Nurturing
Humble	Humble
Empathetic	Empathetic
Sacrificial	Sacrificial
Listener	Listener
Comfortable	Comfortable in role
Uncompromising	Ordered self-love
Compassionate	Pious
	Servicer
	Obedient
	Protective
	Confident

The following are characteristics of persons who are not new persons:

Common Male Characteristics:	Common Female Characteristics
Violent	Inferiority complex
Lustful/Sex Driven	Submissive
Possessive	Gossiper (poor ego)
Controlling	Manipulative
Domineering	Seductress
Protector	Disordered desire for male attention
Competitive	Materialistic
Hierarchical	Egocentric
Egocentric	Controlling
Manipulative	Loving
Aggressive	Nurturing
Superior	Surrendering
Materialistic	Sacrificial
Jealous	Jealous
Loving	Protective of children
Opinionated	

Transformation Flow

- God created woman to be a companion to the man.

- God is brought to the man through the woman because the woman has characteristics more like God than does the man and she was created to be a companion. The evil one through no fault of the woman may "ride her coattails" in order to create sin in the man. Having the characteristics of God she is always under attack by the evil one.

- The woman companion is equal to the man but different and has different characteristics.

- The New Person responds positively to the call from God to seek Him and spend eternal life with Him. The New Person begins the journey on the path that leads back to the Garden where they will spend eternity with God. The New Person follows Jesus and Mary along the path as they are led back to the Garden.

- The New Person is transformed by the Holy Spirit into one who has the characteristics of the New Person.

- God becomes the center of his/her every moment and he/she becomes a Disciple of Jesus.

Companionship

- The woman has more of the characteristics of God and is tasked by God to help the male come back to the Garden.

- The male has more natural sinful characteristics to overcome and the role of the woman is to use her God-given Godly characteristics to help the man as his companion. Many of these male characteristics were needed to "subdue and multiply" but have always been impediments and often killers in his way back to the Garden.

- Companionship is not confined to marriage but includes all Complex Trinitarian Communions.

In order for the male to become the New Person, he must have the following characteristics as well as the acceptance and surrendering to God and being on the journey:

- He must live the characteristics of Jesus as Man!

- Humble—humility makes him very powerful.

- Must be a listener and be patient in order to respond properly to others and to God.

- Must be a benevolent leader in a dominant but ordered way—thinking always of how his words and actions affect others and never willingly committing sin.

- He must love his fellow person.

- He must be a protector of family, friends and the marginalized and show it in his words and actions.

- He must be willing to sacrifice for God and others.

- He must be compassionate.

- He must be nurturing in helping his companion understand and allowing himself to receive information to help him better relate to and help women, children and others that he comes in contact with.

- He must have ordered self-love, i.e. a healthy but ordered ego—ordered with God.

- He must have an ordered sexuality.

- He must believe that women are equals and that they are meant by God to be a male's companion and bring God to him as well as help him return to the Garden.

- He must temper the male disordered characteristics below continuously in his life with the help of the woman as companion:

  o Violent behavior
  o Jealousy
  o Lust/Sex Driven
  o Possessive
  o Controlling

- o Domineering
- o Hierarchical
- o Manipulative
- o Egocentric to the extreme
- o Materialistic
- o Aggressive

- He must always cherish the woman as a true gift from God and acknowledge and accept her Godly characteristics and her divine mission and see these as divine grace!

The New Person Woman's *role* is to assist the male in tempering or modifying these male disordered characteristics with her characteristics and qualities that are more like God. This makes her the companion she was meant to be and for which she was created. The new woman's role as companion to the male are the following:

- To be the New Woman and all that it entails on a personal basis with Mary as the model.

- Think of herself as an equal and a companion of the male, yet different from the male.

- If she engages in the negative characteristics above that are contrary to the New Person Woman, then she will create schism between herself and the male in any relationship. She must not

o   consider herself inferior to the male and act infe-
     rior;
o   be submissive as though one of lesser value;
o   deliberately manipulate the male to get her way;
o   be totally obsessed with the male's response to
     her in everything and not allow her obsession to
     direct her life instead of God;
o   use sex to seduce the male to get her way. Sex
     should be sacred to her;
o   she must help to modify the male's disordered
     characteristics above;
o   should not engage in deliberate actions that would
     in a disordered way create anger, jealousy, etc. in
     the actions of an ordered male.

The Journey Back to the Garden

The Journey

Reflect on: *You show me the path of life. In your presence there is fullness of joy; in your right hand are pleasures for evermore.*

—Psalm 16:11, NRSVCE

Natural law, natural philosophy and natural theology suggest that the world God created is logical and deductive. Man is naturally created to seek God. Therefore, God has given man the ability to logically respond to his inner core desire to seek God within his culture and to do His will. When man chooses not to seek God he goes against the very core of his nature.

Man has a naturally given knowledge of what is right and wrong. Man may do what is right or not through God's grace of personal free will. Man naturally responds to God by choosing to do what is right or not. There are even universal norms adhered to. There are actions never taken. If one does violate these universal norms then one naturally separates himself from the rest of humanity as well as God and is put into a category despised by all.

The "journey" is man's natural response to a call from God to respond to Him in a deep and personal way of obedience or not. It is an invitation to travel forward back to the Garden of Eden, back to an intimate relationship with our Creator, back to a righteous relationship with God; the relationship of our Blessed Mother. It is the fulfillment of natural law, being the reason that we were born to begin with and why we were never meant to leave the Garden. It is a response by each of us to the success of the new Adam, the Christ and the new Eve, Mary. With freewill we decide to journey back to the Garden, our true home. We feel it in our inner being, our heart, our soul. It is so natural to be on the journey. As the new person we naturally hear the call of the journey and our soul naturally leaps to seek God.

Are all on the journey? No. Are all called? Yes. Are there any exceptions? No. Does one have to consciously be "on the journey" to be saved? Only God knows. We do know from Scripture and Christian tradition that all are not saved. Universalism is not true. There is free will and the corresponding responsibility. Not all will be willing to listen for the call and to join the journey. Jesus says this over and over in His parables. The gate is narrow and those who enter are few. To hear universalism promoted is to deny the true presence in the Eucharist. Christ was God incarnate as a human and reconciled us. We must manipulate the Holy Spirit's language and falsely qualify it to meet our feelings to believe in universalism. We blaspheme by superimposing our human will on the divine. None of us want to hear that all are not saved by a loving and forgiving God but none are lost by this same God. The decision is ours alone.

God has given us the intellect and the freewill to respond to His complete love with our love. Scripture and Tradition make it clear. Even Mary had to say yes.

Who is on this journey back home? Only those who with their human freewill respond positively to the call of the Holy Spirit to become the new person of the Beatitudes. You must want in the depths of your soul to truly want to "seek" God and be willing to want to leave your egocentric behavior behind and surrender to Him and obey Him. You must want to become a disciple of Christ who as God incarnate is the only one capable of saving us and of giving us a guide to take us back to His Garden. The journey is a serious life-long conversion.

Many may not hear the call because they are not listening for the call, too occupied with themselves and the secular world to care or listen. In every generation, there are those who simply say no to God and the call, and many may not over time want to make the effort to be on the journey. Many may not even believe that such a thing should or can exist, too totally absorbed in humanism to have time for the Creator of it all. The journey is very much like the parable of the seeds.

And here we are not talking about those who have not been introduced to the saving power of Christ and do not know Him. We are talking about those whose hearts are known by God and reject Him in favor of their own selfishness. Even if we profess to be Christians as Catholics we believe that one can lose salvation and negate the gift of the cross if one chooses. This is free-will. To think otherwise is to be presumptuous and negate Scripture. Christ's death was not carte blanche to anyone who just says yes—the yes has to be an attempt at having a deep and continuous conversion, a surrender, an obedience.

The Church believes that to reject the free gift of salvation requires very disordered intentional action on the part of the individual. We do not really understand why one would negate the reason for their very existence. But only our souls are truly known to God and the fate of others is not within our domain to fully understand nor forecast. For we do not think as God thinks. Therefore, we cannot be judgmental of others. Disordered comparison as we will learn later has no place in a Marian and new person perspective. It is not we who determine who else is on the journey. Our personal journey will suffice in difficulty, hardship and Divine Grace. However, we do believe that some lock themselves out of eternity with God.

We do know that if we respond to God and that we say "yes" we have the ability and the logic to know. It is a conscious effort on our part to respond to God. The journey is not a quick jolt of salvation that makes everything right forever. It is a real conversion, over time *as God sees fit* and *as we are able to handle His grace*. The journey may at times seem that "all is not well" and that we are "not doing well" but we are on the journey anyway. That is what is important. *That is God's grace.*

Since the response to the invitation to the journey is between the person and the Triune God we are and self-serving to think that we, ourselves, are able to convert others to join us on the journey. This is not to say we as journeymen do not have a responsibility for the salvation of others. But it is not just always in our hands to enlighten others. We are just facilitators of the Holy Spirit that offers the free gift. We are commanded to pray, to respond, to do inquiry, to witness to others but the victories are not ours, they are God's.

So what does it mean to be "on the journey" as a new person? There is a particular journey that one has to be on in order to become and sustain the "new person" required by Jesus over and over. There may be "other journeys" that lead to salvation in some sense but not to the new person. How Jesus judges the fate of those on these journeys cannot be judged by us. However, the other journeys are not the one of transformation required by Jesus in the Sermon on the Mount. When we are on the journey inaugurated by the Holy Spirit we know by logic in the mind and grace in the heart that we are on it. There is no question. We are embracing Jesus' command, taking it seriously, and being transformed every day. We show inwardly and outwardly our understanding of the command and we show commitment to it. For we are on the journey seeking God through Jesus Christ, God Incarnate, and our Paraclete, i.e. the Triune God.

If one is on the journey you will know it. Not by just the number of rosaries, masses, novenas, etc. but by a transformation of their heart in how they deal with you and others. They are overcoming themselves and giving part of themselves to you. Can you recognize this when it happens and why is there so much fear?

"They will say we are Christians by our love, by our love, yes they will say we are Christians by our love."

To "love thy neighbor as thyself" and to respond to Christ's new commandment "to love your neighbor as I have loved you" is a true transformation of the entire person—body, mind, heart and soul to become the new person required of us in the Sermon on the Mount. The new person who is ready to bring the Garden to others and to inhabit the Garden. This "transformed" is the one on the journey seeking the Trinity and being led by the Holy Spirit with the help of his spouse, Our Blessed Mother. This is deep conversion that results from allowing Christ to lead us back to our Garden, by showing us how "to be Holy as our Lord God is Holy" with our Blessed Mary as our human and spiritual model. To understand this transformation we need to experience what it means to be the new person of the Beatitudes, to understand how we make our way on the path and the many experiences of good and evil we will encounter on the way. What better way to prepare us than to let our guide, our Blessed Mother show us what to expect as we are transformed on the journey, as we imitate her model of humanity without sin, as we understand how "to love others as I have loved you": her Marian Spirituality.

Where the Journey Takes Us Interiorly As We Move Away From Self-Centeredness and Serious Sin

What can the new person expect as he is slowly transformed for eternity? Interiorly, we are being transformed in a subtle but supernatural way by the Holy Spirit. We may not be able to note the times of the changes but we slowly become aware and are less oblivious to God's working in us. We are somehow subtly different and our experiences in thoughts and words and interaction with others take on a different perspective. The lenses of our view of others is somehow different, we subtly see the world differently, God becomes more the focus than ever before, not just in big decisions and big events but in the small things of continuous life.

We are now slowly becoming open to all of creation and all sensual communication with God. Somehow things are different. We focus more on not only God's creation of nature but on our fellow humans and their creations. We begin to see them as the Beloveds of God and more of our brothers and sisters and less as strangers and, "just other competitors." If we are with other new persons we feel a closeness never felt before, more like a beloved family member and less of an irritating sibling. Our focus is not just ocular but is now emotional and emotion is now "okay."

We notice now, sometimes after the fact, of how God has communicated with us in a situation easily resolved, a prayer answered in some way, a change in our view of a situation, a feeling inside; maybe a concrete communication or maybe a sensual communication with God. Our open readiness tries to match God's expectations. We are open to the expectations of whatever God has for us. We are expected to try to be clear-headed, normal, knowledgeable and intelligent and dedicated to God's will. We seek a natural and supernatural equilibrium in our lives.

Interiorly, things in life become clearer and more serious with minds that are not clouded. Serious, not in the dire sense but in knowing what is around us and caring about it and those we encounter. In a real sense we "already know without words being necessary" what has been communicated. If we are aware of it God does not force anything. Everything is a part of our development in God's hand. He controls it and we respond in a loving child-like manner. We surrender as does a bride to her bridegroom.

We begin to see this in daily life, we pursue it in prayer. All prayer is more natural, we are more aware and it becomes a natural part of every moment—"we pray without ceasing." We need the discipline of particular spaces and times for prayer because we are novices, we are not there yet in prayer, and we will never quite be there in this life. In prayer and thoughts and life we add contemplative prayer to life and we hear God without words! Something we never even thought of! We are now opening ourselves to a deeper prayer life with greater risk. We ask God to do everything in us according to His will. We open ourselves to not having human assurances, security and protection. We open ourselves to an even greater existence of which we know nothing.

Exteriorly, we are transformed by the interior. Exteriorly, we strive to attain what we can through learning, other persons, the Church, etc. but interior understanding supersedes [all] learning.

On the journey we strive continuously to let nothing be permitted to be an obstacle between the person and God. The battle with our self-centeredness is a continuous one to accomplish this as we move down the path interiorly and exteriorly.

> *We have set our hearts for the way; this journey is our destiny. Let no one walk alone. The journey makes us one.*
> (Roy Cooney)[52]

Sin Remains

Reflect on: *If we confess our sins, he is faithful and just, and will forgive our sins and cleanse us from all unrighteousness. If we say we have not sinned, we make him a liar, and his word is not in us."*

—1 John 1:9–10, RSVCE

In our hearts and minds and souls we are on the journey and seeking God. There is no doubt in our minds. We are on the path. We would never go back to a previous time. We know God has called us "by name." We embrace the God imaged by Nouwen in whom we each are the "Beloved of God," a God who is always with us, who continually forgives us, who blesses us each day and who guides us. We have seen His work in our lives in the fog of times passed, and we feel it at the moment as we journey toward eternity with Him. He is mostly subtle but altering us in all cases. Our heart and our mind pursuing God is like the unfolding of a flower as we grow in our understanding of the theology of our Catholic faith. We are versed in the Scriptures, we completely embrace the sacraments, we have a spiritual prayer life, we love our Church, we look to Our Mother for a model, we hope for our soul's eternity with God and we attempt to pass on the faith to others.

But…we continue to commit grave sin, even mortal sin.

Our heart is totally given to the pursuit of God but we sin over and over. Yes, we are told that we are "all sinners" and yes we can accept the fact that we will continue to sin in many subtle, venial ways, "but grave sin!" How can that be? We are not questioning our being one of the "elect" but as Catholics we know our vulnerability to the loss of salvation if we work at it. How does that black spot of sin in our gut continue to be there and overly influence negatively our relationship with ourselves and with God? How is it that we are giving into the strategy of the evil one? How can this be? We don't fear God in possible damnation in order to obey but we embrace God in love by wanting to obey.

Then why do we betray Him and support the evil one? Where is our prayer life in removing this grave sin? Where is our prayer life in helping our venial sins to not become mortal in nature? Are we kidding ourselves about our laundry list of virtues in our pursuing God? Is our prayer rote and are we deceiving ourselves through our own self-centeredness into believing that we are "right" with God in our lives. Sure, there are notable examples of the "righteous" sinning such as David. There are many notable Saints who themselves were not virtuous before conversion. But in many of these historical examples and in the lives of many today a critical conversion experience so changed their lives that they no longer sin. We understand they were tempted and in the thoughts of St. Frances de Sales they were tempted but in that "moment" of temptation they did not "entertain the pleasure of the temptation" and therefore commit the sin. So if we know about the "moment" before we say "yes" to the evil one in the temptation and do not seize that moment to not sin then we are in fact sinning by entertaining the temptation and possibly its overt action.

The sin is always thought to be enjoyable to us no matter how destructive to ourselves or our souls. We want to do it and, as with addiction when we do not have it we feel deprived. This may be psychological or physical or both. Yet when we commit the sin we may loath ourselves and begin in small or large ways to question that we are God's Beloved. We have once again betrayed "the God we should love above all else." We are now in the camp of the evil one.

Our journey in pursuit of God will through progression give us all the resources we need to help us with our concupiscence. Since the journey is a progression in time as well as spiritual growth we each will be at different points in our journeys and since journeys are different and determined by the Holy Spirit comparison should not come into play. Despite where we are on the journey we face the evil one and our sins. These never leave us. However, we also have the Trinity always there helping us to the degree that we allow.

The resources to help us overcome grave sin as well as venial sins are always there. We often do not recognize them because we do not recognize the role of the "executor" of our spiritual journey, prayer, and how prayer in its solitude, community and action provide the grace to overcome the sin. Prayer in all of its forms is necessary and our dependence on God in our state of belovedness must be always a part. Truly grave sin in which the evil one is well entrenched behind our battle line may require even a lifetime to overcome. If the nature of the sin is deeply rooted in psychological issues that may go back to childhood the sin may never be conquered in this lifetime. The same may be true if the effects of the sin are physical in nature as well as psychological.

But the Trinity will never abandon us no matter what the physical or psychological issues, the origin of the sin or the severity of the sin. The Trinity is always with us and we never cease to be the Beloved of our God. One must be on the journey and pursuing God to truly understand this phenomenon. If God would sacrifice His Son to bring us back to Him then He is certainly capable of not shunning His goal of our companionship with Him through eternity. He is always there to help! He never leaves! We can sin on the hour every hour with the same sin but He does not leave.

We have no idea why some are called to the journey. We suspect that all are but some because of self-centeredness never hear His call to get on the path. Predestination has no place here. God is the Beloved of all! Yet we are all weak by spiritual nature. By weak we mean we find it very hard to become as non-self-centered as possible in order to give the running of our life over to God. We have trouble living the life of our model, Blessed Mary.

To overcome sin to the degree we are capable we must rely on the Trinity for graces. We must first surrender to God as Mary did and be willing to accept whatever comes. Again, we must be able to accept whatever comes. This is the hardest part of the spiritual journey away from grave sin. If we are to fail it will really be here whether or not we realize it even if that realization does not come until farther down the journey. We must be willing to suffer through the depravation of not having the sin. This giving up of the sin to God and the "whatever" outcome is the big "moment" when our whole being inches toward the side of God. Here we are saved by Our Beloved in a mystery that truly surpasses all of our understanding!

> *Repent therefore, and turn again, that your sins may be blotted out, that times of refreshing may come from the presence of the Lord…* (Acts 3:19)

> *For we have not a high priest who is unable to sympathize with our weaknesses, but one who in every respect has been tempted as we are, yet without sinning. Let us then with confidence draw near to the throne of grace, that we may receive mercy and find grace to help in time of need.* (Hebrews 4:15–16)

Life on the Journey:
Passing Through the Narrow Gate

What Does This Mean?

Reflect on: *Let your light so shine before men, that they may see your good works and give glory to your father who is in heaven.*

—Matthew 5:16, RSVCE

"Passing through the narrow gate," what does this mean? To try to be a new person and be on the journey and to be following our Lord and Mary down the path back to the Garden does not include everyone. As we previously said with great sadness there are far too many that either do not listen to the call or reject the call as if there are no consequences for doing so. So the narrow gate is not the narrow gate of God but the one we as humans have constructed. Except for free will and Him making us, "in His likeness," He would have destroyed it a long time ago. For love has to be reciprocal between the creatures and their Creator.

So by grace we are called and by free will to accept the journey and the other graces and crosses that go with it. As we say "yes" to the journey we are willingly trying to surrender to God with complete faith, giving up control and asking Him to direct our lives while trying to obey Him.

Our first task on the journey will be what He tells us. It will always be about sin because sin is the evil one's way of running us off the path. Even though he knows that he will not win. He knows that being on the path puts us in his cross-hairs and makes us even more vulnerable to sin. Why would the evil one waste his time on those who are already following him instead of joining the journey.

The Saints have all told us that this is what we have to rid ourselves of first. Remove the fog and the ear plugs so we can begin to see and hear God.

After beginning the journey we can no longer accept our mortal sins. Don't kid yourself, we all have them and we have to begin to control them. We have surrendered to God. He now asks us to surrender our past mortal sins through good confessions and to try to move down the path without them. We now have Him to help us and we better learn to rely on Him because we cannot do it ourselves. If we do not acknowledge this we will very soon quit the journey. It may take into eternity to rid ourselves of these rebellions against God but we have to try and learn from example how the great one's before us captured their sins and locked them up forever—all the while knowing that God loves us anyway, unconditionally, and is there to help.

As we move away from ourselves and our egoism we realize that the spiritual warfare of the supernatural is now our spiritual warfare fought daily in small skirmishes. These are our venial sins. We win these, we win the spiritual war. We lose these; we put our salvation in danger. They push us off the path and slow our journey. By renewing our objective we fill the empty spaces on the path with spiritual awareness as we seek redemption.

Whether we like it or not this is "confession." This is "confession" to God and the Priest and confession to our neighbor followed by true penance in thought, word and action. But what was unwinnable before is now winnable today through daily skirmishes with the evil one because we have surrendered to the Creator and He will always protect us if we ask/allow.

This all requires one difficult concept that we must really and truly understand and believe. That is: supernatural spiritual warfare is real and the evil one does actually exist and he actually and overtly is trying to do us in.

Please, no confusion here! Surrendering to God and obeying Him now that we are on the journey does not mean we are off the hook to be responsible for ourselves! We still have free will to obey or not and we are not free from concupiscence. It means that we have to, even if painful, show heroic virtue through self-imposed discipline. Learn to say "no" to the evil one and "no" to ourselves. The difference now that we are on the journey is the same difference as before. It is that the Trinity is there to encourage us and see us through. The Trinity is on the journey with us and our spiritual health is the paramount virtue of and the focus of our life.

Health then takes on a different meaning for those on the journey. We are of course talking about spiritual health, i.e. the right relationship with God and our fellow man. But we are also talking about health that extends to every area of our being. We are now becoming disciples of Christ. We are true soldiers in the spiritual war and we have to train and by training we become more the new person and therefore able to do God's will in our lives.

Communication means everything. Prayer is our communication with God. Prayer is essential for good spiritual health but also affects our psyche, our mind and our body. Prayer has to become the "executor" in our life, i.e. the means to all of our spiritual and bodily ends.

A discussion in depth will follow on "prayer as the executor." Suffice it to say that at this point understand that one must have a rule of prayer, a daily route to praying without ceasing to hear God's voice and develop us into the new person. And this is not just personal. We have to combine, we have to always combine, with our spiritual mates in the corporate prayers of the Church and in the Divine interface of the Eucharist.

Giving ourselves up to God's control transforms us into being in a "right relationship" with God through prayer. We follow Mary down the path and we progressively move beyond ourselves into caring for others. The old, "prayer, fasting and alms" to righteousness now looks to us in a different light. The prayer part we may have previously "got," and maybe even the alms part we understood before, but the fasting part in today's world is less popular, burdening the concept with denial of specific items or activities or the taking on of odorous ones instead of the simple classical denial of normal amounts of food. Our evolving moves away from self-serving attitudes and leads us to rediscover classic fasting. There is something spiritually rich in the denial of food for the deliberate purposing of another. Coupled with the giving up of money for another's welfare oddly moves our thinking and our being away from ourselves and more fully into another in not just a spiritual way. And oddly it feeds ourselves with a "well-being" that transcends ourselves and makes us feel good inside. The Saints were right. Prayer, fasting, and alms giving does bring us closer to God through the righting of our relationship with our fellow man and therefore Him.

This is real training for the new person! This is always real training for the new person, even years later as we continue being molded into disciples.

A result of our moving down the journey's path is a growing feeling of certainty of the "other" as we move away from the "I." We can almost in a sense feel and taste the other's personhood and spirituality. We are so unfocused on ourselves that we begin to see the beauty of the individual tree despite the vastness of the forest. We see the entirety of the person and as we do so the little chinks in the bark of their tree become less and less important. No matter what fungus grows on them or how many bugs threaten their existence or how little nourishing water they are getting, they are just a mirror of me, a Beloved of God and a fellow child in Christ. I want then to love them despite themselves and look for any opportunity to heal their wounds, to nourish them with that water of the Holy Spirit that never ceases to flow and to pick the bugs off their bark throwing these sins away as God has thrown away my sins. And yes, I feel good inside, a good that does not come from me but an affirmation and validation that God is in us and that the supernatural has severed time and space.

As we journey down the path we very quickly become thirsty, thirsty for the charism of knowledge and understanding. Not just for our own benefit but so that we can share the truth of the universe with others close and far. This is God influencing us. This is God, this is religion. When we sense the truth and then begin to know pieces we yearn for the whole. We want to study, we want to understand, we want to pursue God as a man's passion pursues a woman. And we can never get enough. So we read, read and read not to stroke our intellectual ego but to change our thinking and our doing and to change the thinking and doing of others. Why? Just to win some philosophical or theological argument? No, to know the "other" more completely with knowledge that is never self-serving but exists for the "other" serving only.

And first where is our fervor and where is our immediate focus but on the eternal church known as our family. The Church started in homes of families and the home is still the Church. We are its pastors and our sheep are those closest to us in family and friends. We never want even one to stray and if we do we want to get them back before the nightfall of eternity.

This domestic church often provides us with our greatest challenges. But this is where our buck stops and where we must first be the new person with as many of and as quickly as possible the characteristics of the new person. This is where we often fail but this is also where we, if we are being converted, ask for forgiveness and seek redemption often. This is where we can truly make a difference and truly bring others to Christ. Hard yes, but doable if we are seriously surrendering to God and seeking beyond all of our own baggage.

As we expand beyond our domestic church to our Parish we begin to find ourselves at Church for the right reason—the pursuit of God in the role of a disciple, a disciple in solitude, in community and in service. We are not there to stroke the ego but to serve God by serving others. We participate. We are never the source of friction. We help others no matter how difficult they may seem.

The new person will never do anything that might impede anyone from coming to a closer relationship with our Triune God. And are we loving others and putting them before ourselves? These are the measurements for our Christian

Catholic community and important measurements of the quality of our journey.

The steady state of the new person on the journey then is one of comfort in the role of "becoming," becoming a disciple and therefore becoming a listener to God, becoming a member of Christ on earth—the Church, and becoming a lover of God's other Beloveds. We, "pass through the narrow gate, hand-in-hand as new persons."

> *When the morning comes, solitude greets solitude and community is formed. It's remarkable that solitude always calls us to community…The symbol of the dawn is the awareness that we are all related, connected, and interdependent.* (Henri Nouwen)[53]

> *The definition of the saint is a person who wills what God wills; he is forever leaping into the abyss of God.* (A. von Speyr)[54]

The Parable of the Squirrel

Dan was driving his car down a typical street in The Woodlands. As he rounded a curve a jogger moved down the jogging path and frightened a squirrel sitting close to the road. The squirrel jumped and in fright and ran full speed head-on into the side of the wheel of Dan's car; killing the squirrel. Dan did not know what happened. The squirrel was to the side of the front of his car and out of Dan's line-of-sight. Nor was the squirrel heavy enough to make any sound on the car when it hit the wheel.

As a Catholic on the journey what could be true?

Since Dan was unaware of the occurrence that killed the squirrel did it actually happen?

Did Dan know he had killed the squirrel?

Was Dan responsible for the death of the squirrel?

Was Dan guilty of killing the squirrel?

Did Dan commit a sin?

Eliana was driving behind Dan in route to the same destination. Eliana had seen the death of the squirrel. When they both arrived at their destination, Eliana told Dan that she had seen him kill the squirrel.

Did Dan have any responsibility or remorse now that he knew that his car had killed the squirrel?

It was a squirrel, not a person or even a utility dog. Who cares or who should care?

And what does the death of this squirrel teach us about Mary and what does Mary and the Parable of the Squirrel teach us about relationships?

The fact that Dan was not aware of the death of the squirrel before arriving at his destination and hearing the words from Eliana does not matter. Not knowing of an occurrence does not negate its happening. The fact that the squirrel died from the incident and that Eliana witnessed the event means it happened. If Dan's car had not been there the squirrel would not have been killed at that time. Dan cannot act as if it did not occur just because he was not aware of it.

Dan did not know he had killed the squirrel at the time of the incident. This does not mean he is not responsible for the squirrel's death.

Dan was responsible for the death of the squirrel even if unknowingly. There are many precedents in law with events that are considered "non voluntary" in nature.

Dan did not commit a sin. He did not try to kill the squirrel and since he did not have prior knowledge to the occurrence he did not have the opportunity to choose a course of action. Is killing a squirrel even considered a sin? Killing a man is a sin, killing a squirrel is not.

Dan was not guilty of killing the squirrel. Guilt supposes the opportunity to choose to do or not choose to do something regardless of whether or not killing a squirrel is even a sin.

Did Dan have any responsibility after learning from Eliana that he had killed the squirrel? Does it matter if a squirrel is killed by a human? The Bible tells us that for one, God does care that the squirrel was killed. If He knows when a sparrow falls from the sky He also knows when a squirrel dies. God chartered us to be masters of His creation, to subdue it and care for it. We can make a clear decision to take an animal's life for the purpose of essentials considered needed for man to live or for the welfare of the animal. But when we accidentally take that animal's life and we are aware of it as custodians of God's Earth we should experience some remorse. Guilt is not involved nor sin committed. However, if we deliberately move our car to kill an animal whose life we had the alternative to spare are we being custodians of God's Earth? This is disorder and shows disorder in our view of life not only for animals but maybe for our fellow man. Is this not really pride and egocentric disrespect for our Creator?

If the squirrel is important to God are not our relationships with other human beings even more important to God! With our fellow man we are asked to love one another, not subdue and manage the other as we do with animals.

Mary's pondering was not reactive but proactive and what difference does it make.

In relationships and more so in the intimacy of friendships we must "try" to understand the other so well that we know when the other deliberately kills the squirrel, or accidently kills the squirrel knowingly or unknowingly. The death of the squirrel is merely a metaphor for our relationship with one another. Likewise we need to understand how the metaphor applies to our own motivations and actions.

The squirrel is unimportant and tiny in the environment yet to God even the squirrel is important. We may feel at times just as the squirrel, unimportant, tiny, unknown, and vulnerable to our culture and the world at large. We, like the squirrel, could instantly cease to exist. We may even think that our existence if extinguished tomorrow would be as uneventful as the death of the squirrel and of only some importance to a small few. We are merely the small things of life that as Scripture tells us flowers into the mornings of our years and withers in the afternoons of our years.

But if we understand the vast Earth of God's love and if we see God in our relationships and particularly in our friendships then we see the responsibilities toward them, the responsibility for sins and guilt committed by ourselves and them and we pursue our responsibility to God and our friends in a way that makes us truly human and as grand as the squirrel in the eyes of God.

When we are made aware of our effects on others we encounter responsibility. We have a duty, an obligation that should be complete love in helping the other no matter whether we were aware of our action or whether or not we should have guilt. As the squirrel invokes the metaphor of smallness, in the context of all the little things between two people we find the things that often matter most. It is these little things that matter and bring joy and hurt.

We are not asked to be just reactive to those who matter to us and others who are tiny in our parochial view. As people on the journey we are asked to consider all "squirrel" humans as important. We are further asked to consider those close to us and particularly friendships as providing us with responsibility to go beyond being "reactive" to being proactive. We are asked to understand the other, their cares and concerns, their sins, their love language, their little things in their lives and make sure we anticipate their needs and not just react to them. Most important God is calling us to care about them, not us, them. We are being called to be remorseful and care about the deaths in joy, in actions, in words that we perpetrate on others. We are asked to be truthful, loving, forgiving, and patient with others in creating that Trinitarian Communion. We are asked to care about the "squirrel." He also, is part of God's plan.

We must not think for a moment that Mary's "pondering" was reactive. She had to be a woman of action, a woman of action based not on her own egocentric needs but on the needs of her Son and the needs of others. She was proactive, not reactive! She loved others to such a great extent that she took the role of the "squirrel"—tiny, unimportant in the world, humble, but always knowing that she was a child of the loving God that cared for her as well as the squirrel. She took care of the little things in people and actions. She cared about her responsibility to see other's needs before they became known as Scripture shows us at Cana, the Visitation and Pentecost. As with Mary we are asked to know enough about our friendships, care enough, and know what others need before they know. We are asked to care that we affect and may affect others. We are asked to care about the squirrel. Mary would have.

Our Crosses Are Gifts

Reflect on: *Whoever does not bear his own cross and come after me, cannot be my disciple.*

—Luke 14:27, RSVCE

"Suffering is such sweet sorrow!" Not exactly what we think of when we think of suffering is it? Nothing very sweet about physical and/or mental suffering and anguish as most of us think of it. Our own crosses seem to always have a negative connotation to them with suffering as the effect. As Catholic Christians we have for ever been separated from our Christian brethren in understanding that Christianity requires us to go through our crosses as the only way to salvation. Jesus never suggested that all would be well in this world by following Him. We must go through our crosses to get to His cross.

Our crosses are usually negative, being natural afflictions beyond our ability to change, often self-inflicted, inflicted by others or family or by society. As we mature in our journey we begin to understand that the negative crosses we are given to bear may often result in positive results and blessings" in this life" as well as prepare us for the next. They are in fact, graces.

The challenge in understanding and action is how we unite our personal cross and sufferings with Christ and His suffering on the cross. We share in the passion of Christ on the cross in some way through our suffering and therefore appreciate His sacrifice and begin to understand it to a human degree.

And where is the one who is not on the journey? He may find himself mired in disappointment of his place and plight in life and therefore may blame God for his struggles. He constantly struggles for control, personal control, in some ways even control of hatred by not understanding that his salvation in this world and in the next is giving up his sacred personal control to God and removing it from himself.

But can these sufferings truly be "sweet sorrow." Can the Holy Spirit give us a cross that is not a negative but a true positive in its nature and a truly wonderful gift even though we suffer as a result of it? Could this cross be a person or circumstance deliberately put there by God to aid us in our salvation? Is the consolation for the wonderful suffering bringing us closer to God than moving us further away from God? When we realize that we cannot control an aspect of life and if we are on the journey we give it to God and the more we do so the happier we become.

Was not Jesus's day-to-day suffering while He was with us this type of wonderful cross? He suffered over His love for all those who forsook Him, the lost sheep of Israel, He suffered over His love for the leaders of Israel who rejected

Him, He suffered over Jerusalem, He suffered for so many in His earthly existence and for those for all time that would/will not accept the free gift of salvation. Only God can purely love like this.

What happens to us when we are so blessed by God that we are given a wonderful gift of a cross that could only come from God through the Holy Spirit? We welcome the suffering with open arms and enthusiasm. We embrace it with anticipation. It is worth it in all of its anguish. We can never have what we desire nor be freed from the cross but to have it is immeasurably better than to not have it. We feel truly blessed that God would love us individually so much that He would give us this gift. And then where are we? We are to a greater degree hanging on the cross with Christ, suffering with Christ and feeling the truly blessed warmth and love of Almighty God! Thank you God for the unique gift of suffering that you have given me!

What happens when the Holy Spirit boxes us in to a situation in life that we cannot control without destroying ourselves and others? We acknowledge it as a wonderful situation and a blessing despite our suffering daily. The Holy Spirit only gives good to His children, never a snake or a scorpion.

To be on the journey is to carry your crosses no matter how negative and to make them positive for the glory of God. To feel the ultimate love of God is to be given the wonderful gift of blessed suffering.

For to this you have been called, because Christ also suffered for you, leaving you an example, so that you should follow in his steps. (1 Peter 2:21)

Let us run with perseverance the race that is set before us, looking to Jesus the pioneer of our faith, who for the sake of the joy that was set before him endured the cross, disregarding its shame, and has taken his seat at the right hand of the throne of God. (Hebrews 12:2)

Trinitarian Communions

The Trinitarian Communion

"Every true Christian relationship has to triangulate with God."

> **Reflect on:** *You shall love the Lord your God with all your heart, and with all your soul, and with all your mind. This is the great and first commandment. And a second is like it, You shall love your neighbor as yourself.*
>
> —Mathew 22:37–39

The Trinitarian Communion was the relationship between God and mankind at creation and is the manifestation of the redemption in God's economy of salvation for mankind for eternity. As God's children we begin life in the Garden of our mother's womb in perfect harmony with God. As did Adam and Eve from the Garden of Eden, with birth we move out and away from the perfection of the Garden womb into the world as we begin our journey to death and the Garden. This is life as given to us by our Creator to glorify Him through His creation and His perfect love for that creation. This is pure redemptive love given to us by our Triune God whose overwhelming, indescribable love for us allows us to choose our own redemption. We either choose to accept or we choose to reject. His love is so great that we have the free will to follow or not.

We often spend a lot of this time between womb and tomb in periodic rejection of this Divine love. The child moves out from the womb and away from the mother into greater independence and into self-centeredness and egocentric behavior, i.e. sin. The Church gives us baptism and the Holy Spirit to help us begin the process back to God but through free will we may or may not respond.

Yet, God continues to unceasingly call us to follow His Triune nature and our mortal mother Mary back to His Garden for eternity. If we can move beyond ourselves long enough we hear His call and make the decision to follow Him on the journey, not away from the Garden, but back to the Garden. Our hearing His call begins our process of re-creation into the individual new person God meant us to be—the Beloved Child of God. We surrender our lives to Him and seek to obey Him. As we are transformed as individuals through conversion we truly seek God with all of our heart, soul and mind. This transformation allows us to begin to see others as God sees them, Beloveds of God. Relationships now become God-centric for the new person no matter who the "other" is.

A Trinitarian Communion implies a "relationship" and is associated with the new person. It is formed as each new person man or woman choosing to seek God has an individual relationship with the Triune God. In turn each new person man or woman has interpersonal relationships with other men or women, e.g., Man/Woman to God in Heaven, God to Man/Woman from Heaven. (CCC 249–256) These relationships may be between new persons or a new person and a non-new person. The key is that one of the persons must be a new person seeking the "right relationship with God." This is a, "loving God with all your heart, soul and mind" relationship. The Man/Woman to Man/Woman on Earth is the, "love your neighbor as yourself relationship."

We can see this visually in the figure of an isosceles triangle. An isosceles triangle has an apex with two opposite but equal sides and a base. This symbolizes the Trinitarian Communion. God is always at the apex in each relationship, with man or woman and woman or man being equal in all ways yet residing as individuals on the different sides. They are always sloping up to God, looking up toward Him in surrender and obedience. The base represents the relationship between the man or woman and the woman or the man. (See Diagram A below).

Why is this Trinitarian Communion important? Because in interpersonal relationships with new persons we approach a reality of, "loving our neighbor as ourselves." This is a commandment of our Lord! (John. 15:12–17)

Note to reader: The following triangular representations are generally based upon the lecture discussion of Sean Innerst in the Pillar I course on "The Creed" (see Bibliography).

Diagram A.

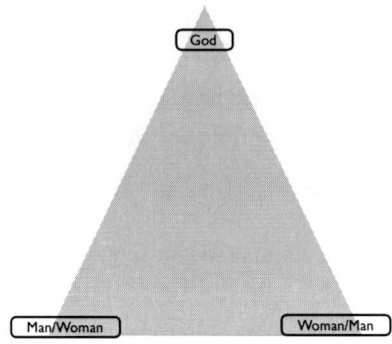

Diagram B.

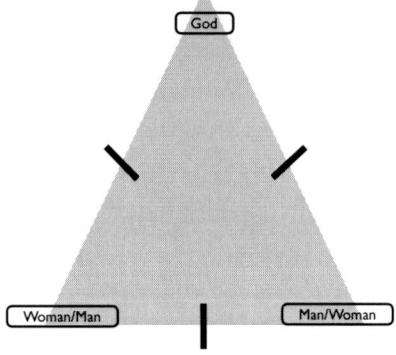

Trinitarian Communions with uninterrupted lines represent healthy relationships between God and the man or woman and between the different possible combinations of men and women. When there is no Trinitarian Communion then one or more of the sides are fractured/interrupted by unbelief or sin (Diagram B.). If the man or woman or both do not have a personal relationship with God, either through unbelief or non-interest there is no Trinitarian Communion. The Trinitarian Communion always involves God and the new person in the "right" relationship with God. There will be times that through individual sins the new person man or woman will interrupt their relationship with God. But if it is a Trinitarian Communion then these are interruptions that will be short-lived and redeemed through prayer and the sacraments.

If the fracture (Diagram B.) is in the base line of the Communion then this represents a state of disruption in the relationship between the new persons or a new person and a non-new person. This redemption of both as new persons requires immediate discussion of the issues between the individuals with prayer and possibly the sacraments. This reconciliation needs to occur as quickly as possible for the evil one not to enlarge the fracture. Never should this fracture between new persons move from issues to personal attacks.

Diagram B.

In the case where there is a fracture in the base line and one of the persons is not a new person, then we are dealing with a fracture that threatens even the possibility of an eventual Trinitarian Communion. The new person hopes that the other will be eventually open to hear God's call and respond appropriately but it may be that the other will never "will" to become the new person. For the new person this is a relationship that may not work out no matter the degree of attempt on their part. If this is a marriage relationship then one's journey on the path back to the Garden is a difficult one. The new person must never compromise being the new person to the other, and must pray and seek help from a spiritual companion and/or clergy. A spiritual friendship cannot exist in this scenario at all.

There is a potentially wide spectrum of possible Trinitarian Communions. In the broadest sense if you are a new person on the journey seeking God then each person you meet represents an opportunity for a Trinitarian Communion. Immediately, if the other is not a new person then the Trinitarian Communion in spontaneity most likely evaporates immediately. Regardless the stage of the journey and if time permits it is possible if both desire to develop a Trinitarian Communion. If both are new persons then in spontaneity a Trinitarian Communion is formed even if time does not allow its continued development. If time does allow then a Trinitarian Communion can develop that allows us to love the other in the way that Christ meant for it to be in the Sermon on the Mount—not simply a concept but a concrete reality!

The concept of the Trinitarian Communion particularly describes the relationship of God to His creatures and the relationships between women and men in their mutual relationship with the Creator. These triangular concepts also help us to understand what God intended in terms of relationships and what He did not intend.

We see the intentions of God and the results of sin on those intentions in the triangular relationship of how the Holy Trinity is within our human bodies. This is a "mini-trinity" of God's creation as in the Garden and how this "good" relationship within us was perverted by sin through the Fall. And, we see how in the Garden that there was a threefold harmony of exterior relationship between man and God which was destroyed by the same sin.

The Catechism of the Catholic Church (CCC) speaks of this mini-trinity as the Trinity of the human body, soul and spirit (the highest part of the soul). The body is how we are in the "image" of God, gendered, and made for love. The spirit is intellect and will. The soul is our human spiritual nature which is immortal. This is seen diagrammatically as:

Mini-Trinity

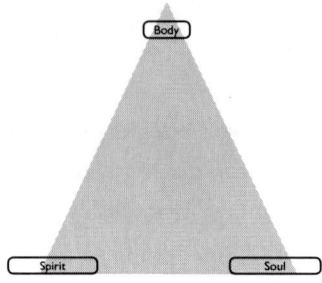

The new person is called by God to live differently, to "master himself." This brings him to have the ability to be the master of his body, spirit and soul in an ordered way in surrender to God. When a person is unable to master himself, he succumbs to concupiscence and we see the encouragement of evil influencing the person in his willingness to sin and not master his own body, let alone his spirit and soul. The result is that the body sins through lust and passion, the spirit is one of pride instead of humility and the soul covets (lust of the eyes). The result is the fracture in relationships leading to the inability to form a Trinitarian Communion or the ability to sustain an existing one:

Effects of Concupiscence
on the Mini-Trinity of the Individual

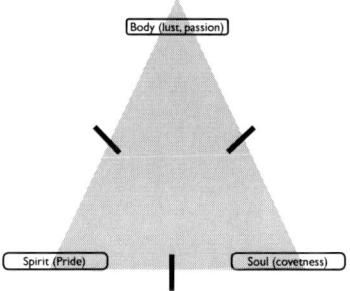

The new person is on his journey back to the Garden where there existed a threefold harmony between God and man. In the Garden there was "original justice" or "integrity," a harmony of the human person, i.e., the right ordering of the internal powers of the person, "communion," harmony between man and woman, and "dominion," harmony between the first couple and all of creation.

Threefold Harmony
between God and Man in the Garden

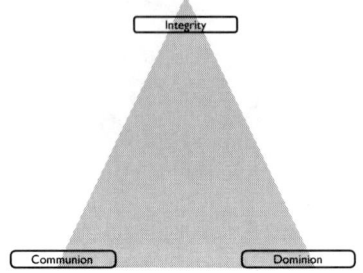

In our fallen world this threefold harmony is fractured. Integrity becomes concupiscence through rebellion against God and a false understanding of freedom, dominion becomes travail or the groaning of creation through a lack of respect for God seen in greed toward all of God's human and natural resources, and communion becomes strife, most apparent with the almost war that is raged between woman and man. Despite our yearning for and the cry for "intimacy between man and woman we also in the same breath tell each other to, "Stay at arm's length."

Original Harmony's Threefold Fall

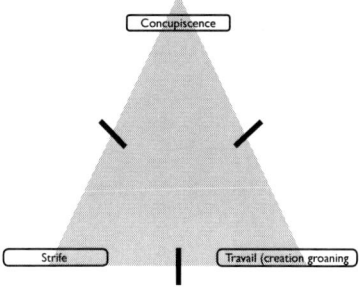

The two theological images of the Trinitarian Communion is "The Church as the Bride of Christ" and "marriage." But the more ultimate and mystical experience of the Trinitarian Communion is when heaven meets earth in the Eucharist. This supreme sacrifice of God for man is the perfect real relationship between God and man in its purest possible form.

> *Human body and soul is created by the Father, Son and Holy Spirit. The Son incorporates us into it as members by means of the Eucharistic mysteries. The Holy Spirit is residence in our bodies as the "temple" built by the Father and sanctified by the Son. The Holy Spirit takes us as new persons into a different realm in the Eucharist.* (Bob/ Sherri)

The Eucharist

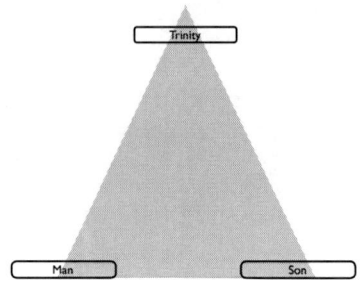

In the mystical but real union of man with God in the Eucharist, the Son replaces with success the failed Adam. The new person in an intimate, almost sexual union in the Eucharist leads us to a Trinitarian Communion with our fellowman and into that same Trinitarian Communion when we pass to the next life. This return to the Garden is not a return to the old Garden but to a new Garden beyond our imagination as we become sons and daughters of God. (A. von Speyr)

Trinitarian Communions that have time to develop become friendships of various degrees. Trinitarian Communion friendships may vary from those who are occasional to more active friendships to very close gender friendships to complex Trinitarian Communions such as intra-family relationships, marriages and even a unique relationship, cross-gender Trinitarian Communions.

This is not to say that friendships outside of the Christian Trinitarian Communion cannot develop. They do develop but they are by nature tenuous since they are often not based upon God as the apex and the values and actions that characterize new persons. We see more easily creeping into relationships the disorders in God's intent at the personal mini-Trinity level and as well as in the threefold harmony originally envisioned.

Let us visit the aspects of various Trinitarian Communions to better understand how our Triune God plays out in the economy of salvation in our daily lives and begin to understand our future as new persons.

> *The suggestion is that a Trinitarian Communion requires a "new person" with a "new mind-set" of thinking, feeling, acting and doing in the model of Mary as required by God in loving Him and our neighbor. Anything less than this means we do not take the words of Jesus seriously.* (Bob/ Sherri)

The Trinitarian Communion of Marriage

Reflect on: The body in its final end is for loving God and he [the man] must draw his wife into that Trinitarian Communion. The gift of God's love is the woman in the eyes of the man and she becomes his body.

—John Paul II[55]

In Christian marriage we hope to find the ultimate ordered expression of the Trinitarian Communion. Although all marriages are meant to be a Trinitarian Communion not all marriages are. Only in the context of "new persons" is it possible to have a true Trinitarian Communion Marriage. The ideal relationship is when the man and the woman are both new persons and discern together to have the vocation of marriage and it be a Trinitarian Communion Marriage.

More problematic is when one new person is married to one who is not a new person. Those on the journey have gotten there in many different ways and many different times in life. This means that if our vocation is one of marriage we may not have discerned at all in choosing it. More often or not this is the case. We rarely review our potential spouse in the context of their dedication to the characteristics of a new person, let alone evaluate them as Catholic or Christian at all. Somehow we view these considerations to be optional or secondary at best. The result is often that one of the spouses may not be on a journey seeking God at all and if so has not responded to God with the interest of becoming the new person. As we have seen, one who is initially on the journey responding to God's call is like the seed cast on the ground. It may or may not take root and become the new person.

> *Or an individual has entered upon a good Christian marriage. Then difficulties arise that, with the best will in the world, he is unable to overcome. Perhaps he is unable to both satisfy his wife and his children because their demands are different and even antithetical. And it is all the harder if the individual sees no way of dealing with it, yet must say to himself that he has gotten into the situation by reason of an honest assent to God.* (A. von Speyr)[56]

Thus a Trinitarian Communion Marriage, the true intention of God for marriage, is a challenge with a degree of difficulty that challenges the best of marriages.

God is complete love and we are made, "in the image of God" so love, as Christians, should define us in all that we are. We all experience love and particularly the love between a man and a woman as the ultimate human experience. As we experience love in all its ways we thus become lovable and capable of loving another in return. Loving is a natural human characteristic and proof of divine interaction that moves us away from the other animal species. Although loving is natural to the person, in the Catholic sense of the "new person" asked by Christ it becomes theological in the "sacrament" of the "new person," making visible the invisible, the spiritual and the divine. We transfer into visible reality the mystery of God.

And, the environment for all of this is the Trinitarian Communion of Marriage. Our bodies are made for love in all ways, physically, involuntarily, mentally and emotionally. Human sex supersedes ourselves and our finiteness and moves us into the infinite realm to give us a glimpse into the incomprehensible mystery of the Trinitarian love of the Divine Persons in a spiritual and eternal communication of love. Therefore, love becomes the unity between the mystery of the body and the mystery of God.

But to have true love as understood by new persons we must separate true love from lust for the other. In the Trinitarian Communion of marriage the new person man's desire for a woman should be beyond the physical, into a love and sex act that incorporates the entire woman, physical, emotional and spiritual, transcending just the physical and focusing on the desires of the "other" above all else. All his desires must be there for both so that the "two" can become the "one." Anything less than this in any marriage or any cross gender relationship ceases to be ordered and human, thus becoming the "use" of the other. Only in the Trinitarian Communion marriages does it become what God intended and ordered—it happens nowhere else! Other attempts show in some way a distortion in the triangular relationship between the man, woman and God.

The physical only, by either sex in any relationship including marriage is just "lust," not love! Even in marriage if the man is only engaged for the physical then he lusts and therefore according to our Lord, commits adultery (Matthew. 5:27–28).

Jesus made that statement directly to men. When it comes to lust, the responsibility rests heavily on the man in an ordered relationship because he is sexually driven with an intensity in the way the woman is not. Then, does that mean women do not lust? Yes, they lust too. The woman may "use" the man for her on ends, be they physical or material. This "use" of the other by either party is still the sin of lust since the love for the other is conditional on their "use" not their personhood.

Why is lusting a sin? Long before psychology and sociology Jesus knew that the sacred bond of marriage and even the ordered attraction between the sexes had to be more than clinical psychology and sociology and be rooted in the type of love only showed by God. All else is rooted in sin. Nietzsche called lust, "the pride of life" or as the new person would say, selfishness. Marx talked about the lust of the eyes and Freud the lust of the flesh. Jesus knew that these future "masters of suspicion" in defining lust were rooted in deception, self-interest and devoid of the "good" of God's creation to explain the physical respectively. Jesus presents the alternative motive to "lust" and the "use" of the other, an appeal to the "heart."

As Jesus made clear, lust is not just a physical act. It is a mental thought also. Both are sin. For men and women only a new person with the help of the Holy Spirit can succeed in making the sexual attraction good and ordered. Both Jesus and John Paul II (Theology of the Body) says this is actually doable for the new person. Noting an attractive woman or a handsome man in the new person's mind is ordered, having sex with the other in his/her mind is disordered and a sin. God provided sexual attraction for both men and women as a gift to humble relationships and within this context and within the new person's mind it is ordered and most wonderful! Beyond that, having sex with the other in his/her mind is disordered and a sin.

When the man becomes the new person he receives as "new" his consciousness and regains the lost fullness of his humanity. He desires the mutual relationship of persons, man and woman (Matthew 5:27–28) This is the Trinitarian Communion in marriage.

In the Sermon on the Mount in discussing the Beatitudes Jesus is speaking of a change in the man's heart. The body is not the problem. The problem is the heart.

Man must realize the nuptial meaning of the body. He must feel called to express in this way the interior freedom of the gift (the body), that is, of the spiritual state and that spiritual power which are derived from mastery of the lust of the flesh.

These words from Jesus are not addressed to the man who is completely absorbed in the "lust of the flesh." This man is unable to seek another form of mutual relations in the sphere of attraction. All concupiscence depersonalizes and makes for this disordered view.

In the new person the body is the manifestation of the Spirit. In interior mastery the freedom of the Spirit is expressed. Therefore, Christian "ethos" is characterized by a transformation of the conscience and attitudes of the human person both man and woman. And therefore in its ordered state the Eros attracts man to what is true, good and beautiful opening an interior force. This call to what is true, good and beautiful in the Eros also means at the same time the same thing in the ethos of redemption, i.e. the necessity of overcoming what is derived from lust in the three forms noted above. The Christian ethos also means the possibility of the necessity of transforming what has been weighted down by the lust of the flesh. The ethos hints at the vision that man has the possibility of overcoming lust. In a new person the Eros and the ethos are called to meet in the human heart. We are often content with the erotic as being exclusively a "prohibition" instead of an "ordered grace of God" which we understand to be at a, "greater depth of love."

A blending of the ethos and the Eros in the new person consequently is a noble gratification and an example of ordered response while just sexual desire is something else. But when sexual desire is linked with a noble gratification, it differs from just desire pure and simple. Similarly, as regards the sphere of the immediate reactions of the heart, sexual excitement is very different from the deep emotion with which not only interior sensitivity, but sexuality itself reacts to the total expression of femininity and masculinity.

For the new person it is necessary to discover continually what is erotic in the nuptial meaning of the body and the true dignity of the body as a gift. This is the role of the human spirit, the role of an ethical human nature. It is precisely at the price of self-control that the new person, but certainly not the carnal man, reaches a deeper and more mature spontaneity within his heart and mastering his instincts, rediscovers the spiritual beauty of the human body in its masculinity and femininity.

Our Failure to Hear God's Voice in Marriage

None of us wishes to be rejected, we do not want to be left alone and we find this basic human desire most pronounced when young and driven by nature and physical reasons to propagate. We choose mates and marry based on criteria of physical and emotional attraction but not necessarily congruent with God's ultimate Trinitarian Communion of Marriage. For fear of rejection we are not listening for or to God. We believe we will make it all, "work out okay" in the end. We forget that it is He, not us who has the ability to make it all "work out" if it is His plan! We have been programmed to be self-centered and self-preserved as individuals and as a species. We are individualized as we seek independence from our parents and whatever else might fit our disordered definition of freedom.

Sometime we may seek a common faith as a marriage criteria in an effort to somewhat involve God but this rarely supersedes the physical and emotional issues that draw us to our potential mate. Typically, we are ill equipped to fulfill God's ultimate directive in a Trinitarian Communion living a life-long commitment blessed by God. When we marry we are typically not new persons, surrendered and obedient to God and on a deliberate path and journey back to the Garden.

Marriage as a "vocation" is rarely acknowledged yet understood and only in the case of a religious vocation discernment do we see spiritual maturity and some degree of clarity in decisions of this kind. We need God in discerning a religious vocation to help us move beyond ourselves long enough to listen.

As noted earlier many of us in our marriage vocation come to conversion and transformation to new persons at a later point after the total commitment to the marriage vocation has already been made. We have not planned from the engagement to choose a mate as a part of a Trinitarian Communion let alone deliberately planned a Trinitarian Communion Marriage. We are retrofitting our marriage at best even when we desire such as a result of both of us becoming new persons. If both are not on board as new persons the marriage potentially will be loaded with difficulty and stress.

Although Jesus made very clear His teachings on divorce in His earthly life the Church with the aid of the Holy Spirit has left the door open to what might not be a marriage "made in heaven." There are very visible actions such as birth control, abortion, adultery, etc. that form the basis for many potential annulments of marriages. But the root cause is always the destruction or the unwillingness to build the Trinitarian Communion in marriage that causes it to never become or ceases it to be sacred and therefore the basis for not being a true sacramental marriage. These outward disordered sins are always the result of some distortion in the triangular Trinitarian relationships.

We are asked to love the ultimate neighbor, our spouse, as we love ourselves and to bring that person to Heaven. If we are not willing or our spouse is not willing to move beyond themselves despite all efforts then where can there be this ultimate Trinitarian Communion on earth that we call the Sacrament of Marriage. "Have I then rejected God's divine plan for my life and my spouse's life? I have said, "no" to the new person and no to God." God gives each one of us the freedom to choose Him and become the "new person" or not. How do we fulfill our required mission from God if we have based our marriage union on something else? Are we asked to persevere and to what end? There is only one earthly life that provides or not the ticket to eternity. How are we to live or can we live in a Trinitarian Communion in a marriage without reciprocity?

> *Jesus had in mind above all the indissolubility of marriage (except by the Church) but also every other form of the common life of men and women, that common life which constitutes the pure and simple fabric of existence. By its nature, human life is "co-educative." Its dignity and balance depend, at every moment of history and at every point of geographical longitude and latitude, on which she will be for him, and he for her.* (John Paul II)[57]

As a new person we are to surrender to and obey our Lord and Savior. We are to love our neighbor as ourselves. We are to be new persons following Him and Mary back to the Garden and we are to do so if our vocation is marriage in a Trinitarian Communion no matter what.

Or are we? As compared to a non-Trinitarian Communion marriage the Trinitarian marriage can build, re-build or transform a marriage into what God meant it to be. God is transforming but the new person is a participant in the transformation and his cooperation with God creates miracles in marriages whether or not we have chosen a mate at a time when we were His disciple and no matter the circumstances along the way.

When we commit any sin we have severed the triangular relationship between God and ourselves and usually between ourselves and another person. The marriage commitment is broken when we commit adultery and this seems so onerous to us since a spiritual, emotional and legal commitment has been broken and we often feel real personal pain. However, how is this mortal sin any different than when we sin against God in any way at all, mortal or venial? Are we not breaking the ultimate commitment even more so than in marriage? A death has occurred, a human physical death, an even greater death, the death of God, Jesus, for that very sin whatever it may be!–And that death, the ultimate death in all human history. With that sin we have been forgiven but at the price of His death, the death of an innocent person. We destroyed the ultimate commitment. Yet, through grace, we are forgiven in Confession for adultery just as we are for forgiven for any mortal or venial sin. The implication of this for a non-Trinitarian Communion marriage is problematic and worrisome. The implication is that adultery in a new person context for those in a non-Trinitarian Communion marriage is problematic when the act itself is totally an expression of love for another as the whole person and not use.

Questions in a Trinitarian Communion Marriage and in Non-Marriage Trinitarian Communions:

- Would the ability of the partners in a marriage to get along be easier and more flowing versus manual and difficult if their common faith and their level of faith were more aligned with one another?

   > Yes, but only if both are new persons even if not at the same point on the journey seeking God and believe in the Trinitarian Communion and God's dictum.

- Would their reactions be more of the "new person" despite their frame of reference of the other person?

   > The negative effects of any frame of reference concerning one another would be less in the number of issues and the importance of those issues. They would better understand and believe the other and accept things that are of less importance in the other. The more "one" the two became the more they would unite their "self-less" nature with the full knowledge of each other.

- Would they allow the other to be "our self" and think of the other's welfare in terms of God's divine plan for the other?

Yes, the humility and the self-less elements of the new person in the Trinitarian Communion would allow this to happen if the Trinitarian Communion began before or early in the marriage. The frame of reference and the degree of the issue requires heroic virtue to overcome human lust and domination particularity in spontaneity. Confession and renewal of vows might be needed to reorient the marriage. However, both must be on the journey with the Holy Spirit to achieve this. This rising above the "human nature" is not just confined to marriage.

- Would lust and domination still play its key "human role"?

    Lust would progress or evolve and move to a combination of Christian ethos and Eros that would combine into a "mutuality" without the negative connotation of domination being felt by either. The domination of the male moves to a spiritual level making the female completely comfortable. He makes love to the complete woman. Both give fully of themselves so there is no domination.

- Could the Trinitarian Communion be unilateral or does it have to be reciprocal?

The Trinitarian Communion may have to start off as unilateral and the one who is the new person and on the journey must try to move the other to a journey and the new person. If the Holy Spirit is not acting in the other or the other does not hear or want to hear the Holy Spirit the new person and the journey cannot take place in the other. At some point the relationship must become bilateral to have a Trinitarian Communion. Remember what we are talking about in the Trinitarian Communion—the two new persons and God. Both must be seeking God actively for a Trinitarian Communion even if at different levels. If God has intended the union of the persons then the Holy Spirit will take over the other so they are on the journey.

Will the other allow the Holy Spirit in? Are they capable of being less self-centered to hear the Holy Spirit? Is it a case in the other person of "not knowing how" or is there "no desire" to allow God to transform them? If the other cannot be reciprocal then the Trinitarian Communion cannot exist and it means the other does not love you in the way defined by God for marriage. We are asked if we are called by the Holy Spirit to become new persons even if this means overcoming our personalities or whatever keeps us from God.

- Is there spiritual gratification in this Trinitarian communion that resembles mutual sexual gratification? What is sexual in a Trinitarian communion?

  > Yes, there is sexual gratification in the spirit of the Christian ethos in the Trinitarian Communion of marriage which is not unlike the mutual oneness of the Trinity and like the mutual exchange of bodies in the Eucharist. The sex act is the ultimate expression of the giving of both. Sex becomes very important as the validation of the Trinitarian Communion in the relationship and flows naturally from looking after the welfare and divine plan of the other.

- If the spiritual is not there or if it is only unilateral is there a point in the union?

  > No, there is no point in the union for a Christian in a spiritual sense or in a Trinitarian Communion sense. Other factors may come into play to keep the divorce and annulment from happening but the marriage is basically invalid in the eyes of God and probably in the eyes of the Church. Children or the economic impact on and the protection of the woman may keep the two together but that means that one is choosing "things" over God's

command! A non-marriage Trinitarian Communion will have the full Trinitarian Communion graces less the sexual component but must result in a nuptial relationship that bears spiritual fruit. God will validate this union through the Holy Spirit in the pure heart! This non-marriage relationship is rare and is brought together by God!

- If the spiritual is not there then what is the point other than the nurturing of children is this union providing?

   There is no point in the relationship. The protection of the woman and her children economically even in a marriage is the only possibility in a union without both on a spiritual journey.

- What happens when one spouse changes over the span of many years, i.e. devalues the marriage by moving away from belief?

   The Holy Spirit was in the person to begin with and the person chose other than God in his freedom. It would appear the person is not on the journey seeking God. They operate from self-centeredness and do not choose a spiritual communion.

- Is it possible that all elements cannot be realized in a marriage, i.e., children, best friends, lovers, helpers in a marriage that only has one new person and might never have the ability of becoming a Trinitarian Communion Marriage?

     Yes, it is possible that all elements cannot be realized in this marriage. If both are not on a journey seeking God or if one is unable or chooses against God and therefore unable to become the new person and divorce and annulment do not occur then some elements, even significant ones, can be achieved outside of marriage in intra and intergender Trinitarian Communion(s).

- Can some of these elements of marriage come from cross gender relationships and is this compatible with the "new person" requested by Christ or is this moving toward just another version of adultery?

     Yes, they can come from new persons cross-gender relationships but these may be rare because they require the change of mind that creates the true new person. If both are new persons or striving to be then this is not adultery. This does not mean that one or both will not be dealing with temptation and conflict in the heart regarding the other as they draw closer. The evil one is always with us but so are the Holy Spirit and our Blessed Mother. Remember all that was said earlier regarding the characteristics of the new person, male or female. Although to grow in this type of Trinitarian Communion both must be reciprocal and say that God's command to us is not an abstraction and is obtainable/doable. Hope for completeness and happiness in life is always there for the new person in Christ.

- Is this Trinitarian Communion in a marriage possible at all even with the Holy Spirit as a helper?
- It is absolutely possible as is the cross-gender, intra-gender Trinitarian Communion. God is not a liar. We are the only ones that limit ourselves in our response to God. He gave us a commandment and as loving disciples we are to carry it out in its full intention.

All new persons are equal, in or out of marriage and therefore in the Trinitarian Communion of marriage. They are companions with subordination more of a result of personalities than God's design.

For the woman to be subject to her husband as Paul discusses in Ephesians is not something new because it has already been demanded of us all to subordinate to one another. We are subject to the Lord as individuals and in a unity of obedience.

Paul uses "fear" [awe] to describe the duty of submission of the new person to his fellow believer as we are asked to love thy neighbor. This is a reciprocal subordination that allows one to consider the word of another as more important than one's own because the word of the Lord is reflected and acknowledged in it.

The archetype of the Lord and the church is the wooing of the woman by the man and the willingness of the woman. The woman has a unique respect for the man in the way both have respect for the Lord, waiting and anticipating the shaping of love. This reverential fear (awe) of the woman before the man is not a quality in its own right but, among new persons, derives from the Church's reverential fear before the Lord. The woman naturally looks to the man for leadership, hoping and anticipating he will guard and nurture her best interests always as the Lord does (Psalm 23).

The woman's actual passage from virgin to bride is after all due to the choice and courtship of the man. She should not consider the courtship to be a thing of the past. The woman should be authentic with herself and convey authenticity to the man so that she is the woman he chose and not an unrecognizable version. She should always be in a state of, "becoming a bride," as the new person will never let that state go stale.

The clinging has to be done by the man. The man has to commit the bond first and then the woman may accept. The woman does not have to submit herself on her own initiative. The man must bind himself even before the woman does. He has to take the risk first, since he does not know whether the woman will accept his courtship. This is his humiliation, while the humility of the woman will consist in the submission that follows.

If the man patterns himself after Christ he cannot arbitrarily use and misuse the subjection of the woman for his human ends. He must form her with her help in the same way that the Lord uses the subjection of the church to form her. She will again and again find a normative mirror of herself in the various manifestations of the Church's life

The possibilities, the grace that God can bestow then is when each person in the marriage places God at the apex, strives to be the new person in all areas of their life, sees themselves as equals without subordination except to God and companions on the path on the journey headed back to the Garden. Then, the Trinitarian Communion Marriage is a possibility whether planned as a vocation or adopted. Then, the marriage simply imitates the Trinitarian Communion and the state of oneness between Adam and Eve given by God to mankind in the Garden before the Fall.

> *The very need for spousal love, the need to give oneself to a person and to unite with him, is deeper, is connected with the spiritual being of the person: Marriage….[is] fundamentally [a] spiritual affairs.* (John Paul II)[58]

A Problem
in Complex Trinitarian Communions

"Are we as new persons who we say we are at all times?"

> ***Reflect on:*** *Put off your old nature which belongs to your former manner of life and is corrupt through deceitful lusts, and be renewed in the spirit of your minds, and put on the new nature, created after the likeness of God in true righteousness and holiness.*

—Ephesians 4:22–24, rsvce

The "Parable of the Squirrel" brings too well to mind the feelings we may sometimes get when we are with those closest to us. Do I really understand how others affect me and how I affect them and are my thoughts, words, actions, and persona helping them to get back to the Garden? Do I have clarity in my relations with them or am I in a fog when I am with them and has the fog been there for a long time? I may not even know how my actions and words have affected them and when I find out that in some way my words and actions have been negative or disturbing I don't know what to do. The new person may find these close but maybe complex relationships to be one of the greatest challenges on the path to the Garden.

We may be able to adapt ourselves and our view of others to the proper ordered approach in spontaneity with many people we meet and acknowledge that the other is also "the Beloved of God." But those closest to us may provide a challenge that various degrees of spontaneity do not. Our frame of reference, our egocentrism allows us the opportunity to fail as new persons in Christ even though we most want to be the new person in these complex Trinitarian relationships. With the evil one leading the way, we may be less humble, sympathetic, pliable, adaptable, etc., because these are those closest to us, and we may not truly understand the truth and honesty surrounding the relationship with them.

Our frame of reference of ourselves may be the worst impediment of all vis-a-vis the other as we are unable to see ourselves in a new person relationship with those close to us. We may also have a problem understanding which persona of these individuals has come to the "party" and which persona we are using on that day.

We are speaking of those relationships we probably believe we know well, i.e. parent/child, sibling, marriage, and certain friendship relationships that fit and represent complex Trinitarian Communions. These are often long-standing relationships that are somehow hierarchical in nature.

These relationships are the ones in which we have the greatest potential to love our neighbor as ourselves because we develop them over longer periods of time. These are the relationships that "should" help make us "children of God" and are the ones that we create and re-create as we move down the path on the journey back to God. These are the relationships that should be the most meaningful as the new person.

However, if these relationships are not ordered i.e., with both having a common shared view of God and His actions in our lives and if in particular we have shown the other a persona that is not the new person in our past relationship then the triangle of unity of the Trinitarian communion is compromised. For example, in our relationships with the members of our families—in this case, mother, father, siblings, cousins, spouses, etc.—do we, as new persons, provide them with a persona of our actual new person selves or do we bend to anticipations, desires, expectations, perceived hierarchy, and create a persona that is really not us? Maybe we display a persona that is stuck in time at some point in our past or maybe a created persona of someone we are not. Conversely, is the other really who their persona says they are or are they trying to create a perception to us of someone they are not?

Are we on both sides of the triangle creating who we really are? In these venues are we meeting people and are we being met where we/they are at this moment in time and situation? And who are we really are in the eyes of God? We care about God, but does the other? Can there be a Trinitarian Communion in these complex situations without God?

There has to be a triangle, the Trinitarian Communion with God at the apex, or the relationship will not be ordered in the way God meant with perceptions and problems real or imagined. And, are we (both parties), believing God or not, treating the other as an equal or are we trying to impose a hierarchy or succumb to an existing hierarchy in the relationship?

Or are we, the new person, in these situations being who we really are in all venues? To do otherwise is to lie, a sin and then possibly sin again through a "use" of the other.

The following represents a perplexing situation that occurs often in complex Trinitarian Communions. When we talk about venues we are speaking about private, family, expanded family, group and public venues.

When we are with a complex Trinitarian Communion person we expect a certain type of behavior out of them and visa versa. We expect them and ourselves to act in a manner we both are familiar with when we are together. Sometimes one may use a group or public setting to convey a message to the other that would be difficult in private. If we then are thrown into a group with them and a second persona emerges from either of us then relationships may be damaged. The second persona may be used by the other person or us because the situation/environment may invoke fear or a need to control or both on the part of one. Therefore, the one may treat the other differently as they attempt to respond to the environment's challenge. One may be in some way an impediment to the other in that venue. They may also use this venue to react to their relationship with you. This change in persona and behavior may be perceived by you as an "inconsistency" in their behavior. You may perceive that one of the following is happening:

- You may think you are being punished by the other in this public group venue because they do not feel comfortable doing so in private.

- You are being reprimanded in a passive public/group venue for your actions in the same public/group venue.

- The public/group environment may be being used to plant little "hints" to you through things said, body language and other actions that seem incongruent with what you experience with them in private. These may occur over a period of time and be deliberate or subliminal. The other hopes that you will eventually pick up on these and connect the hints accordingly to get over to you the point that you are not acting in your relationship the way the other thinks you should be acting. In this way you ascertain the point/points yourself and the other does not have to confront you in the private. They are trying to tell you something but do not want the confrontation that might go with it.

- The other's actions may be completely benign!

It is so easy in complex Trinitarian Communions, whether private or public to over think and over feel the other side of the triangle based upon history and frame of reference. The problem always arises when we are unable to easily discern what the different behavior on the part of the other means. Then you may take the hints of behavior on the part of the other in the public/group environment and connect them incorrectly. This may lead to an incorrect perception of what the other is trying to or not tell you. If the behavior of the other is benign this may lead to all kinds of issues between you and the other.

The new person replaces perception of what any hints mean and the observation of different behaviors in different venues with honesty and straightforwardness. The new person will take different thoughts engendered above concerning the group situation and discuss the group situation in a loving way with the other to confirm or remove the observations. Even if this might be embarrassing or seem petty or selfish to the other it brings resolution to the issue and honestly lays "all cards on the table" so they can be dealt with in a mature, new person way. It also does not allow the perception to continue which opens the relationship to damage by the evil one. Any delay may allow the new person to draw wrong conclusions. Then, "perception divides, honesty unites!" God wins, the evil one loses and the difficulties of the more complex Trinitarian Communions are mitigated.

The new person willing to listen to and be guided by the Holy Spirit will have an innate sense of how to act in different types of complex Trinitarian Communion relationships. The assumption by the new person will be the same no matter what the relationship type. The new person must set aside frame of references and history of the other, they must not think in a hierarchal way concerning the other and they must start from the point that all are Children of God and all are beloved. The key to new person behavior in these relationships is that "truth and honesty must always be." No personas, no legacy feelings, no legacy. The other is a person of "this day," not of some other day and is to be treated as a Child of God, a Beloved of God, with complete honesty and truthfulness in all ways now.

The other may slip in and out of various personas but the new person does not. They are real, truthful, and who they are. This is "witness" and can do more to help the Holy Spirit create true Trinitarian Communions than all the words, gifts, hugs and kisses! We want to be able to trust those closest to us. They want to be able to trust us. Only the Holy Spirit can overcome the past, place us all in the present, and help us show others the journey and the path back to the Garden.

> *God never ignores even the death of a squirrel. Those closest to us should never be left at the side of the road of our journey back to the Garden.* (Bob/Sherri)

To "ignore" the other person is to consider them a non-person, not a Child of God and this is a sin in every way, small or large that it might manifest itself. It shows that our journey is still too stuck in our own self-centeredness and cannot be answered away before God as a lack of conscious perception on our part. (Bob/Sherri)

Trinitarian Communion Friendships

> ***Reflect on:*** *I therefore, a prisoner for the Lord, beg you to lead a life worthy of the calling to which you have been called, with all lowliness and meekness, with patience, forbearing one another in love, eager to maintain the unity of the Spirit in the bond of peace.*
>
> —Ephesians 4:1–3, rsvce

In the world of new persons relationships develop between two new persons in different degrees of closeness. The characteristics of the new person throw a completely different dynamic into the inter-relationships between individuals. God being at the apex of the Trinitarian Communion relationship brings non-egocentric love and behavior into the relationship. Natural competition that existed before moves away in favor of "a spirit of caring for the other." As allowed, some of these relationships will become deep interpersonal friendships that are so unique in our world that they are almost hard to believe as being possible. But our Savior in the Sermon on the Mount says that we are not fabricating relationships but we are building deep eternal friendships that will extend beyond the grave.

Deep Trinitarian Communion Friendships

With deep Trinitarian Communion relationships or friendships between two new persons we have the development of the way a relationship "can be" when both are on the journey actively seeking God with Mary as their guide. In this ordered relationship in keeping with the characteristics of the new person we experience the demands of our Lord in the Sermon on the Mount as well as taste of Heaven.

Above all else the relationship, its origin, its entire sense of being and its characteristics are rooted in the Triune God who is first in the individual relationships and in their relationship. Their communication is easy through the trust in God and the trust in each other. They are holy in their relationship and more open to the Spirit and therefore can communicate more easily. The two people have a home in their hearts for each other and for Him.

In their outward relationship they enjoy each other's company which helps both of them in their spiritual life. Each knows how to surrender and submit to the other but with personal integrity. They both have a holy anxiety about each other's welfare and particularly their spiritual welfare. They both want good things for the other.

They identify with each other. They are on each other's mind from time to time. They feel sorrow when separated from one another.

In these deep Trinitarian Communion friendships they give up nothing of their masculinity or their femininity but instead they feed on the one bond of God that makes them a union of friendship and enhances the ordered power of both in everything else in their lives. Their friendship only continues to grow as they help each other follow our Blessed Mother back to the Garden where their friendship will continue for eternity.

> *You [Lord] are the source of all, and without You there can be neither true peace nor union....Therefore, from You alone, O God, comes perfect union, and where there is disunion, confusion reigns because of sin and the devil.* (*Divine Intimacy*)[59]

> *It is a grace when God brings two who are struggling on the journey together to form one friendship that grows and grows within ordered fidelity well past death into eternity.* (Bob/Sherri)

The New Person and the Concept of Charitable Interpretation

Reflect on: Some friends play at friendship but a true friend sticks closer than one's nearest kin.

—Proverbs 18:24, NRSVCE

Henri Nouwen reminds us that no person can be God for us, because we will be disappointed and so will they. Yet, often we seem to have difficulty distinguishing between "our will" and "God's will." Even as new persons we have problems when others and particularly our fellow new persons and friends act in a manner that is bewildering to us and not in the way we anticipated and expected. We are disappointed! But, maybe they are too! We are more like silent boats passing in the night in a fog than friends and disciples of Our Lord.

As new persons we are trying to think of the other more than ourselves and it is reasonable to assume the same of the other. After all we are of the same belief system and we are both a Child of God so therefore communicating with one another should have communication that is, rational, honest, truthful, and as transparent as possible.

However, we may feel hurt at the other's words and actions and our attempt at being rational, honest, truthful and as transparent as possible with them may fail causing hurt to both. Again, we are bewildered. In line with the philosophical and the Ignation concept of "charitable interpretation" we at least in general, respect and may even love the other, and therefore believe the other's statements and actions to be rational in nature, truthful, using words in an ordinary way, have something interesting to say or do, and believe that they in general have valid arguments.

"But, why did you not respond the way I anticipated and expected you to respond?" We are brothers and sisters in Christ! We are not talking about differences in opinions here. If so, then we could easily fall back on the concept of "charitable interpretation" and say with charity that if I were in the same place as the other, in the same circumstances as the other then I might very well look at the issue before us in the same way that the other has looked at it. I could easily have the respect and love for the other and see them simply being as rational, truthful, honest and transparent as possible with their view, even though I could not agree with nor accept it. But I can deal with it and the other on a "non-personal" level without hurt or disordered division arising.

"Why do you not respond the way I would respond?" We could also easily say that we are all different with different frames of reference and influences and therefore the other may not respond to the same situation as I would and I should not assume they will do so. Okay, well that's life and no reason for disorder and division. Right? But as relationships become friendships and develop more deeply between new persons, the anticipations and expectations regarding the other are more important and the possible hurt is more deep. It seems we would have a common understanding but very well may not.

The frames of reference do affect how we respond to the other but our self-centeredness also may influence our words and actions and our interpretation of the meaning of things like friendship, love, honesty and transparency. With self-centeredness come fears of being too transparent with another or too honest or a willingness to love and trust the other to the degree that the initiator would anticipate and expect. Our fear is being hurt and this is only enhanced by our experiences in our frame of reference and the tampering of the evil one.

The real problem lies, though, in whom it is that is being self-centered. Surely it could be very well the receiver and responder. But just maybe the initiator is expecting the other to respond/act in exactly the same way that the initiator would react. "I expect you to act in the manner that I would react."

When it comes to friendship and love the failure of the other to act in a manner anticipated and expected by the initiator may say to the initiator that, "I do not want to spend time with you," or "maybe I don't want to be seen in public with you," or "maybe I am afraid to tell you that I really don't care for you" or "maybe." One or even more of these might be true but probably are not! What is true is that the initiator is being self-centered and not meeting the other where they are at and anticipating responses from them that they may not be capable of providing or understanding in what format the initiator wants the response. It does not mean these possibilities from the other are true and as we state in this book, "perceptions and assumptions divide; honesty and reality unite."

The new person cannot assume that the other will respond in the manner that they would respond. But they can anticipate and expect certain actions from the other in friendship and love and when they do not see the basic components of friendship and love in terms of respect, rationality, honesty, truthfulness, and transparency from the other then the new person needs to care enough about the other, and be focused enough on the other to try to meet the other, "where they are," and discuss the differences in anticipation/expectation so that there can be an understanding of the relationship that allows them to, "love thy neighbor as thyself" and both grow in their relationship as disciples of Christ. The other then has the responsibility to be as truthful and as transparent as they are able to be with the initiator and to forge unity through understanding and mutual love for a brother or sister new person in Christ.

> *Friendship requires reciprocity of affection and mutual benevolence.* (Divine Intimacy)[60]

Spiritual Friendship

Reflect on: A relationship held in a "state of virginity" like Mary and Joseph or Adam and Eve before The Fall—where gender doesn't get in the way of a true Trinitarian Communion and where the result is the bringing forth of spiritual fruit.

—Bob/Sherri

A Trinitarian Communion Marriage reflects what would seem to be the ultimate ordered relationship between the new man and the new woman, it by nature being the sacramental bond between God, a woman and a man. Jesus' dictum to love thy neighbor as oneself means that the new person on the journey back to the Garden will encounter other new persons who are not spouse nor gender. That represents roughly 50 percent of the population if new persons are divided roughly equally between women and men. As new persons we are expected to have new person relationships with all others and those that are new persons to include those of the opposite sex in and out of marriage. As we have seen earlier to various degrees, depending on the depth of the relationship with the opposite gender, the new person forms Trinitarian Communions.

We are well trapped in our current overwhelmingly sexually oriented culture believing "hook, line and sinker" everything our media tells us. We have been bought and sold by the evil one concerning the relationship of women and men. We truly believe that men and women cannot get along very well and cannot be trusted to be other than sexual playmates.

We even see this attitude in churches of many Christian denominations. We just feel we have to, "separate those boys and girls or sparks will fly!" With thought it is not hard to conclude that this attitude reflects our society's degraded image of women, the evil one's propaganda gone mainstream!

What a lie! Catholic Christianity, in reality always ahead of the rest of society, made women important as had Jesus with convents and orders as an option to marriage for women. Schools, hospitals, and social agencies for the poor and marginalized realized and celebrated the importance of women to the betterment of all mankind. During the Middle Ages, often viewed as the epitome of discretion forced upon society by the Church, we find men and women more routinely in spiritual friendships able to hurdle the sexual magnetism and be friends. Maybe, even more so than today, women were held to a value greater than their bodies for use for the sexual pleasure of men. The result, also somewhat amazing to us in our era, is that they could be friends with men without the sexual component and without marriage! Although not an everyday occurrence there were many instances of men and women in spiritual friendships outside of marriage with no "hanky-panky"! People believed in relationships and the primacy of God and they were not victim to the lies of "romantic Hollywood lore."

Starting with Mary and Joseph's relationship as a model we see the reality of Spiritual Friendships—friends in celibacy, in reality, acknowledged by the Protestant reformers despite Protestantism today. We see classical examples of spiritual friendships coming out of Catholicism down through the ages such as St. Hathumoda and Agius and Fortunatus, St. Radegunde, and Agnes, Queen St. Margaret of Scotland and Turgot, Blessed Jordan (Order of Preachers Minor) and Diana (Dominican nun), St. Francis and St. Clare, St. Teresa of Avilla and St. John of the Cross and Francis de Sales and Jane de Chantal, and others.

Spiritual Friendship builds from a non-physical foundation of intimacy that incorporates the transcendentals of truthfulness, goodness and beauty into the construction of a friendship that puts the "thou" always before the "I." The grace of celibacy in the relationship overcomes the natural growing desire for potentially disordered physical contact between people who love one another, channeling it into ordered expressions of physical contact. The new person flowing in the mind-set of redemption understands the need to adore the beauty of God's creation, the other in its entirety.

Orientation of the relationship is always to God for control, submission and obedience. The new persons are able to relate to one another in friendship, even deep friendship as God meant without sin. We must understand with complete clarity that *only* in the context of a new person cross-gender Trinitarian Communion is it possible for a man and a woman who are unrelated to one another to become Spiritual Friends. This is not a typical relationship between two new persons. The relationship is potentially and particularly a deep one. Spiritual Friendship is a unique grace given selectively by God only, which is particularly true in our era of history. This complete Trinitarian Communion is celibate with each gender celebrating the complete surrender to God of the other as the first order of adoration.

> *Virginal or chaste love enables one to love the other predominantly for the sake of the other rather than for one's own personal usefulness or pleasure. Virginal love does not mean denial of human affection for another but increases caring, tenderness and the other "soft" feelings and virtues. This is something sinners [non-new persons] cannot understand or fathom because there is a tendency to project one's own lack of virtue on to others and thereby fail to understand how the great virtue of chastity does not kill feelings; on the contrary it keeps the physical pleasures of the body in check—close friends sharing the intimacy of the heart.* (D. Calloway)[61]

As one might expect all the characteristics of the new person, either obtained or in formation must come into play to achieve this Holy intimacy between two people who are not married. But the characteristic or behavior of the greatest importance is that of transparency and honesty between the two. Spouses must have complete knowledge and the ability to modify the relationship if they are rightly concerned. With a Spiritual Friendship that friendship cannot, no matter how deep and intimate it might be, take precedence over the marriage relationships of the two. In fact the spiritual friendship should enhance the marital relationship of the two as would any friendship by broadening the example of relationship of the person in knowledge and experience.

Therefore, the cross gender Spiritual Friendship discussed here is only possible when considered as a vocation as in a marriage or a religious vocation. The commitment to the other is a considerable commitment of time and emotion as well as celibacy. This can only occur when both are new persons and when both already understand their unalterable commitment to their vocation of marriage or religious life. Thus the Spiritual Friendship can only occur when the Spiritual Friendship itself is celibate. It is a solemn vow of celibacy even if not made public or written.

Only when one or both of the new person Spiritual Friends are married can Spiritual Friends develop in a vocational celibate relationship. When both new persons are not married and have not taken some form of consecrated vows to include a vow of celibacy, then the relationship has to be viewed as "dating," not Spiritual Friendship. Why? Because the sexual element will always be potentially in the relationship and will hinder the development of the all-important non-sexual elements of the relationship both material and spiritual. Their personal altered personas came into play to decrease transparency. Think how wonderful it is to truly know someone for who they are as a human being of the opposite sex instead of always thinking of them as a potential sex partner.

Celibacy we must remember does not mean nor imply a lack of intimacy or physical contact in the Spiritual Friendship. This is a vital aspect of the relationship that must be worked out in harmony between the two friends in a way that is comfortable to them and their spouses if applicable. The love of one for another always involves ordered "touch" in some ways appropriate in time and place. We are made sensual by God and we are expected to give glory to Him as our Creator in an ordered sensual way.

What a unique and wonderful possibility that a new person man and woman, brought together by God in celibacy, are equal and are shared companions of one another in the way meant by God in the Garden, in a state of mutual love and veneration of God's creation, and in friendship without the sexual element to distort the happiness and grace!

Meditation:

"Despite what our modern culture preaches about sexuality and love, we recognize and celebrate the fact that deep and powerful friendships can exist between men and women

who remain focused on God. Today we pray for the courage to open our hearts to celibate passion, celibate love, to be aware that these Friendships bring challenges as well as blessings, risks as well as benefits. By journeying together in grace, may we discover a new way to relate, a new way to grow, a new way to meet God on the path to spiritual wholeness. " (M. D. Poust)[62]

Spiritual Friends and Celibate Love

One Key to a True Grace

Reflect on: *We are all just seeds in God's hands.*

—K. Mattea[63]

The parable of the seeds has always been a challenging one for many. We see ourselves as the seeds and we may even contemplate ourselves as the sower or the soil depending on our level of "I." As new persons we know well who is controlling the sower and therefore we should be unconcerned about being the seed or the sower.

In cross-gender Spiritual Friendships truly God is involved in throwing the seed in the very special way of bringing two people together in Trinitarian Communion. This unique grace provides the opportunity to bring out all the characteristics of the new persons allowing them in the Spiritual Friendship to enjoy an incredible bond that goes beyond typical human relationships, possibly being as deep as any relationship that exists in the sexual venue of marriage.

But the seeds that God spreads in these Spiritual Friendships are unique seeds, seeds that require celibacy to grow for the individuals without exception. Celibacy has to be part of the Spiritual Friendship. Without it there can never develop the deep friendship between the man and the woman that make this relationship unique. Sex in Spiritual Friendships introduces potential factors that compromise the relationship by introducing disorder in motives, suppositions and actions, making the way clear for jealousy and misconduct including lust and adultery. This is true in all Spiritual Friendships. The relationship has to be celibate to work and the celibacy has to be defined at the beginning of the relationship and understood and accepted by both parties.

The seeds of the God-given grace of celibacy are sown to new persons contemplating how they will relate to the opposite sex in Trinitarian Communions. The new person's level of spiritual maturity, location on the path and the journey may often be the chief factor in their willingness to be open to Spiritual Friendships with the opposite sex. Often, it is the seeds of celibacy that may be the factor that destroys the ability to form, develop and keep Spiritual Friendships.

To some new persons the seeds of celibacy will fall on their ground which may be "hardened ground" not yet softened by the Holy Spirit and they will be unable to even contemplate such a relationship as a Spiritual Friendship. The thought and the action will not be possible for them due to often egocentric natures in transformation that cannot yet love the "thou," being too centered on the "I." They may have not overcome their fear or dislike of the other sex or they may still have somewhat of a subordinated view of the relationship between human women and men.

The seeds of celibacy may fall on new persons who are enthusiastic and eager at first to become the new person but who have not been tested by the path and the journey. Some may rush to try to formulate relationships and love their neighbors and may desire to enter into Spiritual Friendships. Then their patience runs out as they misunderstand the importance of patience in any relationship and its vital nature in a Spiritual Friendship. Or they may not be willing to trust themselves and the other in the relationship bending to the evil one's favorite weapon. Or they may be worried about their image to others in their relationship—too proud, and willing to bend to man's reaction instead of God's call. This hurried approach to failure in Spiritual Friendships usually has as its root cause in self-centeredness, lacking the humility to stay the friendship.

The seeds of celibacy may fall among new persons and encounter thorns that kill the potential friendship before it starts. This might be a spouse or a child who says no to the potential Spiritual Friendship. It might also be that both are not really committed to the relationship because they are not committed or do not want to pursue the relationship. These are valid concerns that hopefully are the result of prayer and discernment.

The other may be an embarrassment in some way to the one and the relationship never starts or quickly dies. The death of the potential Spiritual Friendship may have its root cause in expectations and the acceptance of expectations on the part of one that are too high or need to be negotiated. Or the cause may be the result of where one is on the journey.

To the glory of God and the grace for humans the seeds of celibacy may fall on the fertile soil of new persons far enough along the path and journey to understand the potential of this unique grace. Soil that includes new persons who understand the companionship God envisioned between men and women and the potential for deep friendship between them in and out of marriage. They have great respect for the other and their gender. They have less "I" and more "thou." They embrace celibacy as a way to potentially higher friendship and love. They are willing to be patient with the other and with themselves in the relationship and let God do His work. They would rather have the other as a Spiritual Friend than not have them at all!

Celibacy's seeds on the fertile ground of the progressing new persons creates a true grace of love and friendship between a man and a woman that mirrors God's intention for the interaction of men and women in the Garden, a friendship that supersedes lust and provides a relationship that mimics the transcendentals of God-truth, goodness, and beauty in a holy love.

> *In answer to your question, yes, we have a deep celibate Spiritual Friendship.* (Bob/Sherri)

> *A unique Blessing and Grace.* (Bob/Sherri)

Living the Cross-gender Spiritual Friendship

> **Reflect on:** *Love is patient and kind; love is not jealous or boastful; it is not arrogant or rude. Love does not insist on its own way; it is not irritable or resentful; it does not rejoice at wrong, but rejoices in the right. Love bears all things, believes all things, hopes all things, endures all things.*
>
> —1 Corinthians 13:4–7

This unique form of a Trinitarian Communion, only possible as a special gift from our Triune God offers all of us as new persons no matter what our vocation in life a potential understanding of the true relationship of, "loving our neighbor as ourselves." The word that best characterizes this unique communion of God and a man and a woman is the word "intimacy."

The word intimacy in our sex oriented culture usually is thought of as a synonym for "sexual relations" especially when it is used in the context of a woman and a man. But Christians often speak of an "intimacy with God." Even that intimacy with the Divine can be helped in understanding by relating it to the "oneness" relationship of the ordered sexual union of a woman and a man. But even this intimacy with the Divine does not stop at the sexual act since intimacy with the Divine reveals the other aspects of using the word intimacy in describing the relationship of the Cross-gender Spiritual Friendship since the other synonyms are "close relationship, communion, affinity, friendship, and familiarity." These more accurately begin to suggest the characteristics of the Cross-gender Spiritual Friendship that has as its hallmark, celibacy.

This unique celibate relationship of what we might even institutionalize as a Spiritual Marriage instead of Cross-gender Spiritual Friendship may develop a closeness in the relationship that will never replace but may supersede in some ways the individual marriage relationship of the two individuals. All would hope that a marriage in its best version would also have all of these characteristics but we all fear that with the sexual component thrown in all bets may be off for these same characteristics being in a marriage.

The other key importance other than celibacy in a Spiritual Marriage is the acceptance of each other," just as we are" and being willing to defend ourselves "just as we are" and being willing to defend the other, "just as they are." Only in the context of truthfulness, honesty and transparency that we previously discussed as a characteristic of this type of relationship can this acceptance take place. This characteristic leads to all of the other components that make up the profile of a Spiritual Marriage.

Acceptance allows compassion for the other in a greater degree than we typically think of compassion. This compassion is not only for the other but compassion for the self. Both share in the compassion which allows for thought before words and actions.

With compassion means without judgment as we accept one another embracing our mutuality in the relationship. We are then open to forgive ourselves as well as the other. This is really meeting each other "where we are," whether it be spiritually or another aspect of life. We become, "totally received" by the other in a very deep and personal way.

"The result is that we become free internally allowing for true friendship. We are happy and joyful personally and within our friendship."

We become truly equals as is so possible in relationships that are celibate and not sexually based. Our unique cross-gender friendship transforms us as individuals and in our other relationships including our marriage. The transformation is where we feel true and deep gratitude to God for this unusual gift. We now exercise more patience in all relationships understanding that the source of the gift is from God and we have the responsibility of transforming ourselves not only in our Spiritual Marriage but in all of our relationships. The patience is God's action in our conscious before we respond.

This empowers us to always think of the other more than ourselves and to think of the other often as we see them consciously go through their day. We miss them in an ordered way. We do not wish to control their time or other variables in their lives and we never try to own them. But as the song says, "you are always on my mind; you are always on my mind." There is none of those fears that go along with the sexual component such as jealousy and strategy. We meet them completely where they are in time and space and in every aspect of life.

We desire daily contact in all of its variables with the other. We desire lifelong contact and eternal contact. We do things together to cement the relationship. Above all we pray for one another and we pray together jointly whenever possible. We respect our shared confidentiality. We respect the inevitable changes that occur in either or both of us over the years with changes in priorities and preferences. We don't reject physical contact because the boundaries are already there and irrevocable. Again, we think of the "thou" more than the "I" in all circumstances.

These characteristics create a profile of our Spiritual Marriage that neither sins nor robs anything from our spouses or others close to us because we are always in gratitude and awareness of being the new person and the critical nature of this gift that makes this a relationship from God. In essence our Divine gift and grace becomes institutionalized. It becomes an institution of Holiness as a witness to all we know and come in contact with in a way we could never obtain in any other circumstance. We can only hold hands and praise God for this communion along with all those we know and meet.

Consider the friendship that exists between women and men, between men and women. Human nearness, spiritual kinship, agreement in thoughts and feelings; these are the foundations of friendship. (Rudolph Schnackenburgh)[64]

We are reminded that while everything is temporary here on earth, nothing is temporary where God is concerned. (Mary DeTurris Poust)[65]

Non-marriage Cross-Gender Trinitarian Communions

Spiritual Friendships: Protestant and Catholic Views of Men and Women

Reflect on: *Chaste cross-sex friendships cannot flourish in communities that limit sexuality to sex or to lust management.*

—D. Brennan[66]

Cross-gender spiritual friendships outside of marriage (also called Catholic spiritual friendships, cross-gender spiritual friendships, spiritual marriages, spiritual friends, cross-gender Trinitarian Communions, cross-sex friendships) have historical Catholic basis. We are beginning as well to see potential interest from evangelicals, e.g. Dan J. Brennan's blog.

What is different about the approach suggested in this book's discussion and the comments we see on the Protestant blog from mainly Evangelicals:

Spiritual Friendship:

- There is the overwhelming feeling on the part of the friends that they were brought together by the Holy Spirit.

- Their Trinitarian Communion is a grace that will bear spiritual fruit.

- The Trinitarian Communion helps to develop their individual spiritual lives and their joint spiritual life as friends.

- The Trinitarian Communion friendship is based upon their individual and joint" journeys" in the pursuit of God.

- This Trinitarian Communion is God placing one in a unique situation, a unique grace.

- There are unique circumstances on both sides of the Trinitarian Communion.

- The Catholic concept of celibacy as a gift and grace given by God is fundamental to a non-marriage Spiritual Friendship.

- Spiritual Friendships, Trinitarian Communions are coming from an ancient Catholic heritage of spiritual development in relating to God and from the common belief in the Eucharist and a deep prayer life.

- Spiritual Friendship is coming from a foundation of Catholic Marian focus, i.e. Marian spirituality with Christ/Mary as the New Adam and the New Eve.

- Spiritual Friendship can help to put relationships with others in perspective, i.e. among others it shows the individual distinctiveness of vocational marriages and friendships.

- Spiritual Friendships may help to decrease the divorce rate by providing friendships based upon spiritual and other interests that the spousal partner does not share.

In general, by looking at Evangelical Protestant blog responses concerning non-marriage cross-gender spiritual friendships:

- The Holy Spirit or Jesus is rarely mentioned in the blog responses.

- The emphasis is entirely on "friends" instead of a spiritual communion with a possible spiritual purpose.

- There is no spiritual basis of a "journey" or a "path" in spiritual development or a charism or a specific spirituality as a guide to understanding and direction.

- There is no Discernment of Spirits as we see in Catholicism from the legacy of St. Ignatius. There is no way to determine if the relationship is from God or the evil one?

- The concept of marriage as a vocation never appears. Neither real commitment nor lifetime commitment is mentioned. The sin of dissolution of the marriage union is not mentioned.

- As a Catholic, the consequences of divorce are a helpful barrier to other potential actions resulting from a relationship that is disordered and creates sin.

- The Protestant vs. Catholic view of mankind and man's creation is quite different. Catholics believe that man is basically "good" as is noted in Genesis. Protestants believe that man is permanently and personally damaged. As Luther states, man is dung and the best that he can be is to be covered by the redemption of Christ covering man as if He were snow on top of the dung. The dung can never improve, can never become Holy as stated in 1 Peter 1:16.

- In the Protestant vs. Catholic view, is it possible that in Protestantism a man "can become holy"? In the Protestant view, he cannot become holy. The Catholic view is that according to Jesus, we are unmistakably directed by Him to "become Holy as your Father is Holy" (1 Peter 1:16, Matthew 5:48).

The Protestant vs. Catholic view of women is that Protestantism degrades women as being subservient to the male and not equal. (See below.)

> *Protestantism has a degraded view of women not shared by Catholics. A Protestant has one source of reference for women and their relationship to males and that is Eve. Eve was seduced by the evil one leading to the seduction of Adam through her engendered influence on Adam. This*

influence led to the seduction of all mankind and the Fall from the Garden. Eve was created as Adam's companion in Genesis 3 without procreation mentioned. She was supposed to be like and equal to him in all areas (the rib as the complete copy of the person). But Adam and Eve failed God throwing all mankind into a state of sin. In Protestantism man had now became incapable of being righteous, i.e. in the right relationship with God. The relationship with God and with each other in the Garden meant that man is incapable on his own of not sinning and relies completely on the power of the risen Jesus to wash away all his sins. We are unable to do anything on our own to become holy despite Jesus telling us to, "become Holy as your Father is Holy." (1 Peter. 1:16; Matthew 5:48)

Therefore, a Protestant woman, the daughter of Eve, is incapable of resisting temptation and the evil one. She is without defense physically (God's gift) or morally/mentally of resisting sexual temptation on the part of the male. We are not talking about rape and physical over empowerment but normal relations between a man and a woman. The male can have his way with her due to her inability to not be seduced. Remember, she is the off-spring of Eve who failed God as her Creator and failed man as his companion. She has the ability to seduce in a way unmatched by the male if she wishes as she did to Adam. Man is subject to her seduction because man has little control over his reaction to her seductive female nature.

However, the Catholic woman has Mary as her perfected inspiration and God's gift as pure femininity. Mary is the

New Eve who defeats the evil one and says "yes" to God. She takes on her divine role as "companion," not the victim of the Fall. She is not the offspring of Eve with the "yes" to the evil one and sin and "no" to God. With Mary as the prototypical model we see the most important woman in history as the most important person in the earthly Church. The most important woman, Mary, in Christianity is not the failed seductress who failed mankind.

Therefore, since in the Protestant view women are not capable of "not seducing or being seduced" then men and women must be separated and without mutual friendship because as "snow on dung" it is inevitable that they will engage in sex whether married or not. The foundation of Protestantism reduces the likelihood of being holy and therefore saying "no" to temptation.

As Catholics, women are able to pursue holiness and say "no" to temptation. They are not the fallen daughter of Eve but the full companion of Adam and the holy women descended from Mary. They are daughters of the New Eve. Catholic women and men, since they were created "good" and have the capability to be holy, are capable of non-marriage spiritual friendships. They both do have responsibility and at times may be truly tempted. But if their faith is sincere and they are listening to the Holy Spirit then they will be given the grace by God to have a true Trinitarian Communion.

This requires a surrendering to God and the corresponding obedience that is truly supernatural in nature. One cannot enter into a Spiritual Friendship without a true belief that

God will provide the grace necessary to obtain being "holy" in this regard with the transformation of the new person. Without this belief in the Divine to transform us as Jesus so reminds us in the Sermon on the Mount we are subject to falling into the sin of "use" of the other and the giving into our natural passions that can be aroused between the sexes.

So to many of our non-Catholic Christian brethren and secularists the idea of a celibate deep friendship between married members of the opposite sex, i.e. a Spiritual Friendship is inconceivable, naive and contrary to our nature given us by God. But Jesus tells us differently. He says that, "yes," without Him it is impossible! Man, at the helm of his own life will fail. But with Him at the helm it is possible! The grace is enough! It will enable us to truly, "love our neighbor as ourselves" as we seek to, "be holy," an attainable effort characterized by everyone on "the journey" back to the Garden. Cross-gender Trinitarian Communion Spiritual Friendships then become the physical reality that proves that man is good, made in the image of God and can provide love for another in a way contrary to all the evil one contends is possible.

The Trinitarian Communion is the spiritual foundation necessary for the friendship. The friendship is important but the basis has to always be spiritual and include the Trinity no matter where the relationship goes. Both must be on the path to trying to be holy and seeking God. The real problem for the Catholic cross-gender Trinitarian Communion is the overcoming of one's false self and self-centeredness that keeps the two in communion from having the trusting relationship envisioned by God in the Garden. Woman was really made in the Garden for companionship and not just procreation. The evil one has obsessed our culture and us with sex and the lack of trust; a lack of trust in God to create "good" and man to be "holy" in the pursuit of God.

Protestantism has done unknown harm in denying the ability to have cross-gender Trinitarian Communions by denying the quality of God's creation and created man's ability to spend eternity with the Creator. Therefore in cross-gender encounters we may pursue the wrong companions both in and out of marriage. We punt to the human characteristics of the culture to tell us how to view, select, fear and pursue the other gender. We forget the criteria of the Garden, we don't listen to God, and forget that love, companionship and close relationships in cross-gender Trinitarian Communions, although rare gifts from God, are what Jesus meant when He said to," love your neighbor as yourself." As Catholics on the journey we should not shy away when the Holy Spirit brings us the unique human companion. Remember, we were asked to "love our neighbor," and that neighbor defined as minus approximately 50 percent of the population, plus one.

> *In so many ways our culture trains us to be unfit for friendship.* (Paul Wadell)[67]

> *As spiritual friends, we are bound together by God, the common thread woven into the fabric of our individual lives…* (M. D. Poust)[68]

New Person's Pathway in Love

Jesus' World
Non-dualistic Consciousness
Charitable Interpretation
Mary and Catholic Church and Community

Triune God who loves
us unconditionally
Pure Love
Always there

Able to love another
unconditionally
Spiritual Friendship
Spiritual Marriage

Able to love aothers
as Christ loves us
(all people are created by God)

One's true acceptance
Of God's unconditional
love

New Person
contemplative silence
Characteristics of New Person
Searching to Understand NT & Jesus;
His thinking and meaning of parables

Relationship

RELATIONSHIP COOPERATION WITH GOD
Walking with God in Communion
Moments with God

Past	Present (Now)	Future
Prior moment	Where we meet God	Anticipation
Gone is the moment	Prayer	Unknown
Forgiven by a God who always forgives our sins	Silence Contemplative prayer	Control Celebration of Reconciliation
	Eucharist	

Prayer as the "Executor"

of the New Person

Prayer as Our Executor

Reflect on: But whenever you pray, go into your room and shut the door and pray to your Father who sees in secret; and your Father who sees in secret will reward you.

—Matthew 6:6.

Rising very early before dawn, he left and went off to a deserted place, where he prayed.

—Mark 1:35 NABCE

At several times, we have mentioned that as new persons "Prayer" is our Executor. Great! Expressed with enthusiasm may be one response to such a statement. Great. Expressed with sadness may be another response since at times prayer can seem like a burden, another thing that must be done, or prayer seems like an anomaly. The question arises what is prayer? What does it mean? What are we suggesting? We all understand that prayer is our communication and participation with our Triune God. Prayer is the result and expression of a decision for God on our part as a response to a decision by God to be available to man. Prayer creates for us a state between heaven and Earth of pure love where we meet God in a real yet mystical realm of mutual communion.

Our Model of Prayer

Prayer is both simple and deep, immensely enriching, leading to unspeakable love and delight. Prayer is not complicated, because there is nothing more natural than to converse with your beloved, and most especially with your supreme Beloved. If all grows normally it becomes deep, because it is rooted in your profound human and spiritual reality in who and what you are as a man or a woman. (T. Dubay)[69]

The Definition of Prayer from the Catholic Church

We will turn to the Catechism of the Catholic Church (CCC) Part Four entitled Christian Prayer for the foundation of our definition. There is so much written on and about prayer and so many forms of prayer and a diverse way to practice prayer that it is an inexhaustible subject. So to start with the CCC is prudent and reasonable in an effort to lay a solid foundation on the definition of prayer. The numerical citations indicate where in the CCC one may find the exact quote.

> 2558 "Great is the mystery of the faith!" The Church professes this mystery in the Apostles' Creed (*Part One*) and celebrates it in the sacramental liturgy (*Part Two*), so that the life of the faithful may be conformed to Christ in the Holy Spirit to the glory of God the Father (*Part Three*). **This mystery, then requires that the faithful believe in it, that they celebrate it, and that they live from it in a vital and personal relationship with the living and true God. This is relationship is prayer.**[70]

What is prayer?

> For me, prayer is a surge of the heart; it is a simple look turned toward heaven, it is a cry of recognition and of love, embracing both trial and joy. (St. Therese of Lisieux, Manuscrits Autobiographiques, C 25r)

Prayer as God's Gift

> 2559 **"Prayer is the raising of one's mind and heart to God or the requesting of good things from God."**

(St. John Damascene, Defide orth 3,24: PG 94, 1089C)
But when we pray, do we speak from the height of our pride and will, or "out of the depths" of a humble and contrite heart? (Ps 130:1) He who humbles himself will be exalted: (*CF LK 18:9-14*) *humility* is the foundation of prayer. Only when we humbly acknowledge that "we do not know how to pray as we ought" (*Rom 8:26*) are we ready to receive freely the gift of prayer. "Man is a beggar before God." (*St. Augustine, Sermo 56,6,9: PL 38,381*)

2560 **"If you knew the gift of God!"** (Jn 4:10) The wonder of prayer is revealed beside the well where we come seeking water: there, Christ comes to meet every human being. It is He who first seeks us and asks us for a drink. Jesus thirst; His asking arises from the depths of God's desire for us. **Whether we realize it or not, prayer is the encounter of God's thirst with ours.** God thirsts that we may thirst for Him. (*Cf St. Augustine De diversis quaestionibus octoginta tribue 64,4: PL 40, 56.*)

2561 **"You would have asked Him, and He would have given you living water."** (Jn 4:10) Paradoxically our prayer of petition is a response to the plea of the living God: "They have forsaken Me, the fountain of living waters, and hewn out cisterns for themselves, broken cisterns that can hold no water!" (*Jer 2:13*) Prayer is the response of faith to the free promise of salvation and also a response of love to the thirst of the only Son of God. (*Cf Jn7:37-39; 1928; Isa 12:3; 51:1; Zech 12:10,13:1*)

Prayer as Covenant

2562 **Where does prayer come from?** Whether prayer is expressed in words or gestures, it is the whole man who prays. But in naming the source of prayer, Scripture speaks sometimes of the soul or the spirit, but most often of the heart (more than a thousand times). **According to Scripture, it is the heart that prays. If our heart is far from God, the words of prayer are in vain**.

2563 **The heart is the dwelling-place where I am, where I live;** according to the Semitic or Biblical Expression, the heart is the place "to which I withdraw." *The heart is our hidden center, beyond the grasp of our reason and of others; only the Spirit of God can fathom the human heart and know it fully.* The heart is the place of decision, deeper than our psychic drives. It is the place of truth, where we choose life or death. It is the place of encounter, because as image of God we live in relation: it is the place of covenant.

2564 **Christian prayer is a covenant relationship between God and man in Christ,** It is the action of God and of man, springing forth from both the Holy Spirit and ourselves, wholly directed to the Father, in union with the human will of the Son of God made man.

Prayer as Communion

2565 In the New Covenant, prayer is the living relationship of the children of God with their Father who is good beyond measure, with His Son Jesus Christ and with the Holy Spirit. The grace of the Kingdom is "the union of the entire holy and royal Trinity...with the whole human spirit." (*St. Gregory of Nazianzus, Oratio 16,9: PG 35,945*) Thus, the life of prayer is the habit of being in the presence of the thrice-holy God and in communication with Him. This communion of life is always possible because, through Baptism, we have already been united with Christ. (*Cf Rom 6:5*) Prayer is Christian insofar as it is communion with Christ and extends throughout the Church, which is His Body. Its dimensions are those of Christ's love. (*Cf Eph 3:18-21*)

God initiates the relationship between us and Himself. He waits for our response to His invitation. This invitation coupled with our response creates a new life within us, a life commonly referred to as a prayer life. This life grows and matures within us as we commit to it, nurture it and understand that discipline is not only a virtue it is joy and life. We move from vocal prayer and meditation to contemplation immersing ourselves slowly into the indwelling Trinity and allowing Him to transform us into the divine image.

This defines prayer but what we may not understand it's meaning in the many contexts in which we pray. In its many contexts prayer may be corporate as in worship or personal as in meditative or contemplative prayer which may have also a corporate venue. But the context of prayer is better thought of in the context of the individual who is doing the praying. Prayer may be rote and defined by space and time for some. In the context of one who is or is in transformation as a new person and clearly seeking God on the journey we encounter "prayer as the executor." Here the context is prayer completely enveloping the new person directing all aspects of the lives of the willing faithful.

Prayer like any activity in our lives becomes transformed from a duty that must be completed to a way of living or a lifestyle that is naturally and joyfully entangled within our daily routine. This lifestyle is so entangled within us it is who we are and there is no end in this world or the next. Prayer's pathway leads us to the Reality, that Reality is God Himself.

As a new person we are giving our life to God. We are depending on Him and allowing Him to direct us in each and every moment of our lives. Through prayer we experience conversion and experience the joy of conversion. We are to move away from ourselves and self-centeredness to be more like Mary, i.e., in the "right relationship" with God, i.e. righteousness.

Every genuine encounter with the Word presupposes an accepting and receptive consent on man's part: and Mary in her fundamental orientation to the Holy Spirit and in his descent upon her, this consent became the source of the Incarnation of the Word. In the Spirit she utters that Yes of hers which is the origin of all Christian contemplation, by which she becomes pregnant with the Word and keeps "all these things, pondering them in her heart." (Lk. 2:19, 51) Only now we can see why the Word given and promised by the Father can be something man is able to understand, not only on the human plane but on the divine plane as we; a word which in faith, he actually expects, which finds in him a ready womb in which to develop. This is because the same Spirit who brings the Son to men from the Father has also prepared their hearts to receive him. The feminine, Marian element in faith, which implies fundamental openness and readiness to receive God's "seed" is identical with the contemplative element implanted in every act of faith through the grace of God's Holy Spirit. (Hans urs von Balthasar)[71]

In this context of prayer we must understand and believe in our hearts that our Triune God is always loving us unconditionally and communicating with us no matter who we are. We must understand how this might be so. As von Speyr so simply notes prayer is only necessary because of sin. Without sin prayer is unnecessary. We must remember that God in three persons is pure love. For understanding we look to von Speyr's eloquence of the pure love relationship that exists between the Father, Son and Holy Spirit. We see complete, eternal and simultaneous expectation and fulfillment of understanding, agreement, and compliance between the persons of the Triune God. We see God the Father's Will simultaneously understood, grasped, and executed by the Son and the Holy Spirit. We see a totality of simultaneous expectation and fulfillment. Never in anything other than total love and surrender to one another have we seen the completeness of the ultimate love. The love between the three is overwhelming beyond our mortal conception and like a huge Niagara Falls we feel the power and the fear and the love of that Love cascading down in incredible and unimaginable power from the Trinity to us. We see and feel the freedom of the all-powerful Triune God to love us beyond our comprehension.

For one on the journey we say that Prayer is now our Executor. Prayer is the vehicle that administers our life on the journey that employs the characteristics of the new person that we employ daily that allows us to realize that we are at the foot of these incredible powerful Falls of Love of the Triune God. We through awe and a wonderful fear are open to receive that incredible, overwhelming sense of Love for us. His Love is Everything and we begin to realize and accept that anything less than Everything is not enough. And we willingly begin to fall in love with our Triune God and understand that prayer in all its forms is an "I love you" response to Him. (T. Dubay)[72]

In further thought to say that Prayer is the "executor" means that our lives on the journey are given over to the Holy Spirit to more and more communicate to us the journey itself and what we are asked to do for God while on the journey. It is through prayer that we are administered—by listening to God in all the ways He speaks. This means that above all we must open ourselves to God in total surrender via prayer with no thoughts of fear or second guessing.

God has created us to hear his Word and enabled us with the ability to hear His word. This ability to hear the Word goes as deep in us as being itself; The Father created us as spiritual creatures, and so we are 'hearers of the Word'. To hear and believe the Word of God are one and the same thing. (Hans urs von Balthasar)[73]

Therefore one must continuously discipline oneself and practice prayer in an effort to advance along the prayer pathway learning to be attuned to God's voice learning to discern God's voice from our own self-centeredness or the evil one. Without deep prayer there is no real sustained journey that progresses or does not become stagnate or at least bog down or become cumbersome.

But listening may not be so easy. Here is where our self-centeredness tries to defeat us buoyed in many apparently good ways by the evil one. Our first hurdle is our own lack of faith in the heart and soul given to us by God. We remember, maybe too well, all the times when we are acutely aware we did not listen to God. We recall particular instances. We doubt our ability to listen and we couple our failures with lack of faith and add in that we are told that listening to God in prayer is very difficult. It is but it is possible with persistence and patience. We are told that it is "hard," that it comes "rarely," that we are unable to "make it happen" and we let all this get in the way! What a predicament, we are on the journey, prayer is our executor, it is imperative that we listen to God with expectation of hearing Him, but we are set up to fail at this before we even begin. We are told that even in the best form of communication with God, contemplative prayer, that we cannot orchestrate the communication—it all comes from God, we have no control. Further, it would seem that we must be monks and abbots and spend hours each day over long periods of time to get any communication from God at all! I have to be "selected" in order to be intimate with the Triune God and I am "not a Saint." The evil one tells us what seems to have a lot of realism, "this prayer as the executor is not for us, maybe the best I can do is just to want to be on the journey and realize that this intimacy with the Creator is predestined for others and not for me. Is God the only one capable of calling us to be on the journey? Can we fake ourselves into it? Are we predestined? Am I to make do as best I can with prayer at best in a "space" and a "time"? Just think, I can do good works, I will continue to sin and go to confession as much as I need, or I can decide on my own what is really a sin in the context of my own conscious and situation in life, I can go to Church when it seems appropriate, I can understand that my conscious will be my director and that I will "just try to be a good person." I don't need to think too deeply about these things—I have life to live. I don't really need that ultimate, intimate relationship with God that I am not blessed with to begin with. I am not a Priest, Religious, Contemplative, Spiritual Director, or Biblical scholar or …. If God had meant for me to be intimate with Him, He would have made me one of these. Has that not always been the case!?

It is so easy to fall into this trap of the evil one. Many do in one or more ways mentioned. Pursuing God can be tough in our mortal views of pursuit and failure/success at anything and time. It is so much easier to settle for a "C" in our spiritual relationships. It is so easy to buy the "predestination" myth of Calvin and our self-centered nature when it comes to prayer.

The problem is that we have been called and we just cannot seem to get that out of our heads or hearts. We yearn for God and we want to pursue Him regardless of our inabilities. Something remains missing and we feel it in our souls. It's hard to just discount it as just being emotion or fear of Hell. It is neither of these. It is like being in a state of serious mortal sin and putting off going to confession. It eats at our souls. We are never allowed to forget and we are not allowed to rationalize it away. We have listened to God without knowing it!

We are on the path, we are on the journey, we pursue Him who has pursued us, we long to see His face, we want that intimate relationship with our Creator. We want our communication with God, our prayer, to be without ceasing and we want to hear the "voice of God" in our hearts.

Therefore, we flee to the grace given to us from the beginning of eternity, our Blessed Mary, our sister in humanity, our human liaison to God, our model, the bride of the Holy Spirit and the mother of our corporate presence, the Church. She was in "the right relationship with the Triune God." She did have an intimate relationship with God. She prayed without ceasing. Prayer was her executor. Without sin she could see clearly. She can help us with sin, to see more clearly and help us be led by Him to the clarity of eternity.

> *Mary was beginning in dark faith the eternal contemplative enthrallment of immersion in the Trinitarian beauty seen face to face.* (T. Dubay)[74]

As our foundation of commune with God we go back to remembering that our Triune God is complete love. Each one of us individually is the Beloved of God, He is always present, always with His hand extended to each of us, always looking after our spiritual welfare, always inviting us as individuals to eternity with Him. Therefore, there is no predestination; there are no limitations on our ability to be in right relationship with God. The evil one lies. We are all called. We each have a unique and complete potential relationship with our Creator. Therefore, we begin by knowing completely in our hearts and minds that we can have an intimate relationship with God and we can commune with Him. This is crucial. The past does not matter. Mary calls us to move beyond our past, beyond our limitations, beyond our self-centeredness to allow God to do His work in our lives. This is the foundation He gives us to be on the path on the journey and to realize the grace and peace of prayer as our executor.

As was Mary, in prayer life we mean we progress in our relationship with God so that we "pray continuously," i.e. we understand the ways we pray continuously and understand how God speaks to us in so many diverse ways. Our prayer is without ceasing as is our conversion.

Understanding how we pray without ceasing and how God speaks to us only allows us to move forward in actually praying without ceasing versus going through the motions as "wanting to" but not really "doing so." There is true danger in "wanting to." Wanting to is not doing so. God is real and our commune with Him must be real as it is with any human relationship. The word "pray" listed in a dictionary is a verb—a verb expresses action—as we pray we are actively engaging in a relationship with God. We must not deny this reality in our thoughts or our actions. All must be real and not perceived or manufactured/manipulated. Patience in the activity of prayer is a blessed virtue.

When prayer is our executor and we pray without ceasing then all prayer is worthy—not just contemplative prayer. We continually owe God praise and thanksgiving and we want Him to hear and act on our petitions at all times and in all places according to His Will. Contemplative prayer allows God to speak and must be the true medium of the executor. However, we must look for God's speaking to us in all scriptural, doctrinal and sensual means. We must be awake, aware, attuned, ready to accept Him when He comes, not simply at the end of times but today, now in the ordinary existence of our lives.

To draw on von Speyr, there are aspects of each type of prayer that must be understood from a Triune as well as a human perspective.

Worship is the loving recognition of God. Worship contains much astonishment and gratitude: astonishment that God is so great and gratitude that He allows Himself to be contemplated. In worship the new person must come completely out of her skin of self-centeredness into the realm of the Triune God. As von Speyr puts it, in worship it is the *thou* and not the I. We are asked to worship the Triune God in all of His power, glory and majesty. We are to forget ourselves and fully become engrossed in the Thou in the Eucharist. God is there in the Eucharist in all His glory. We are allowed by Him to completely surrender to Him and to bring into our bodies Himself in all His majesty and to become one with Him in a way that foreshadows our eternity with Him in heaven. It is all about the Thou and because we love God love is always an act of preferring the other. It is nothing about the I. Even in our petitions during Mass we are dwelling on our problems and concerns we are giving them to Him to do with as He feels best. We know He and He alone will do what is absolutely best for us. We need not fear or continue with concern. It is all in the hands of the only One that can meet our needs! And, in staggering amazement He forgives us our sins! The word is "He." He forgives our sins, He takes care of our problems and concerns, He guides us, He makes us one with Him. The "He" is totally "Thou."

In our petitional prayer we have and show our faith in God as our Creator and our Redeemer. The One knows what is best for us eternally. We are asked to trust God completely. The overwhelming love, expectation and fulfillment between the Trinity creates a hierarchy of expectations/fulfillments that move from God to the Son and the Holy Spirit that are simultaneous and in complete mutuality. This is done with the freedom of the Son and the Holy Spirit to freely answer our prayers since the Triune God's will for us is always in complete agreement with each person of the Trinity. To us, God's creatures, these heavenly mutual expectations/fulfillments mean we enjoy God's answers to our petitions in a situation of true freedom. Our freedom is our freedom to do God's will. This means that God's answers to our petitions will always be in the context of His laws and what is right. This means that His answers allow us the freedom to do what is best for us in the context of our salvation. His answers to our petitions will never be in the territory of the evil one and never a danger to our souls and never return us to slavery. This is true freedom—freedom from ourselves' centeredness and our ability to endanger the very reason we were put in this world by God.

And in the Triune God's grace we have the communion of saints and the Saints themselves who in conjunction with the mutual love of the three persons have the responsibility to assist in the answer from God to the petition. Therefore the answer to prayer flowing from God flows to the Son and the Holy Spirit in their freedom to do His will as they have freedom to do so in the context of the mutuality of the Trinity and in turn the Saints may assist in the answer and all those in the greater communion of saints through their prayers also participate in the answer.

Prayers of thanksgiving are certainly a very Marian form of prayer. This is where there should be no thought of "I" since "I" is thanking THOU for what THOU has done for "I." We have completely left our realm of self-centeredness knowing that whatever we are thankful for we do not have the power and ability to do ourselves. We become and show our dependence on God to run our lives. We are in complete knowledge of having surrendered to His will.

Only when disorder enters our hearts do we sin in thanksgiving. Only when we begin to move to motivations that attempt to give us some of the credit do we hint that we have not moved to true belief and dependence on God. However, did we not have a part to play? Could we maybe have accomplished it on our own? God gave us skills and graces and does not God expect us to do our part or to do our part before we turn to Him? Why bother Him with such simple issues? To the new person on the journey this is true disorder. **We are to give it all to God so that He has all the glory. Only if He directs us through the executor do we participate at all and then only in response to the initiative given to us.**

Is this possible? Truly, are we not expected to think and act with the intellect God has given us. Don't we have to have and exercise that intellect to listen to the Holy Spirit and understand what we are to do? We are definitely participants and exercisers of our intellect but only as it relates to our communion with God in prayer and only in a definite ordered way. For the new person "ordered way" means we are listening for and to God at all times, not just in a time and space. Based upon our listening and discernment of spirits we take action. Our apparent passive prayer of thanksgiving becomes as active as other forms of prayer in reaction to God's word to us. We might even contend that our anticipation of God's communication with us is active and not passive. These in-line prayers of thanksgiving with all other prayer makes it more than just words of casual thanks.

But, as we seek a deeper prayer life and as it moves us to deeper conversion we must become aware of the evil one or false spirit and his ability to attack anyone on the journey with ruthless pursuit. He will use our best to do his worst. He will destroy any kind of love if given any opportunity at all. Even our prayers are not immune to his influence. He will make prayer a folly by using our fragile minds and natures.

Only a spirit of joy and happiness internally and externally should grow in us as we move along the journey. We should not become in-bred, judgmental, legalistic, and obsessive with ourselves or with others. When we fall off the path we experience sadness and appropriate penance but only in the measure that God gives it, not in the evil one's measure.

Love creates the joy and happiness and spurs one on to prayer whereas mere virtue without love leaves one cold. Belief in God is not needed to live a mere virtuous life. But involuntarily and without being aware of it the person who loves God is continually opening doors of prayer for everyone who loves Him and shares His life.

When we fall off the path, often in a major way and are awed at our ability to so easily slip and still sin at this point on the journey we must ask in prayer for the frame of mind that makes us really remember that we are the Beloved of God. We ask for forgiveness and try to get back up on our feet and back on the road knowing full well that we are once again being reminded that we are forever fragile and so open to the wiles of the evil one or false spirit who once again has used our self-centeredness. We doubt the ability to ever make progress on our journey, returning to the same sins over and over but often at farther points than before but not necessarily.

We must then ask ourselves why, how, where and when so that we can look to avoid these opportunities that set us up to spiral down in failure and do the evil one's work and not God's. This is our work. We often wait to celebrate or participate in the Sacrament of Reconciliation believing that we have to prove to ourselves that this time we can do a little better than the last time. We must diligently try hard to listen to God in the sacrament because we know that this will do us the most earthly good yet our penance may have us delay.

How We Exalt the Holy Cross

There is a tree planted by God which we call Love.
You there, you I see up in its branches—
Show me where I can begin to climb,
That I might leave this darkness behind.
I climb so slowly that if I stop to speak to you
A puff of wind will blow me down.
I have a long way to go;
Indeed, there's a hard struggle ahead.
The glory of the ascent, I know, is God's, not yours,
But help me work free of this swamp—
If thanks to your aid I come to serve God

It will be you who has won me back for Him.
To the praise of God I tell you,
And as a friend,
That in fear of the Enemy
Was I led to this tree.
I looked at it in my mind's eye
Meditated on it at length,
And burned with the desire
To climb that measureless height.
I could not even guess
How high the branches reached;
The trunk was straight and smooth.
I saw no place where I could get a hold,
Except for one branch
That curved down to the ground;
A poor despised little bit of a branch,
It bore the mark of humility.
I was ready to climb when suddenly
I heard a voice; "Do not touch me
Unless you have first confessed,
Cleansed yourself of all mortal sin."
Contrition flooded my heart,
I cleansed myself with confession
And with the help of God
Made satisfaction.
Coming back to the tree I felt fear and misgivings,
In anticipation of the exhausting effort;
I devoutly prayed to God for help,
For without His aid I could not climb the tree.
"Sign yourself with the sign of the cross,"

Said a voice that came from Heaven,
"And take hold of the shining bough,
A branch that is pleasing to God."
(Brother Jacopone da Todi, +1306, Franciscan poet born in Italy)[75]

Here, also, we must retreat into deep solitude of contemplative prayer and search our true hearts for signs of Divine life. Asking God all along to forgive us without qualification and let us truly believe it, not fake the belief. Then we know that we are back on the path with some progress made. This may take some time or instantly—that is God's wisdom, not ours. This is where we have to pray to listen to Him until we are sure that we have moved beyond ourselves and are ready to enjoy the joys of the journey. Only the supernatural will honestly move us forward after these falls from grace!

As many of the Saints have told us, one must rid themselves of mortal sin first to move at all on the journey. We must be sure we understand what mortal sin means for each of us and why. We must also be completely aware of the potential for venial sins to become mortal ones if we ignore them in confession. When we commit it we may be majorly thrown off the path with recovery possibly being a sad and struggling time.

The executor leads us to community and to service that is in community always. If we fall off the path we must never shy from community prayer. Community prayer is our prayer when we are trying to recover from mortal sin. We find joy in the prayers and concerns of others as we seek it in our sufferings.

In community we must also be aware for the potential of sin. In prayer and worship in particular we must recall our discussion of comparison. There is no comparison of ourselves with others in prayer. This is the height of indiscretion. We do not know what the other is thinking or where they are coming from. We have no right to dwell on the other "I" because then we are focused on our "I" and our "I" should be totally focused on the THOU. Love does not compare, it is totally focused on the THOU.

As noted by Rohr this can be best visualized in the concept of "quantum entanglements." The Holy Spirit flows through all of us into all those we come in contact with creating a mosaic of all believers, non-believers, animals, plants, and the whole earth and the cosmos. To the new person this means that we must be affected by our encounter with the pure love of God and positively affect others as we transfer that love to all those we come in contact with in the world to spread the love of God to all that are possible.

As noted in an earlier chapter individually and in community we train with our fellow brothers and sisters to be true disciples of our Lord Jesus Christ through passive and active prayer. The journey in pursuit of our Triune God requires our whole being and must include body, mind, heart and soul. We train for today's game as well as for eternity.

Training requires us to learn the means to hear God and obey the Executor. We may practice Lectio Divina, Ignation Spiritual Exercises including the Discernment of Spirits, and Marist Spirituality may be practiced and found significantly meaningful and necessary as one progresses on the journey since God speaks to us through the Scriptures. We must feed our hunger for spirituality in important books, Papal encyclicals, retreats, etc., journeying closer to God's will in our lives is an unending education in the language of prayer.

Part of the journey that we cannot underestimate are the graces that we experience as human beings who suffer because we are not in The Garden. As Catholics we embrace suffering as a corridor back to The Garden. Suffering brings us closer to God as we join our suffering to His and closer to an advanced prayer life that brings true joy and happiness. There is no better way! God will give us enough of our own sufferings. His joy from the sufferings of the cross is now our joy as we suffer in our own little way with Him. The sufferings of the cross always lead to the joys of the resurrection.

Only through suffering do we really become dependent on God. We can often do very little about our sufferings; they are beyond our to-do list and our wishing and hoping. His will be done! But by giving up the concerns of suffering to Jesus we are freed and we rest in the security of God's wings, giving us a glimpse of eternity to come and bringing the joy that passes all understanding. We are under His wings where we were always meant to be. As, Our Mother of Sorrows, we become closer to the "right relationship with God" and joy no matter what the adversity. Then we have hit a milestone on the journey. We can endure all things.

But despite the suffering we are reminded that we embrace God in prayer who is there lock stepped with us through the suffering. He hears our prayer and sends us through our own kind those to help us through the suffering as well as the joys of the journey if we allow Him to work His grace. Most notably for half of our species we have previously strongly suggested that the woman brings God to the male. The analogy with prayer cannot be overlooked. The availability or not of the woman to the man is not unlike the availability of the new person to the Triune God. We must make ourselves available to God as the woman does to the man in the act of love. She initiates the availability through her being available. She surrenders of her own free will to the man with not only the element of surrender but with adoration, thanksgiving, and submission as we do when we make ourselves available to God in prayer. And in reciprocity the male in mimicking the reception of God into the human in the Eucharist in turn gives to the woman in the act of love adoration, thanksgiving and submission that is the height of human physical love and the manifestation of God's communion and participation with those who love Him. The results of the reciprocity is the mutual love of the Trinity in heaven played out in Mary's surrender to the Holy Spirit and in the mutual coming together of a mortal man and woman in the ultimate physical and mystical expression of love.

As Fr. Mark Thibodeaux, S.J. so well explains in "Armchair Mystic" there are several recognized prayer types that help us to meet with God at various times and places. Depending on where one is at in their spiritual life ready-made prayers, extemporaneous prayers, meditative prayers and contemplative prayer all offer opportunities to listen to God no matter how far we are in our prayer development or in our spiritual journey or our place in time and space at a given moment. In any of these prayer types we must seek solitude and silence! As new persons we must find these in the privacy of a darkened room, at Mass or even when we are in the noise of a public place. Matthew's sixth chapter does not confine us to a room with a closed door. However, it does call us to find that spiritual solitude and silence, the key to Matthew's room with the closed door. Only in solitude and silence can we find the best opportunity to listen and hear God speak to us. Our listening is a key to prayer. It is so easy for us to just "talk at" or "talk to" God where we do all of the talking and God gets to do all the listening. There is nothing wrong with this. Scripture tells us to thank God in prayers of thanksgiving and ask Him in prayers of petition. But too often we end the pseudo dialogue there. God, of course, is always listening to our prayers. But, we often forget that of grave importance is also what God says to us. Do we listen for Him? Do we hear Him? The Holy Spirit is trying to guide us and answer the prayers and we often don't know how to even listen.

In our effort to hear God's will for us in our lives we must seek that one-on-one solitude and silence with God. This takes the practice of daily prayer in a contemplative way and setting. As we proceed in our spiritual dialogue with God, through contemplative prayer we can even hope to have the solitude and silence with God no matter where we are, how in community we may be and the noise and movement of any time and place.

Contemplative prayer would seem to be the epitome of Marian prayer since we are totally at the mercy of God to one-way communicate with us. Contemplative prayer is all about listening to God to help us do His will. Mary without sin was able to clear away the distractions and cobwebs of her mind and listen to God and we can assume she did it always. For us, contemplative prayer affords the best place to find solitude and silence. As we clear our minds of distractions and place ourselves, at least initially in our contemplative prayer life development, into solitude in a quiet and silent place we are able to hear God as He chooses to speak to us. Remember, it is God who really initiates prayer. In contemplative prayer we offer our hearing to the Lord without any agenda or expectation that He will speak to us.

But if we are to meet Him, to hear Him, if He speaks, to us the new person must understand that the best environment for hearing God is in the current "moment." There is where we truly meet God in monologue or dialogue with the emphasis on His monologue to us. The previous moment is gone, sins are forgiven and that moment is now history. The future moment or the moment after the current moment is somewhat not truly predictable and we do not have control over it. We can celebrate whatever occurred in the current moment. History or anticipated times may allow us to see the works of God and may influence us concerning God but it is in the solitude and the silence of the moment that we truly are with God. We experience this most intimately in the Eucharist.

As people on the journey desiring for our hearts not to be hardened we are aware we are beginners constantly. As Sister Ann Goggin, r.c. asked her Spiritual Direction Institute class in year one "are you willing to be beginners over and over?" I paused, pondered, wondered and accepted that yes I am—in reality I seemed to have lived my life like that. But until she asked the question I felt that beginning over and over somehow equated to a lack of understanding. "Who are beginners in prayer? Novices or veterans, we are all unworthy beggars, unworthy even to appear before the unspeakable beauty and goodness who is our God, let alone to converse with Him. Most people consider it a privilege simply to be greeted by a famous person or to shake hands. Who of us would not feel blessed to have a chat for ten minutes with Augustine or Bernard or Thomas or Catherine or Teresa of Avila or Therese? Yet it is the infinite Trinity, Lord of all the saints with whom we chat at prayer. The Imitation of Christ puts it well:

> *O Lord my God, you are all my good, and who am I that I should dare speak to You?" (book 3, chapter 3). We dare because by his tenderness in Scripture he invites us over and over to have a chat with him. Best of all, The Son of the Father admonishes us to pray "Our Father…" and even to "pray always" (Mt. 6:9–18; Lk. 18:1). The chat may even be wordless, just being with Someone who loves you unspeakably. (For more on Jesus's teaching about prayer, see CCC 2607-15; 2663-82.).* (T. Dubay)[76]

Prayer is communication with God and communication is vital within our relationship with Him. We *need* it. He *desires* it. We have the privilege to choose it. Do not delay in your choice. Do not delay regardless of the state of your soul. He waits for us to return to Him.

> *Come back to Me with all your heart don't let fear keep us apart. Long have I waited for your coming home to Me and living deeply our new life."* (The Hosea Song)[77]

> *Prayer is life!* (Sherri) Return to T. Dubay's quote at the beginning of this section and reread his beautiful description.
>
> *No truth can be found unless there is search for meaning, recognition of human vulnerability and limitation, relationships with trusted spiritual friends,*

and openness to the disclosure of the transcendent mystery of God, before whom all questions cease. (Henri Nouwen)[78]

The important thing in prayer is not to think much but to love much. (Theresa of Avila, Interior Castle)[79]

SPIRITUAL LIFE PATTERNS
(Potential Spiritual Development Phases)

Progress in spiritual development does not look like secular progress being non-judmental of self or others, moving from head to heart

External Phase	**Devotional Phase**	**Meditative Phase**	**Contemplative Phase**
(Talk To/Talk At God)			
Mass - Do's	How do I start to _____?	A truer progressive image of who	The God of Nouwen
Confession - Do's	Read scripture commentaries	God truly is	Solitude and Silence is where
Rosary - Do's	How do I begin to understand	Begin road to being a new person	we meet God
Rote Prayers - Do's	scripture?	Begin moving to non-dual	Listening for God
Novenas/Litanies - Do's	Help me ????	consciousness	Non-dual consciousness
Phase where most Catholics are	How do I interace with God?	Begin moving from head to heart	Charitable Interpretation
Various Images of God	Need anchors to help them	Lectio Divina	Part of the community of
Varying degrees of: Does God love me?	Read scripture commentaries	Developing a sense of "abba"	the Christian Triune God
External actions	Head knowledge	Still involved in Externals	Quantum Entanglements
Bible Studies	Still involved in Externals	Begin to apply to life	links to rest of creation
Spirituality is External	Fear of intimacy with God	A call by God into contemplation	New person characteristics
Dualistic Consciousness	Importance of Community	Spiritual Direction	Less self-centeredness
Strong sense of Community	Spiritual Direction		The "do's" of External Phase
External events may be major influences			are celebrated differently
There is little interior reflection			Continued development as
No meditative or contemplative prayer			a Contemplative
Personal devotion separate from			Continued spiritual direction
community prayer			
Length: till death for many			
Length: till spiritual deepening hunger			
May have ties to external events that			
are major			
Spiritual Direction - maybe			

Internal Working of God throughout the whole process

"Prayer as the Executor"

Spiritual Patterns Overview

- The development phases above represent a typical spiritual progression to contemplative prayer.

- Each phase may be for the individual a progressive phase or one may spend their whole life in a single phase.

- God will call you if He wants you to move to the next phase.

- Spiritual development is done in God's time, not our time.

- Spiritual development is dependent on where He is calling you and your receptivity and capacity to His call.

- What phase you are in may be affected by external influences on your life.

- There are no comparisons or implied comparisons between individuals in the spiritual development.

- One spiritual development phase is not better than another.

- Deep personal relationships with God if you are receptive are forged in the meditative and contemplative phases.

- You do not begin with the contemplative phase. You must progress there.

- Each phase must have some components of the inner, relational, and service elements of spirituality.

The Fulfillment Jesus Wants for Us

Jesus wants me to tell you again…how much love he has for each one of you-beyond all you can imagine. I worry some of you still have not really met Jesus-one to one-you and Jesus alone. We may spend time in chapel-but have you seen with the eyes of your soul how he looks at you with love? Do you really know the living Jesus-not from books but from being with him in your heart? Have you heard the loving words He speaks to you? Ask for the grace; He is longing to give it. Until you can hear Jesus in the silence of your own heart, you will not be able to hear Him saying, "I thirst" in the hearts of the poor. Never give up this daily intimate contact with Jesus as the real living person-not just the idea. How can we last even one day without hearing Jesus say, "I love you"—impossible. Our soul needs that as much as the body needs to breathe the air. If not, prayer is dead-meditation only thinking. Jesus wants you each to hear Him-speaking in the silence of your heart.

Be careful of all that can block that personal contact with the living Jesus. The devil may try to use the hurts of life, and sometimes our own mistakes-to make you feel it is impossible that Jesus really loves you, is really cleaving to you. This is a danger for all of us. And so sad, because it is completely opposite of what Jesus is really wanting, waiting to tell you. Not only that He loves you, but even more—He longs for you. He misses you when you don't come close. He thirsts for you. He loves you always, even when you don't feel worthy.

When not accepted by others, even by yourself sometimes—He is the one who always accepts you. My children, you don't have to be different for Jesus to love you. Only believe-you are precious to Him. Bring all you are suffering to His feet-only open your heart to be loved by Him as you are. He will do the rest.

Blessed Teresa of Calcutta[80]
Blessed Teresa of Calcutta (1997) founded the Missionaries of Charity and was awarded the Nobel Peace Prize.

In Reflection

In reflection Catholic Christendom in our post-modernistic, relativist, secular culture is challenged to provide an alternative to this culture as it fails. Although we may not be able to relegate this failure to the downswing of a cycle to explain its demise so predictably and easily, we can say with the certainty of Scripture that Catholic Christianity has survived and will survive anything else thrown at it. And certainly this post-modernistic culture has and still does in its death throws, throw at Catholicism every attack possible. And with more force than the pagan Roman Empire or the Reformation ever could, it uses weapons of intellectual, moral and emotional deception to confront the Church as never before.

What a masterfully simple strategy on the part of the evil one to sway the minds and hearts of men and women by simply making them believe that the Creator, God, "is irrelevant" and that we can do just fine without Him. I have my own conscious, my own personal "Ten Commandments," and that is all the moral direction I need. I simply don't need two thousand years of Divine moral direction. I live in the twenty-first century therefore I must be more sophisticated, more correct, more moral and smarter! I am "spiritual, I am my own god." I take care of me and my fellow man and that it is all I need. I know and acknowledge that out there somewhere is a god of some sort but He does not hold me responsible for anything. Those ideas are ancient, prejudicial and create bigotry!

The problem with the strategy of the evil one is that it does not work and it did not work. Post-modernism, relativism and secularism does not deliver on its promises. The Church and Christianity survived and once again is there to move the world back from the brink of chaos. The Church is still there despite the failures of its own leaders at times, despite various versions of self-centeredness and selfishness on the part of the "ism's," supposed enlightened and liberating movements toward freedom in all the ways it may be distortedly defined, and despite the false sciences being practiced in the name of empirical science.

What does work is simply what has always worked, Christ, the "Truth" in ancient times and the "Truth" today. Not distortions of the Christian faith as customized by self-centered individuals for their own purposes but the Church founded by and handed down by Christ through the apostles and the Magisterium of the Church. The faith that is not bigoted, not at odds with science, not an antique, but fully ready to step into the void and failure of the "Meism's" and their misunderstanding of the word freedom.

What does work is the quantum entanglements of love that emanate from the individual new person Christian, emanating to the Church, enlightening with experiential Christianity affecting along with an alternative orthodoxy that melds with the orthodoxy of the Church to not change dogma but to expand our understanding of dogma. This ancient institution of sinners founded by Jesus and alive and well is there poised and ready to enter into an entire new realm of human development that brings all into the human experience to allow all to experience the graces of God and the human dignity that He had in His economy of salvation since the Big Bang.

Thus, an alternative for all and a new world within an ancient world will emerge and be available to all. Nothing has changed, Christ and His Church have always been there and with free will as the option for each human individual to either accept or reject the blessings of the Church and the three persons of the Trinity and the salvation for eternity that goes with it.

The new world and the alternative is found in the new persons that now habitat in the Church. They are what makes it new. They will provide the alternative to the failed culture of post-modernism, relativism and secularism. They will reach out as others are drawn to reach in to the Church full of new persons as outlined in this book.

As we have seen in the preceding pages of this book both equal as never before in the eyes of each other women and men together in all configurations will listen for God's call, respond to His call, begin the journey along the path back to the Garden and progressively become disciples of our Lord Jesus Christ. They will know in their gut that God loves them unconditionally, that He is always with them, that He forgives them for all their sins, that He wants them to spend eternity with Him and that He wants to communicate with them in all types and times of prayer, particularly meeting them in solitude and silence. The new person will begin to think more of the THOU and thou and less of the I. The new person will progressively take on the characteristics of the new person and be a safe and loving draw to those around them. The draw for all humanity, wounded by the failure of the "me" culture and post-modernism, will be the happiness of the new persons they come in contact with because they have not wasted their life on the "me." They have given up their lives to the Triune God which brings peace, happiness and joy both in this world and in preparation for the next world.

We will in time see the new woman emerge as the daughter of Mary who with the response of the new man to her will forge the companionship of the sexes in the way that God meant for it to be but has never been. This will renew the face of the earth!

AMEN.

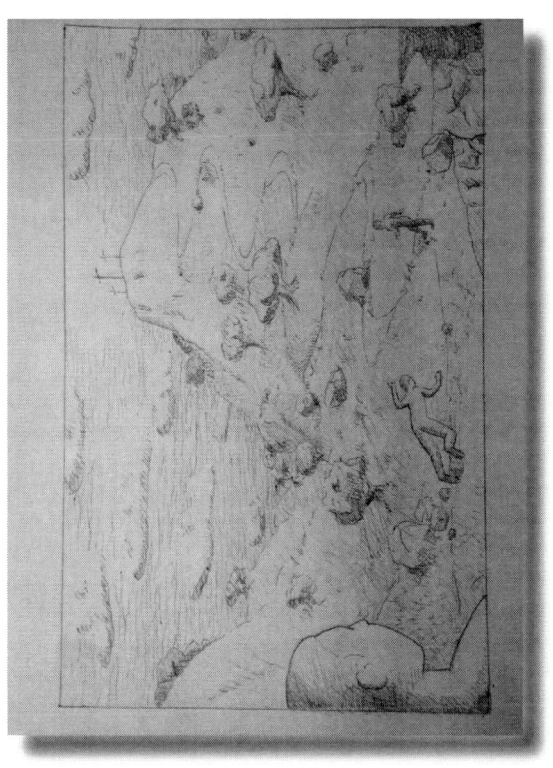

Parting Thoughts

As two spiritual friends and co-authors we have particularly come to realize in the last several years that our society worldwide does not reflect what the Triune God had in mind when He made us as man and woman. Scripture, and Tradition coming from the Early Church Fathers, does not support the current various relationships of women and men that we see today. I am not suggesting that our God's intentions concerning the relationships between men and women have ever existed. However, that does not mean that they were not meant to be by God, and does not mean that God did not mean for them to be His will in a certain time of human development. God works in His time.

One of the precepts of this book is that women have natural characteristics that are more like God than men. I have found few honest men that don't have to "ponder" when I say that to them. Most agree that it would seem to be true with exceptions of course but the exceptions are the minority in any shape or fashion. God sent woman to be the man's companion. She was equal in every way and not subordinate, not a slave, not chattel, not inferior, just different in the way she processes emotions, etc. making us, together, a wonderful image of God as one as we merge the two different natures into one no matter what the venue or circumstances.

The new person, creating the new world within the ancient Church founded by Jesus Christ must enter into a new world of relationships between men and women to be an alternative for the injured of post-modernism. The new person is the experiential of this new relationship between men and women.

As male Christians we cannot continue to treat the other gender in the way we have and continue to do so! Most of us treat them as something other than equal companions on a daily basis if we really give it thought! How are we being Christ-like, how are we being the new person men that are talked about in this book? We are challenged in evolving society into a Christian society of love for all! If we change with the help and grace of the Holy Spirit, they, the women will respond to us with help from the Holy Spirit. They will be transformed. We will then be an alternative to the post-modernistic, relativist, secular culture that we currently stagnate together in as both men and women. Then, and only then, can we proceed to renew the face of the earth!

There is much more to say about this!…Maybe it should be said at a later time? Maybe God's time for this revelation has now come!

Parting Comments

Bob: Well, Sherri, what are you thinking and feeling about the new person now?

Sherri: Feeling? Hmm? Well, feeling wise, I feel a little overwhelmed, yet very hopeful?

Bob: Overwhelmed, yet hopeful? What does that mean?

Sherri: The overwhelmed could be a negative, it requires too much discipline, requires me to not be so selfish and I may have to give up some sins I really like! Can I really be happy by following God's view of what "freedom" is? Do I really want to give up control of my life to God? Do I really trust Him that much?

However, I remember that Jesus asked us to be transformed, or maybe He did not ask us but demanded that we be transformed and to be like new persons to be His disciples, "to love God with all our heart, soul, and mind and to love your neighbors as I have loved you." To believe Him, and yearn to be His disciples is not easy. Yet, the struggle to be the new person gives me a happiness that surpasses all understanding in this world. The joy

434 ～ ～ Robert W. Spruce and Sherri C. Petrek ～

of meeting Him in the moment of solitude and silence in prayer supersedes any of my womanly emotions and brings me into a communion with Him that is indescribable. And, I want others to have that too!

Bob: Sherri, as a woman, does what we say about women having more of the characteristics of God than men resonate with you now? I know at the beginning of this journey you were very skeptical about that. Do you think we can renew the minds of men to God's view of women? Can men and women really be in communion with each other as "companions" that are equal?

Sherri: Bob, that is where the hope comes in. Everything I just said will come to pass as I am transformed by Christ into the new person. But, regarding the man and woman as companions and the other things that are being said, I want to echo one of my directee's comment regarding prayer. It sums it up well. My directee simply said, "It is doable!" And "Yes, it is doable!"

Bob: Well, Sherri, I still have that feeling as I know you do that there is much more to be said about women and men and men and women being in the new relationship that God intended exemplified by the new persons and their cross-gender Trinitarian Communions. Maybe we will talk more again on another day!

About the Authors

Robert (Bob) Spruce has degrees in international studies and economics from The American University and a degree in theology from the University of the South Episcopal Seminary. He is president of S&S Texas Properties, LLC. Bob is a convert to Catholicism. He is a professed lay member of The Society of Mary (Marists), a Catholic religious order, is on the RCIA team in his parish, and is a member of the Men's ACTS Movement, and currently enrolled in the SDI (Spiritual Direction Institute) at the Cenacle Retreat House in Houston, Texas.

Sherri Petrek is an active Certified Spiritual Director within the Catholic diocese of Galveston-Houston. She is a member of the Women's ACTS Team and provides spiritual direction to that community in her local parish. She has provided numerous "spiritual reflections" and has provided spiritual companionship to various Catholic faith communities. She has been on the core team of the Cornerstone Catholic Scripture Study ministry in her parish since its inception. She has a BA in English from The University of Houston–Victoria.

Front Cover: An emblem with the background of the Irish "friendship" knot with the Irish cladaugh symbol of crown, heart and hands meeting superimposed on a cross on the Irish cladaugh knot. This symbol is original and signifies a "spiritual friendship" most certainly between two of different genders as a special grace from our Triune God. These symbols represent the right relationships between God and between our fellow women and men that brings happiness today and eternally.

Notes

1. *Divine Intimacy.* "Invitation to Sanctity" #2, page 6.

2. "Freedom in Not Knowing," *Non-Dual Consciousness.* Richard Rohr's Meditation, Aug. 31, 2014.

3. "What is Non-Dual Consciousness," *Non-Dual Consciousness.* Richard Rohr's Meditation, Sept. 3, 2014.

4. "Freedom in Not Knowing," *Non-Dual Consciousness.* Richard Rohr's Meditation, Aug. 31, 2014.

5. "Being Conscious," *Contemplation.* Richard Rohr's Meditation, Sept. 7, 2014.

6. Henri Nouwen with Michael J. Christiansen and Rebecca J. Laird, *Spiritual Direction*, (San Francisco: Harper, 2006), 74.

7. Adrienne von Speyr, *The World of Prayer* (San Francisco: Ignatius, 1985), 265.

8. Nouwen, *Spiritual Direction*, 27.

9. Henri Nouwen, *Life of the Beloved* (New York: Crossroad, 1992), 45.

10. *Divine Intimacy,* "The Mystery of the Trinity" *#250,* 657.

11. Robert Wise, *Spiritual Abundance, The Quest for the Presence of God in Daily Life*, (New York: Thomas Nelson, 2001), 7.

12. Henri Nouwen, *The Way of the Heart*, (New York: HarperOne, 1981), 96

13. Federico Suarez, *Mary of Nazareth*, (New York: Scepter, 1956), 72.

14. Suarez, *Mary of Nazareth*, 48.

15. Suarez, *Mary of Nazareth*, 45.

16. Joseph Kentenich, *A Life for the Church*, (Cape Town: Schoenstatt, 1985), 70.

17. Donald H. Calloway, *The Virgin Mary and Theology of the Body*, (West Chester, Pa.: Ascension, 2007), 241.

18. Kentenich, *A Life for the Church*, 76.

19. Calloway, *The Virgin Mary and Theology of the Body*, 230.

20. Kentenich, *A Life for the Church*, 78.

21. Religious of the Cenacle, *"To Surrender Oneself"*, (Houston: Cenacle, 2000), 1-2.

22. Religious of the Cenacle, *"To Surrender Oneself"*, (Houston: Cenacle, 2000), 1-2.

23. Religious of the Cenacle, *"To Surrender Oneself"*, (Houston: Cenacle, 2000), 1-2.

24. Kiernan Kavanaugh and Otillo Rodriguez O.C.D., *The Collected Works of St. John of the Cross*, (Washington, D.C.: ICS Publications, 1991), 316.

25. Jose Maria Escriva, *Friends of God*, (New York: Scepter, 1977), 40.

26. Escriva, *Friends of God*, 41.

27. Suarez, "The Call", *Mary of Nazareth*, 33.

28. Suarez, *Mary of Nazareth*, 81.

29. Thomas Dubay, S.M., *Authenticity*, (San Francisco: Ignatius Press, 1977), 26.

30. Dubay, *Authenticity*, 204.

31. Dubay, *Authenticity*, 71.

32. Suarez, *Mary of Nazareth*, 165.

33. Von Speyr, *The Christian State of Life*, (San Francisco: Ignatius, 1986), 107.

34. Nouwen, *Spiritual Direction*, 27.

35. Dubay, *Authenticity*, 153.

36. Nouwen, *Spiritual Direction*, 18.

37. Nouwen, *Spiritual Direction*, 34.

38. Nouwen, *Life of the Beloved*, 41.

39. St. Thomas Aquinas, *Summa Theologica*, (New York: Benziger Brothers, 2006), Part I.

40. Catechism of the Catholic Church (CCC) Second Edition, *"The Church in God's Plan"*, (Citta Del Vaticano: Liberia Editrice Vaticana, 1977), Article 9, para 1.

41. CCC, *"Church Is One"*. Para 818.

42. Suarez, *Mary of Nazareth*, Derived from.

43. Society of Mary, *Constitutions of the Society of Mary*, (Rome, Italy: Padri Maisti, Casa Generalizia, 1988), 93.

44. Pope Francis, "Apostalic Exhortation Christ the King Sunday", *Evangelii Guadium*, (Rome), 24 Nov. 2013.

45. J. Snijders, S.M., *"From the Marist Desk"*, 27th Sunday in Ordinary Time (Oct. 2, 2011).

46. CCC, "Origin of Sin", Profession of Faith, *CCC*, Para 400.

47. Adrienne von Speyr, *Mary in the Redemption*, English Edition, (San Francisco: Ignatius, 1987) 47.

48. Pope John Paul II., *The Theology of the Body*, (Boston: Pauline, 1997), 175-176.

49. John Paul II., "On Catechesis in Our Time, *Catecesis Tradendae*, (Boston: Pauline, 1997) Apostalic Exhortation.

50. J. Budziszewski, "Evangelizing Neo-Pagans", *First Things*, March, 2014. 24.

51. J. Budziszewski, *First Things*, 24.

52. Gather Hymnal, *"Jerusalem My Destiny"*, #390.

53. Nouwen, *Spiritual Direction*, 112.

54. Von Speyr, *The World of Prayer*, 267.

55. Karol Wojtyla, *Love and Responsibility*, (Boston: Pauline, 1960), derived from paraphrase.

56. Von Speyr, *The Christian State of Life*, 113.

57. John Paul II., *The Theology of the Body*, 159.

58. John Paul II.(Karol Wojtyla), *Love and Responsibility*, 78.

59. *Divine Intimacy*, paraphrased from various articles.

60. Divine Intimacy, "The Love of Friendship", *Divine Intimacy* #251, 751.

61. Calloway, *The Virgin Mary and Theology of the Body*, 52.

62. Mary DeTurris Poust, Walking Together, (Notre Dame: Ave Maria, 2010), 120.

63. Kathy Mattea, *"Seeds"* lyrics (CD Musical Album), (General Books, 2010)

64. Rudolph Schnackenburgh, Derived from with paraphrase from various text of Sacred Unions, Sacred Passions, Walking Together.

65. Poust, *Walking Together*, 108.

66. Dan Brennan, *Sacred Unions, Sacred Passions* (Elgin: Faith Dance, 2010), 20.

67. Brennan, *Sacred Unions, Sacred Passions*, 33.

68. Poust, *Walking Together*, 8.

69. Thomas Dubay, *Prayer Primer*, (Cincinnati: Servant, 2002), 15.

70. CCC, Para, *Prayer CCC* 2558-2565, 195.

71. Hans Urs von Balthasar, *Prayer*, (Chicago: Ignatius, 1986), 71.

72. Dubay, *Prayer Primer*, 17.

73. Balthasar, *Prayer*, 33.

74. Dubay, *Prayer Primer*, 27.

75. Brother Uacopone da Todi, *"How We Exalt the Cross"* (Pocm, +1306)

76. Dubay, *Prayer Primer*, 64.

77. Gather Hymnal, "The Hosea Song", (1952)

78. Nouwen, *Spiritual Direction*, 8.

79. St. Theresa of Avila, *Interior Castle*, (Madrid: Wilder, orig 1615, 4.

80. *Magnificat*, "The Fulfillment Jesus Wants for Us", January 8, 2015.

References

Alighieri, Dante. *The Divine Comedy*. Mobile Reference Electronic, 2014.

Brennan, Dan. *Sacred Unions, Sacred Passions*. Elgin, Illinois: Faith Dance Publishing, 2010.

Calloway, Donald. *The Virgin Mary and Theology of the Body*. West Chester, Pennsylvania: Ascension Press, 2007.

Catechism of the Catholic Church. Second ed. John Paul II., Pope. "Promulgator." In *Catechism of the Catholic Church*. Second ed. Citta Del Vaticano: Liberia Editrice Vaticana, 1977., Vatican: Liberia Editrice Vaticana, 2000.

Coutinho, Paul. *How Big Is Your God?* Chicago, Illinois: Loyola Press, 2007.

De Sales, St. Francis. *Introduction to the Devout Life*. Electronic ed. Wyatt North Publishing, 2012.

DeTurris Poust, Mary. *Walking Together, Discovering the Catholic Tradition of Spiritual Men and Women*. Notre Dame, Indiana: Aves Maria Press, 2010.

Dubay, S.M., Thomas. *Prayer Primer, Igniting a Fire Within.* Cincinnati, Oho: Servant Books, 2002.

Escriva, Josemaria. *Friends of God.* New York, New York: Scepter Publishers, 1977.

Francis, Pope. "Apostalic Exhortation." Address, Christ the King Sunday, Rome, November 24, 2013.

Gabriel, Fr. "The Love of Friendship." In *Divine Intimacy,* 251. Rockford, Illinois: Tan Books and Publishers, 1964.

Gallagher, O.M.V., Timothy M. *The Examen Prayer, Ignatian Wisdom for Our Lives Today.* New York, New York: Crossroad Publishing, 2006.

Hahn, Scott. *Hail, Holy Queen.* New York, New York: Image Books Doubleday, 2001.

Innerst, Sean. *The Creed.* Pillars I Study Set ed. Vol. Pillars II. West Chester, Pennsylvania: Ascension Press, 2012.

Jerusalem, My Destiny Lyrics. United States: Gather Comprehensive Choir Edition, 1952. Musical Lyrics.

John Paul II., Pope. "Homily Daily Mass." Lecture, Catholic Caucus from UCCB, , June 2, 2003.

John Paul II., Pope *The Theology of the Body.* Boston, Massachusettes: Pauline Books & Media, 1997.

Kalb, James. "Sex and the Religion of Me." *First Things* 248 (2014).

Kavanaugh, Kieran, and Otilio Rodriguez. *The Collected Works of St. John of the Cross*. Washington, D.C.: ICS Publications, Institute of Carmelite Studies, 1991.

Merton, Thomas. *Contemplative Prayer*. New York, New York: Image Books Doubleday, 1996.

Monnerjahn, E. *Joseph Kentenich, A Life for the Church*. English ed. Cape Town: Schoenstatt Publications, 1985.

Nouwen, Henri. *Life of the Beloved, Spiritual Living in a Secular World*. New York, New York: Crossroad Publishing.

Nouwen, Henri. *Spiritual Direction, Wisdom for the Long Walk of Faith*. San Francisco, California: Harper, 2006.

Nouwen, Henri. *The Way of the Heart, The Spirituality of the Desert Fathers and Mothers*. New York, New York: HarperOne, 1981. 96.

Of Mary, Society. *Constitutions of the Society of Mary*. Rome: Padri Maristi, Casa Generalizia, 1988.

Rievaulx, Aelred of. *Spiritual Friendship*. Kalamazoo, Michigan: Cistercian Publications, 1977.

Rohr, Richard. *Everything Belongs, The Gift of Contemplative Prayer*. Revised 2003 ed. New York, New York: Crossroad Publishing, 1999.

Rolheiser, Ronald. *The Holy Longing, The Search for a Christian Spirituality*. New York, New York: Image New York, 2014.

Rohr, Richard. *Silent Compassion, Finding God in Contemplation*. Cincinnati, Oho: Franciscan Media, 2014.

Rolheiser, Ronald. *The Holy Longing, The Search for a Christian Spirituality*. New York, New York: Image New York, 2014.

Rolheiser, Ronald. *The Shattered Lantern, Rediscovering A Felt Presence of God*. New York, New York: Crossroad Publishing, 2004.

Scruton, Roger. "Is Sex Necessary?" *First Things* 248 (2014).

Seeds (CD Musical Album). Performed by Kathy Mattea. General Books, 2010. Musical Lyrics.

Sri, Edward. *Men, Women and the Mystery of Love*. Cincinnati, Oho: Servant Books, 2007.

Sri, Edward. *The New Rosary in Scripture*. Cincinnati, Pennsylvania: Servant Books, 2003.

Sri, Edwards. *Walking Wit Mary, A Biblical Journey from Nazareth to the Cross*. New York, New York: Image, 2013.

Suarez, Federico. *Mary of Nazareth*. New York, New York: Scepter Publishers, 1956.

The Cloud of Unknowing. Brewster, Massachusetts: Paraclete Press, 2006.

Thibodeaux, S.J., Mark E. *Armchair Mystic, Easing Into Contemplative Prayer*. Cincinnati, Oho: Franciscan Media, 2001.

Thibodeaux, Mark. *God's Voice Within, The Ignatian Way to Discover God's Will*. Chicago, Illinois: Loyola Press, 2010.

Urs Von Balthasar, Hans. *Mary for Today*. San Francisco, California: Ignatius Press, 1987.

Urs Von Balthasar, Hans. *Prayer*. Chicago, Illinois: Ignatius Press, 1986.

Von Speyr, Adrienne. *Handmaid of the Lord*. English ed. San Francisco, California: Ignatius Press, 1985.

Von Speyr, Adrienne. "1985." In *The World of Prayer*, 311. San Francisco, California: Ignatius Press.

Von Speyr, Adrienne. *Mary in the Redemption*. English ed. San Francisco, California: Ignatius Press, 2003.

Von Speyr, Adrienne. *The Victory of Love, A Meditation of Romans 8*. San Francisco, California: Ignatius Press, 1990.

Von Speyr, Adrienne. *The Christian State of Life*. San Francisco, California: Ignatius Press, 1986.

Von Speyr, Adrienne. *The Letter to the Ephesians*. San Francisco, California: Ignatius Press, 1996.

Whitehead, Evelyn Eaton, and James D. Whitehead. *Christian Life Patterns, The Psychological Challenges and Religious Invitations of Adult Life*. New York, New York: Crossroad Publishing, 2003.

Wojtyla, Karol. *Love and Responsibility*. Boston, Massachusettes: Pauline Books & Media, 1960.